SKELETONS IN THE CLOSET

A Sociological Analysis of Family Conflicts

Aysan Sev'er and Jan E. Trost, editors

Wilfrid Laurier University Press

[WLU]

This book has been published with the help of a grant from the Canadian Federation for the Humanities and Social Sciences, through the Aid to Scholarly Publications Programme, using funds provided by the Social Sciences and Humanities Research Council of Canada. We acknowledge the financial support of the Government of Canada through the Canada Book Fund for our publishing activities.

Library and Archives Canada Cataloguing in Publication

Skeletons in the closet : a sociological analysis of family conflicts / Aysan Sev'er and Jan E. Trost, editors.

Includes bibliographical references.
Also available in electronic format.
ISBN 978-1-55458-265-5

1. Families. I. Sev'er, Aysan, 1945– II. Trost, Jan, 1935–

HQ519.S54 2011   306.85   C2010-905176-9

ISBN 978-1-55458-318-8
Electronic format.

1. Families. I. Sev'er, Aysan, 1945– II. Trost, Jan, 1935–

HQ519.S54 2011a   306.85   C2010-905177-7

Cover design by David Drummond using an image from istockphoto. Text design by Catharine Bonas-Taylor.

© 2011 Wilfrid Laurier University Press
Waterloo, Ontario, Canada
www.wlupress.wlu.ca

This book is printed on FSC recycled paper and is certified Ecologo. It is made from 100% post-consumer fibre, processed chlorine free, and manufactured using biogas energy.

Printed in Canada

CONTENTS

INTRODUCTION

Opening Closets, Rattling Family Skeletons:
What Will They Say?

AYSAN SEV'ER

JAN TROST

We welcome you to a moving collection of narratives about unresolved, and sometimes unresolvable, family conflicts. First and foremost, we thank every colleague, whether our graduate students or peers, for participating in this amazing collection. A few others expressed interest in our work and offered their encouragement but did not agree to write a chapter.

Many participated, however, and we are deeply grateful for their enthusiasm. Anne Michaels, in her widely popular novel *Fugitive Pieces* (1998), reminds us that writing is an act which has healing powers. "Write to save yourself ... and someday, you'll write because you have been saved," she asserts (p. 165). We do not know if our contributors were writing because they were still grappling with their family skeletons or writing because they had managed to rise above their family secrets. Whatever the case may be, and in a world where family issues are still privatized, being able to share one's most intimate family quarrels is nothing short of social heroism. We are certain that our readers will be amazed at our contributors' candid stories.

After reading the narratives about the family struggles of our authors, our readers may also develop insights into their own family conflicts. Moreover, the narratives in this book turn upside down what otherwise is the most common pattern of the sociological study of families. In our judgment, the personal intensity captured in the narratives in this book will expand the "safer" and "more distant" methodological boundaries of traditional family research, such as studying families though the census, or through surveys, or even through interviews and observations. As social scientists, we are mostly—one might say exclusively—trained to study "others." In this book, however, we turn the table around. We asked social scholars (including ourselves) to focus the inquiring lens on what they consider to be *their* family conflicts. The journey each of us took is unique, and we will venture to suggest that none has been easy, because "skeletons" come with or bring about a closet full of emotion. However, examining and sharing these narratives have their own rewards, whether by providing relief to others who may have similar family issues or by providing the authors themselves with insights and new perspectives. Giving voice to parts of our lives that have remained silent (or silenced) has its own redemptive qualities. Reading about the struggles of others may provide vicarious relief to our readers.

Shortly, we will delve into an in-depth discussion of the metaphors we use in our title, introduce a critical discussion about the concepts and terms central to this collection, and launch our views about different theoretical positions on the family and methods of study. However, before we do, we would first like to share with our readers how the idea for this book about family skeletons emerged. In May 2008, some ISA (International Sociological Association) members attended a conference on aging and families organized by Lasell College in Newton, Massachusetts. We (Aysan and Jan) were two of the 50 or so attendees. Aside from an interesting intellectual exchange, the host college had organized an afternoon tour of the Boston and Newport regions. During the relatively long bus ride to and from our conference destination, we happened to share adjacent seats and had an opportunity to discuss the conference in general. Our unstructured chat about the sessions we had already attended led us to an equally unstructured discussion about what types of sessions to include in upcoming sociology of the family conferences. Because her area of expertise is intimate partner violence, Aysan expressed a desire to incorporate more sessions addressing family conflict. "Conflict," Jan said. "If you are interested in conflict, I have a story for you!" Within the evening shadows of a moving bus, Jan told a version of the story which now appears as Chapter 2 in this collection. This initial narrative, told by one colleague/friend to another, led us to the phrase "skeletons in the closet." Soon after, Aysan also shared a family story, a version of which now appears as Chapter 1. During the remainder of the Lasell conference, and through countless emails that followed our return to our respective homes (in Toronto and Uppsala), we started to talk about how important it is to tell, write, share, discuss, collect, and analyze narratives of family conflict. Through our increasing interest, we came to the conclusion that, as unique as each family conflict may be, skeletons of some kind reside in most family closets.

Initially, we mentioned this idea of "skeletons" to a few close colleagues. Although we brought up the idea casually, we were amazed and emboldened to see a resounding interest. Almost every colleague we talked to was eager to share a riveting story considered to be a "family skeleton." Some of those narratives, along with their authors' perceptions and analyses, have been presented as chapters in this book. During our interesting journey of collecting narratives, we also heard about many other skeletons from many other closets. Some of those narrators chose not to submit a written version of their stories for reasons that are important for them. We truly respect their need for privacy, and we respect their choices. We wish them well in their personal attempts to find alternative ways of finding a restful place for their skeletons.

We believe that family conflicts, feuds, and grudges are common; they probably date back to the origins of humankind. They also form a common thread in religious teachings. With long-accumulated wisdom about the devastating effects of conflict among different generations, prophets of all major religions have stipulated tolerance and respect among people who are closely related. These religious stipulations reach their absolute clarity in prescribing respect toward one's parents. It is no coincidence that religious teachings repeat the obligations to love and honour one's mother and father. Love-and-honour themes (with the frequent addition of "obey") have also been applied to husbands and wives. From Cain and Abel to Siddhartha, themes of family conflict can be found in the stories and teachings of all the major religions. And, of course, Freud built his whole theory of personality development on the basis of the tragic ancient Greek myth of Oedipus.

Strife between parents and children, siblings, husbands, wives, and in-laws also serve as the backdrop of many Hollywood movies—be they within the comic, adventure, thriller, and drama genres. Sometimes funny (*Meet the Fockers, Are We There Yet?*), sometimes tragic (*The War of the Roses, Burning Bed, American Beauty, Gone with the Wind, Kramer vs. Kramer, Sophie's Choice*), stories of family conflict form a staple of the silver screen. Despite the efforts of screenplay writers to make these stories palatable for mass audiences, and despite a humorous edge often thrown into such stories for good measure, conflict among people who are (or are normatively expected to be) part of a family group spells trouble. However, unlike the ratings-hungry mass media, our interest in working on this collection is not about feeding the appetite for social voyeurism. We are interested in finding out in what different forms family conflict manifests itself, how different strategies may help resolve or end up fuelling conflict, and how conflict transforms individuals (for better or for worse) and strains family relations. Thus, the following is a summary of our goals for this book:

- To show that family strife happens in many families. Not only people in general but also people who are highly educated, highly trained social scholars may be caught up in the conflict.
- To show that the sources of conflict can be different but the trajectory of conflict often coincides with sociological variables of interest (gender, age, race/ethnicity, class, sexual orientation, culture).
- To show that once the conflict starts, and without a mutually satisfactory solution, the intensity of the conflict is likely to increase.
- To show that the original conflict is likely to spread over time and that it will possibly taint the relations of members who were not party to the original struggle.
- To show that families often form cliques. Cliques sometimes balance the distribution of power and influence, but at other times they create long-lasting family fragmentation.
- To show that, although conflict can pave a way for heightened sensitivity, mutual respect, and new forms of trust and intimacy for some members of families, other members may be hurt and isolated.
- To show that family members may utilize different strategies to resolve the original conflict and that some of these strategies may work in the short or long term. However, despite the initial goodwill, some strategies may actually intensify the original conflict.
- To show that conflict is often a hard-to-address part of family skeletons but that airing out these skeletons may have a transformative effect on both the teller and the reader of the stories.

Having listed our goals, it is also important for us to tell our readers what we are *not* trying to do:

- We are not trying to suggest that this book is the ultimate authority on conflict within families. We only want to pave the way for much-needed focus and debate.
- We are not suggesting that the authors of this collection have a particularly privileged position in conflict resolution, despite their important academic credentials. On the contrary, we would like to suggest that

family conflict is a powerful phenomenon that sometimes can overwhelm an individual, despite his or her many accomplishments.

- We are not presenting this book as a self-help book. Although we hope that many of our readers will find the narratives insightful, it is possible that some may not find these stories helpful for their own lives. We trust that many will.

- Last but not least, we did not rank the severity of family conflicts presented in this book in any way. We hope that our readers do not rank the conflicts either, because family turmoil is not a contest. Obviously, our authors have found these stories important enough to write about. As their audience, we can learn from their stories without judging the characters or the events that the narrators have shared with us.

Most particularly, we are interested in finding out about how conflict transmutes into skeletons in family closets and how people deal with their skeletons. At this point, we would like to explore what the metaphors we have chosen as part of the title of this collection—skeletons and closets—mean to us and may also conjure up in most minds.

Metaphors of Closets and Skeletons

Dictionary definitions of *metaphor* specify a figure of speech where a name or a quality of something well known is attributed to something else to which it is not literally applicable (e.g., an *icy* glance, a *rainbow* coalition, *thunderous* applause). By the nature of the above definition, metaphors cannot be (and are not meant to be) taken literally; their strength is in their ability to hone in on a generalizable quality or aspect. In social contexts, and when not taken too literally, metaphors can bring clarity to otherwise hard-to-grasp complexities. However, upon careful inspection, the apparent simplicity of social metaphors is somewhat deceiving, inasmuch as they highlight hidden complexities of the social reality to which they have been applied.

So, let us explore the metaphor of *skeletons in the closet* as it applies to family conflict that is not publicly divulged. The literal meaning of *closet* conjures up a confined space, generally for the purpose of storing clothes, that is closed or that can be closed. A closet also implies a storage area for objects that clutter our day-to-day lives by their sheer, unruly presence, although some, if not most, of these objects have particular import, and are thus retained, if relegated to a peripheral space. What one needs to remember, however, is that what is closed and closeted can also be opened up and aired out. So if skeletons are in the closet, like clothes in the more literal sense, the closet can be opened, the skeletons revealed. It is also possible that more than one person—maybe a whole family—may be sharing the closet. Some skeletons may exist over generations. Moreover, skeletons, like clothes, need not always be confined to the closet; they can be taken out (one by one, or a few at a time), aired out, and used (discussed). At a later time, they can be put back in the closet, and the closet can again be closed, even locked. Family members may collude to stash skeletons in communal closets, with the intention of keeping them closed. Therefore, any one member's decision to open the closet may cause substantial angst among others who may be reluctant to face these skeletons, let alone display their secrets to the world. This is exactly why some of our colleagues interested in this edition were nevertheless reluctant to contribute personal accounts. They feared that, by opening the closet, they might face new family turmoil and possibly even create new skeletons.

The ingenuity of the skeleton metaphor also forces us to consider other possibilities. For example, if the skeleton is left in the closet for too long, it may cease to be a skeleton. It may transform into something else, even something which has some positive value for the person or persons who initially stowed it away. Like forgotten outfits from a long-ago era that again become fashionable as "vintage," some family skeletons may turn out to generate personal growth, shared intimacy, and insight for some family members. How many sons and daughters of famous people have achieved their own fame and fortune by writing a book about a famous (or infamous) parent, especially when the parent may not have gotten an A+ for his or her parenting skills? Christina Crawford's *Mommie Dearest*[1] provides a striking example of this pattern. At other times, skeletons that are stored too long may appear forgotten or discarded, but may end up stinking up everything else in the closet. Even new clothes (or relationships) can be tainted by their close proximity. The violence literature is full of the revelations of people who were sexually or physically victimized in childhood. The secrecy of past violence often inhibits them from building trust or intimacy in adult relationships. What is important, then, is that even when skeletons are securely closeted and appear to be discarded or forgotten, they are still there, and they often exert significant influence on the closet-keepers. Occasionally, skeletons may become obsolete, like the belongings of a person who has moved or passed away. They may also be inherited by a new generation. Sometimes, skeletons may instigate new conflict, inasmuch as one person's skeleton may be another's treasure (or nightmare). Some of our readers will recall President Clinton's skeletons, which turned into public spectacle and engendered an impeachment trial. Others will be more familiar with Michael Jackson's or Tiger Woods's skeletons.

So far, we have been concentrating on skeletons in the closet, but what about the metaphor of the skeleton itself? As a metaphor, a skeleton is something that was alive but is now dead. A skeleton has lost its flesh and blood; it has lost its ability to have a body or a mind of its own. The metaphor also implies a loss of animus, drive, and efficacy. But the skeletons in family closets are not necessarily dead—they may just be dormant. At times, they may be animated at will, or they may become animated indirectly through the acts or deeds of other people. At other times, skeletons have a latent (as opposed to a manifest) life of their own, in the form of a bad conscience, anger, or guilt in the person who keeps them. Skeletons may also be the source of resentment, fear, or blame. After airing, they may return to the closet peacefully, or they may lead to a new bout of personal or interpersonal havoc.

In this book, we are starting from the assumptions that nothing is written in stone, everything is subject to change, and anything can be changed. Therefore, although some may think of skeletons in closets as a cause for stagnation and despair, we will argue that they can also be seen as agents for new ideas and change. The change may come through examination of the skeletons and examination of the power of secrecy that has been imbued in them. Through this examination, individuals may find that the issues were not that detrimental after all, or they may find new sources of courage, support, and empathy to combat whatever the original problems may have been. We believe all the authors in this book are seeking alternative ways of addressing the past or presenting conflicts in their families. Visiting skeletons may be a way of disempowering what originally consumed the authors' energies and drained their personal relationships. By taking this courageous route, the authors in this collection are also acting as role models to other keepers of family crypts and custodians of family skeletons. In families, it is sometimes silences that chain the participants to their skeletons.

Conceptualization of Conflict and Family Silences

Silences

Throughout this book, we will see examples of skeletons taken in and out of closets. As awkward as it may sound, people sometimes choose to air out their skeletons, just as they may periodically revise their wardrobe. Early sociologists have theorized that humans are "active" agents (Mead, 1934;

Parsons & Bales, 1960; Strauss, 1956/1977). Even "not using" something, ignoring it, or forgetting it can be seen as an "activity" which involves choice.[2] In more recent years, feminist theoretical developments have taken the idea of "active" a step further and have underscored the importance of "agency." In its most basic sense, agency can be interpreted as determined, goal-oriented activity. Debates about agency can be found in the gendered violence literature, which contrasts agency with passive victimization. Even under the most dire circumstances (such as long-term victimization by an intimate partner), women make choices: leaving or staying with the abusive partner, calling for help or suffering alone, protecting their children even when it means more suffering for themselves (Sev'er, 2002, 2010a). Thus, even remaining silent can be considered an activity involving choice. For example, witnesses to a crime can stay silent or can register a complaint, and people who have skeletons can choose to lock them up in closets or talk or write about them. So, in reality, silence can be a noun or a verb—*to silence*. Of course, the latter also involves power-based tugs-of-war. Who imposes silence on whom is of the utmost sociological significance: Is it men silencing women? Adults silencing youth? The affluent silencing the poor? Custodians of skeletons silencing those who want to air out those secrets? Those who have done wrong silencing their victims?

Heinrich Böll's short story about Dr. Murke's collected silences (1966) provides us with food for thought. Dr. Murke was working on editing tape-recorded speeches that were to be sent to a radio station. At the time, speeches were recorded on long strips of magnetized tapes, and his job involved cutting out the long pauses (silences) and splicing the tape together in order to make it seem as if the speaker had been more fluent than he or she actually was. Dr. Murke decided to collect the "pieces of silence" discarded from the taped speeches and splice them all together into a new tape that could be played on its own: a tape where one can actually listen to and "hear" other people's silences. In this example, the silences themselves, the collecting of the silences, and the listening to the silences can all be seen as activities. Similarly, silences that are documented in this book can also be looked upon as an activity. Silences can be used as tools, as when someone wishes to avoid a confrontation by keeping unpleasant memories or recollections at bay. They can also be used to exclude others from one's own emotional territory. An individual may also attempt to silence his or her own conscience or to use silences to challenge the legitimacy of other people's thoughts and actions. In short, people who use (or abuse) silences are exercising agency.

Conflict

In North America, as in many other societies, the word *conflict* conjures up negative emotions (Folger, Poole, & Stutman, 2009). In dictionary definitions, the first associations with *conflict* are "war," "warfare," "military warfare," and "armed struggle." In contrast, social scientists define conflict in many other ways (Eidelson & Eidelson, 2003; Folger et al., 2009; Coser, 1956). Some define conflict in terms of the incompatibility of activities and behaviours (Deutsch, 1973), and others define conflict as incompatability of goals (Pruitt & Rubin, 1986). Yet others define conflict as an interactive phenomenon, where the behaviours and goals of one significantly transgress the behaviours and goals of another (Folger et al., 2009; Tedeschi, Bonoma, & Schlenker, 1972). Arguably, the last conceptualization comes closest to capturing the complex nature of conflict among family members. It is also important to point out that the goals and behaviours that lead to family conflict may not be overt. Moreover, conflicts may occur because of the divergent interests of the individuals or from the divergent interests vested in their social positions, or they may arise from both levels simultaneously (Ford, 1994). In families, these complexities are frequent.

Although social sciences—especially sociology—have taken up as their subject matter the study of different forms of struggle (for example, class struggle), the study of conflict within the family literature has been segmented. At the micro level, scholars of group interactions have studied conflict and conflict resolution as an unavoidable aspect of group dynamics (Simmel, 1950, 1971). For example, Simmel (1908/1923) claims that humans have a double nature, which means that people live in some sort of conflict with their social surroundings. On the one hand, we generally feel positively toward individuals and may even like them a lot. On the other side, we may harbour negative feelings toward the same individuals, disliking them at times. These colliding feelings and emotions can be conceptually separated, but empirically, they may be overlapping and concurrent. For example, a daughter may like and respect her mother but may also at times be exceptionally angry with her and may even hate her for interfering in the daughter's personal life. A son may love and respect his father but may feel unhappy about the father's domineering ways and may deeply resent the way his father belittles his mother. Simmel (1908/1923) claims that the conflict people feel toward their surroundings also reflects a deeper inner conflict: although people have contradictory feelings toward others, they nevertheless want (or need) a more consistently positive regard from others. In other words, although they may feel bouts of love and hate, what they yearn for is love and appreciation.

According to Simmel (1950; 1971), small, intimate groups, such as the dyad (a group of two), are fragile entities. In the dyad, all it takes for the group to break up is one person to say that he or she does not want to continue. Of course, either of the two may take such a stance, adding to the fragility of the dyad, and high divorce rates in industrialized societies are a testament to this fragility (Sev'er, 2010b). Fortunately, family groups often consist of numerous people and thus are much more robust than a dyad. Simmel (1908/1923) claims that because of the closeness people feel, because of the emotional bind that exists among them, families can often cope with great contradictions without disintegrating. However, it is still possible that inner conflicts that go on for a prolonged time will threaten the very important ties that keep families together. In the face of intense conflict, different members of families may form coalitions, and thus the original conflict between two or among a small group of individuals may spread.

Early sociologists also saw the importance of conflict as a unique way of increasing group solidarity (Durkheim, 1951), as long as the conflict did not involve the fundamental foundations of the group's existence (Nixon, 1979). In other words, as long as the members of a group agree on the highly valued principles that carry moralistic and normative overtones, lesser disagreements are expected to be tolerated and even seen as beneficial. To give an example from the business world, the executive leaders of a company may agree on increasing their profits but may disagree on which particular project may help them to reach the desired profitability. They may try one, they may alter or combine a few, and they may discard some other ideas. Although conflicts may arise, they are likely to be resolved as long as the group agrees on the main goal (profitability). Because family groups are often cradles of vested interests—some very long term—they may appear like business groups. However, this similarity is misleading, because families are also cauldrons of high levels of emotion. Therefore, conflicts among family members have the potential to be intense.

The ultimate goals of families are overlaid with abstract moral values rather than being clearly definable goals in and of themselves. It is much more difficult to define love and loyalty as goals than to sell so many products or make so much profit per year. Thus, benefiting from conflict as a pathway for positive change is harder in family relations, where conflict strikes at the heart of highly valued norms and expectations—as ambiguous as they may be. For example, in a family where fidelity is held to be the most important moral value, a wife may manage to overlook her husband's drinking and gambling habits as long as she is certain that her husband's transgressions do not include extramarital sexual affairs. In another family, where the highest moral value is that of financial sacrifice for the children's advanced education and upward mobility, a husband who has gambled away the family savings may find himself in an irresolvable conflict.

Because conflicts among family members are intense and tend to be emotionally laden, they have the tendency to divide the family group into factions and can end up creating fissures even among people who were not part of the original conflict. For instance, in the preceding example, adult children may intervene by either defending the victimized mother or sympathizing with the father. In general, some family members entangled in the conflict may remain unscathed and may even become stronger and more insightful in the process. Other members may give up, crumble under pressure, or become bitter. It is our hope that the honest narratives in this book will give us clues about how to increase the probability of positive outcomes while also cautioning us against negative strategies.

Family

Up to this point, we have used the term *family* without attempting to provide a definition. Some may claim that everyone knows what a family is and a definition is not necessary. Moreover, the definition of the word can change when the word is used in a given situation. For example, when a physician asks a patient to bring his or her family to the next meeting, what is usually meant is one's spouse, parents, or adult children. In such cases, the patient is not going to show up to the next appointment with an infant or a great-grandfather in tow. However, social scientists have not been comfortable leaving the definition of such an important human institution to commonsense. Therefore, before we attempt to bring clarity to the inclusive conceptualization we use within this book, let us start with the definitions of family in the sociological and social-anthropological literature.

In the literature, we find legal definitions (these identify what a marriage is, who can marry whom, rules about inheritance, who can be claimed as a dependant for taxation purposes, etc.), formal definitions (such as those used by censuses, the World Health Organization, and the UN Human Development Index), and social definitions (such as calling one's girlfriend "family"). In general, the legal definitions are the most binding, the formal definitions set the stage about what is commonly considered to be a family, and the social definitions are the most dynamic, flexible, and even contradictory. There are also populist usages of the term. Sometimes, the term is used for things that are not even human. For example, the Simpsons (bright yellow cartoon characters) are referred to as a "family." Popular restaurants may offer generic "family discounts" to any two adults with a couple of children. In such definitions, there is no requirement for blood, conjugal, or residential connections. Two adults and two children who may be neighbours can order a meal together and get their family discount. What is important to underscore is that all definitions are temporally and geographically bound and that all definitions are subject to change as the social milieu and conditions change.

From the outset, sociological and social-anthropological definitions of the family have captured bits and pieces from the legal, formal, and social aspects. However, due to the complexity of the subject matter (social interaction at micro and macro levels), conceptualization and definitions have been challenging for sociologists. Not only is the social phenomenon they address multi-dimensional, it also changes and shifts across time and place. Thus, the concept of "the family" or "families" is problematic for a variety of reasons (Ambert, 2005). The question "What is a family?" is a legitimate sociological inquiry, but the answers sociologists (and other social scientists) have provided have not always been free of the values and biases of the Western societies these scholars are a part of (Baker, 2006; Eichler, 1997a). For example, although families have always been widely varied in their form, inclusivity, and structure, Western scholars have habitually erred on the conservative side by giving primacy to certain dimensions and overlooking others. The prerequisite dimensions in most definitions have been (a) heterosexual marriage between *a pair* of adults, (b) social and/or legal approval of the union, (c) economic obligations, (d) commonality of residence, and (e) the presence of children. One look at an early social-anthropological definition such as that of Murdock (1949) will bring these points into focus. Murdock defines family as "a social group characterized by common residence, economic co-operation and reproduction. It includes adults of both sexes, at least two of whom maintain a socially approved sexual relationship, and one or more children, own or adopted, of the sexually cohabiting adults." Stephen's (1963) sociological definition echoes similar prerequisites, defining family as "a social arrangement based on marriage and the marriage contract, including recognition of the rights and duties of parents, common residence for husband, wife and children and reciprocal economic obligations between husband and wife." Of course, social scientists have also been intrigued by various other forms of the family and have come up with hyphenated terms to refer to them. Lone-parent families, reconstituted families, stepfamilies, same-sex families, and so on, are terms that bestow a qualified family status on families that fall outside of what is considered to be the "normative" form: the nuclear family (Eichler, 1997a).

Formal definitions of the family are problematic for different reasons. When they are rigid, these definitions exclude large groups of people who live in familial relations but face the possibility of seeing themselves and being seen by others as illegitimate. For example, in a society that shuns or criminalizes same-sex unions, a lifelong same-sex partner may be barred from visiting his or her spouse at a hospital and may be barred from being legally included in his or her estate. In many patriarchal societies, children born out of wedlock are legally barred from carrying their father's surname and may be barred from inheriting from their paternal lineage. Moreover, and just as importantly, how families are defined has serious policy implications. Division of property, inheritance, marriage prohibitions, immigration access, tax exemptions, and health insurance coverage, for example, are all closely tied to how families are formally or legally defined. Implications of the definitions also extend to the ways in which responsibilities, obligations, and access to social benefits (apportioning of pensions, eligibility to housing, etc.) are configured (Ambert, 2005; Baker, 2006).

It is true that the rigidity of formal definitions of family have changed over time, especially in the West. For example, lone parents and common-law partnerships have been increasingly included in formal definitions of family. In 2001, the Canadian census (Statistics Canada, 2001) defined family as a "married couple (with or without children of either or both spouses), a couple living common-law (with or without children of either or both partners), or a lone parent of any marital status with at least one child living in the same dwelling." The 2001 census also stipulated that grandchildren living with grandparents where no parent was present constituted a family. Since 2006, the Canadian census (Statistics Canada, 2006) has included same-sex partners and their children in its definition of a family. However, in most parts of the world, the "intact" forms of families continue to hold a preferential status among other forms. In Canada, only about 40 percent of Canadian families fall into the category of intact or nuclear (Baker, 2006).

An additional problem in traditional sociological research has been assumptions about the functionality of the families on the basis of their structure

(Eichler, 1997a). For example, rather than making relations among family members a point of inquiry, traditional sociological research has frequently started from the assumption that certain forms of the family are more prone to problems (e.g., families headed by women, families created outside of legal marriage, same-sex couples, mixed marriages). So, when it comes to families, it is not that sociology has avoided conflict per se but that most traditional research has sought conflict within what society considers to be non-norma-tive forms of the family. This tendency has created a double bias: (1) after endless scrutiny, actually finding conflict where it was assumed to exist in the first place (problems in single-parent homes; problems among the different— be it in terms of race, ethnicity, immigration status, or sexual orientation), and (2) not looking for—and thus not finding—conflict where it is assumed to be absent, thereby tautologically reinforcing the original position (traditional reluctance to study violence and incest that take place in "intact" families).

In the minds of ordinary people, the perception of family is much more elastic. For example, Trost (1988) used a list of various combinations of peo-ple and asked representative samples of respondents which of the combina-tions they considered to be a family. Results showed an enormous variation. Some respondents saw an adult and a child living together as a family, but others did not. Some perceived a cohabiting couple as a family; others did not. Some defined a married couple as a family; others defined only a mar-ried couple *with children* as a family. Some included same-sex couples as a family; others did not. Trost (1988) also asked respondents to write down whom they considered to be members of their own families. Again, the find-ings were varied. Some respondents considered only one other person as their family; others, dozens of people. Some confined their affinity to parents and siblings (the nuclear-family idea); others included aunts, uncles, and in-laws (the extended-family idea). Some respondents in Trost's (1988) study were more creative. They included cats, dogs, and other pets as part of their fam-ily; others included deceased persons, music, and even God. The exclusions were also interesting. For example, some people included some brothers or sis-ters on their family list but left out other siblings. Likewise, some, but not all, aunts and uncles made the list, adding to the picture of the complex ways people define their families. Thus, families are defined by inclusions but also by exclusions and cliques. Regardless of their configuration, however, what all families have in common is that they can be fraught with—and fragmented by—passion, intensity, and conflict.

Summary of Theoretical Orientations That Address Family Conflict

Different disciplines, especially those closely related to the helping professions (social workers, therapists) or those that address the self (psychology, psychiatry), have dealt with family strife through their own theoretical perspectives. For example, both psychologists and social workers have routinely dealt with the aftermath of family pressures, conflict, and strife, and some of their insights have been translated into shared knowledge. However, in most of these works, the individual—his or her problems or suffering—is the focus of interest. Possibly starting from Freud, psychiatry has also developed ways of analyzing how conflicts (in that case, between parents and children) can and do have lifelong repercussions (Freud, 1951). Through the conceptualizations of terms such as *complexes, identification, fixation,* and so on, Freud's theory has addressed the after-effects of unresolved and unresolvable conflicts among closely related people—especially the father/mother/son triangle. Without giving our unwavering sign of approval to any of the intrapersonal perspectives, we are suggesting here that in some social scientific approaches, the crucial nature of family-based conflict is already well established. Their locus of interest, however, is the individual. In contrast, sociology's focus on conflict has been within the clearly defined boundaries of its subdisciplines (e.g., stratification, social movements, race relations, gender relations) rather than within the sociology of the family. This limited focus is the result of a number of factors.

Sociology's Positivist Roots

From its inception, sociology has been deeply rooted in philosophy/logic on the one hand and history/economics on the other. This early skew has made sociology a discipline that is particularly well tailored to the study of macro-level issues and problems: inequality, stratification, crime and deviance, religion, social movements, education, and politics, to name a few. Moreover, from early on (Comte, Durkheim, Spencer traditions), sociology has struggled to establish itself as a legitimate form of science by borrowing models and concepts from other sciences, and it has developed a thirst for generalizable rules. The quest for a scientific identity has pushed the discipline toward looking at structural and social processes through the lens of hard sciences that have already proven their legitimacy (biology, chemistry, mechanics, physics). Undeniably, the remnants of these related disciplines are very much part of some theories that sociology calls its own (e.g., Darwinian biological determinism in Spencer (in Perdue, 1986, pp. 56–62); historical/economic determinism in Marx, 1978). One particular result of modelling after hard sciences has been the continuing dominance of the positivistic/consensus paradigms in sociology. For example, the analytical sociological gaze driven by consensus models starts from the assumption that social entities, like their biological or mechanical counterparts, exist within boundaries and seek balance, equilibrium, order, co-operation, and interdependencies (Durkheim, 1933; Parsons, 1968). Thus, sociological inquiries often attempt to find general rules, predictive models, explanatory factors, tests of causality, and so on, in social processes to explain how and when order (rather than conflict) is possible.

Functionalist and Interactionist Expansions

The original sociological study of the family as an institution (or as a small group system) has evolved within the consensus paradigms. In North America, family sociology has been rooted in the Parsonian functionalist tradition (Bales, 1953; Parsons, 1968; Parsons & Shils, 1962; Parsons & Bales, 1960). Like other consensus paradigms, Parsonian functionalism starts from the study of order and looks at the interconnectedness of institutions, the division of labour, and the differential specialization as healthy or normative manifestations of social systems. Conflict, although not ignored, is looked upon as a trigger for the resolutional attempts of a social system, resulting in incremental change and new forms of adjustment. Like Durkheim, Parsons also underscored the moral value systems that serve as a glue to keep the system intact, noting that disintegration of any kind (such as divorce) is seen as problematic (Parsons, 1968). Functionalists have never been able to grapple with continuous conflict and rupturous forms of change. Moreover, functionalist approaches to the study of the family have basically glossed over some of the destructive power imbalances and ingrained inequalities that often cloud family life. In reality, patriarchy, conflict, domination, and inequality are very much part and parcel of family life, often setting men against women, young against old, the able-bodied against the disabled, and heterosexuality against variations in sexual orientation.

Borrowing from social anthropology, early sociologists also concluded that families are universal. However, the attribution of universality to families, assumptions about the functionality of their existence, and the expectation that families are necessary for the survival of the species have sometimes come at the cost of diverting the critical gaze away from the conflict and the turmoil experienced in some family-like structures. This does not mean that early sociologists were oblivious to conflict. Certainly, they were not. Nevertheless, conflict was almost always seen as a non-normative or destructive state that had to be remedied as quickly as possible in order to return the social organism (be it a small group, a large collectivity, or a state) to its more desirable, conflict-free level of functioning. The traditional emphasis has been on avoidance, rather than prevention or skillful resolution of conflict.

In more micro, interactionist variations of sociological thought (G. Simmel, G. H. Mead, C. H. Cooley traditions), where the units of analyses are smaller social groupings (dyads, triads, families, small groups, organizations), we find a more focused interest in families. In the Cooley tradition, the emphasis is mostly on interactions and meanings rather than just outcomes or frequencies. Of course, family interactions may be smooth and positive, or they may be riddled with conflict. Clearly, Simmel (1908/1923) captures the complexity that is present in small groups when he suggests that dyads are the most vulnerable of all group relations. Moreover, the complexity of relationships exponentially grows as the size of the small group expands. For example, in a triad consisting of ABC, there are four possible relationships—AB, AC, BC, ABC. In a group of five persons, 10 dyadic, another 10 triadic, five quadruple, and one five-person relationship is possible, for a total of 26. In a group of 10, the total of just the possible dyadic and triadic relationships is 165. Thus, it would be naive to think that all these subgroupings can function smoothly; instead, there will be tensions and complications.

Simmel (1908/1923) was also cognizant of the differential needs and wants of individuals in small groups and the different ways in which they might see or interpret events. Amazingly, almost 100 years ago, he suggested that a kiss is not the same for each of the two people who kiss. Many years later, Jessie Bernard (1972) expanded this idea and claimed that the experience of marriage is greatly different for men ("his" marriage) and women ("her" marriage). In Bernard's feminist version, the difference that is highlighted is not only a nominal differentiation (such as different sensations and meanings) but is due to the tensions arising from the uneven distribution of resources, power, and vulnerability. Ann Goetting (1986) has utilized a similar analysis in looking at "his and her" divorces.

Perhaps, more than others, it was Goffman (1959, 1961, 1963, 1967) who provided us with the most powerful conceptual tools to interpret face-to-face interactions in groups. Through his dramaturgical approach, he theorized about the public ("front stage") versus the private ("back stage") variations of behaviour and both the impression management and the team work required to keep the two separate. He also introduced us to the crucial importance of saving face and the collective effort to restore face when someone has lost face. In Goffman, personal relations are likened to a well-choreographed dance, where all members partake in a social drama with relatively well-understood scripts. It is important to understand that Goffman's dramaturgical perspective is *not* about lying, misleading, manipulating, or deceiving. Instead, all interactants are seen to gain by partaking in the socially acceptable performance, because failing to preserve social boundaries is seen as embarrassing to all. However, this choreographed "social dance" has its limits. For example, in his ingenious analysis of stigma, Goffman (1963) identified circumstances where people or categories will be transformed into the stigmatized other in order to differentiate them from the self. Unfortunately, those who are stigmatized also learn to fit into the stigmatized role, where their actions and self-presentation come to reinforce and legitimize the accusations of the stigmatizers. In asylums, the selves are lost in an increasing level of negative homogenization (1961). Goffman calls these types of places "total institutions." All forms of "othering" are sources of conflict among individuals and between people and institutions. The conflict puts a wide wedge between those who are stigmatized and those who are doing the stigmatizing. It is not surprising to see the applicability of Goffman's analytical theories in the conflicts narrated by many of our contributors.

Feminist Contributions to the Family Literature

Powerful as they are, interactionist theories can best work at understanding families at the micro level. However, both the literature and personal experience show that there are also macro-level and power-based factors at play in engendering family conflict. Therefore, although micro factors are crucial in understanding conflict, macro determinants are also significant.

Since its beginnings in the early 1970s, second-wave feminism has contributed much to sociology at both the theoretical and methodological levels. At the theoretical level, feminists have started dismantling traditional assumptions about the functionality of families by asking, "Functional for whom?" Thus, feminist thought has engendered a new vision of families as collections of diverse individuals who may be bound by intimacy and affection but are also differentiated in power, influence, and access to resources (Friedan, 1963;

Lorber & Farrell, 1991; Luxton, 1980; Smith, 1974). Rather than accepting that the division of labour is necessary and desirable—a functionalist assumption, starting from Durkheim (1933) and finding its apex in Parsons (1968)—feminist scholars have critically evaluated the gendered division of labour as a conflictual form of oppression of women (Armstrong & Armstrong, 1982; Fox & Luxton, 2001; Frye, 2000; Nelson, 2010).[3] Feminist theories, especially of the Marxist or socialist types, have also questioned the role of the state and challenged states to shoulder more responsibility for their citizens.

More recently, feminist thought has more effectively combined with traditional conflict theories in what is called the feminist political economy position. In feminist political economy, it is argued that clusters of social and political institutions and social relations disadvantage individuals and groups. Moreover, feminist political economy is concerned with untangling how dominant and powerful social processes empower certain groups while creating disadvantages between men and women, married and non-married people, heterosexual and same-sex couples, and whites and non-whites. In a way, then, political economy invites us to focus our critical lens on class, power, political ideology, gender, and even conceptualizations of morality (Armstrong & Armstrong, 1982; Mandell, 2010). Although individual problems may appear to be due to individual circumstances, feminist political economy shows us that they are irrefutably linked to social, structural, political, and economic conditions, as well as the ideological milieux from which they spring.

Methods

Research methods are ways to establish links between different social concepts and to find causal patterns, assuming there are such patterns to be found. Research methods are a way of generating novel, reliable, valid, and generalizable knowledge about socially meaningful topics. What questions we ask and how we ask them, what we study, how we draw our samples, and how we present the collected data are all part of methods (Babbie, 1986; Lofland & Lofland, 1995). Although we do not wish to argue that there is a one-to-one correspondence between the theoretical positions and the research methodologies investigators use, there is nevertheless a link between the two.

Quantitative Research
Mainstream sociology's dominant methodological outlook has been positivist. Positivism is slanted toward the collection of "objective" evidence or

facts that are carefully quantified, or at least quantifiable. The samples used in positivistic research are often randomized to prevent any form of systemic biases from tainting the collected data. The data are often in the form of numbers (quantitative) or are easily quantifiable (percentages, ratios). In quantitative research, the "objectivity" of the researcher from his or her research is of prime importance. The goal of positivistic research has been to discover general "truths" that can be applicable in a variety of settings, which is called "generalizability." The workhorse of positivist sociology is the survey, where respondents are asked a host of questions that researchers have pre-selected and, through increasingly sophisticated analyses, probabilistic or statistical expectations and inferences are produced.

Positivistic, quantitative research often uses deductive reasoning, where hypotheses (testable statements) are generated from existing theories. This type of research has generally worked well for many sociological quests, such as the macro studies of inequality, social or global stratification, and studies of crime and deviance.

Qualitative/Observational Research

Social interactionist research has mostly utilized either quantitative or qualitative observations of small group interactions. In social interactionism, meanings, values, and styles of interaction are important. The creation of norms and how they change (or resist change) have also been topics of interest. Although many variations are available, William Whyte's *Street Corner Society* (1943), Bales's small group interactions (Bales, 1953; Bales, Strodtbeck, Mills, & Roseborough, 1951), and Goffman's studies of *Stigma* (1963) and *Asylums* (1961) are the prime examples of qualitative/observational methods. Some of these studies are theory driven (deductive), and others include observations which have eventually contributed to theory building (inductive). With the exception of a few (e.g., Bales et al., 1951), most interactionist studies are qualitative (Berg, 1989; Denzin, 1997, 2000).

Feminist Research

Feminist scholars have expanded sociological methods in order to make them better equipped to the study of "sensitive topics," "power dynamics," and the exploration of "multiple truths" (Eichler, 1997b; Luxton, 1980; Smith, 1974). Feminist theorists have repeatedly demonstrated that positivism's insistence on objectivity and overreliance on survey methods and quantification make it much too blunt a tool for the study of more sensitive topics. Feminist researchers have rightly argued that the study of interpersonal conflict and strife that is based on such sensitive topics as gender, race, ethnicity, faith, or sexuality requires methods that give context to events, that level off the power differences between the researcher and the participant, and that give voice to the historically silenced. These researchers have called not only for a reconceptualization of theoretical orientations and a refocusing of research questions, but also for a reconstruction of data-gathering strategies. Thus, feminist methodologies question the assumptions (and even the desirability) of objectivity. Instead, they insist on the importance of subjective meanings and of the contextualization of events and recollections. Feminist methodologies are also cognizant of the role of power, not only in the social phenomenon they study but also within the research environment (e.g., researcher versus participants; those who fund research versus those who carry out research). In a way, there is a surprising similarity between some of the methodological tools used by interactionists and the methodological innovations of feminist research, although traditional interactionists are not feminists, and most feminists are not interactionists. Nevertheless, participant observations and ethnographic research rather than pencil-and-paper responses are now frequently utilized methods for sensitive topics.

In general, most feminist research is inductive, rather than deductive. This means that, rather than deriving rigid hypotheses from what are considered to be general truths (traditional theories), feminist research focuses on the gathered information, with the possibility that many observations taken together may lead to a theoretical formulation. Moreover, because feminist researchers give context its due importance, knowledge generated from meticulous observations is expected to lead to partial truths. Rather than seeking an all-encompassing theory, feminist research starts from the assumption that multiple realities, rather than a single truth, are possible. For example, it is acknowledged that depending on one's multiple positions (locatedness) in the world—being a woman versus being a man, white versus non-white, rich versus poor, heterosexual versus lesbian/gay, and so on—social relations will be perceived and experienced in substantially different ways. Therefore, rather than privileging one type of research (qualitative), feminists often use multiple strategies, such as in-depth interviews, participant observations, open-ended questions, historical documents, and narratives. In feminist research, one of the main goals is to find out how power and influence are configured in social relations, and in turn, how power and influence differentials end up determining social meanings and interpersonal outcomes. Feminists also see an undeniable link between what are considered personal troubles and the social/structural conditions that fuel those troubles.

Within the new methodological tools introduced by interactionists and feminists, we are increasingly seeing the use of narration or autonarration. The latter is not new, and it has frequently been used as a methodological tool in the humanities, especially by historians. Ellis (2004) defines autoethnography as "research, writing, story, and method that connect the autobiographical and personal to the cultural, social and political" (p. xix). For Reed-Danahay (1997), autoethnography is both a text and a method (p. 9). An oral or written narrative is considered both an instrument in personal growth and a source of knowledge for others. It is argued that both the listener/reader and the narrator can be enriched through the experience (Schettini & Aiello, 2004). The applications of autonarration in the social sciences are still rare, but growing. Ellis (2004) explains this relative absence in the following ways: "It's amazingly difficult. It's certainly not something that most people do well. Social scientists usually don't write well enough. Or they're not sufficiently introspective about their feelings or motives, or the contradictions they experience" (pp. xviii). We would like to add that most social scientists are trained in observing others from the relative safety the researcher role provides. Opening up their skeletons for the world to see may be particularly hard for them. We are exceptionally grateful to the 10 authors in this book who dared to tell their own stories, in their own words.

Generally, autonarrators tell their own stories according to how they see the events in question playing out in their own lives, in the time frame they choose, and in the order they deem important (Reed-Danahay, 1997). This is especially important in studies of people who have not been adequately heard in more traditional studies utilizing more traditional (especially, quantitative) methods. Women, children, the aged, non-whites, immigrants, and other members of historically marginalized groups thus have an opportunity to add their voices to the creation of knowledge without being harnessed by the preconceived disciplinary requirements or biases of researchers (Schettini & Aiello, 2004). Narration allows the nuanced realities and the context of social processes and events to be captured in their full complexity. Moreover, although narratives may be highly individualized, qualitative researchers argue that it is still possible to garner insights from different stories that can be generalized beyond each unique story. It is our contention that the narratives in this book will add depth, context, and colour to the studies of family conflict, without forcing the narrators to fit their experiences into preconceived categories.

The Unique Contribution of This Book

In this book, we do not start from a pre-set theoretical position. Likewise, we do not have a specific hypothesis to test or any vested interest in proving or disproving theoretical positions. Neither did we restrict the theoretical position our contributing authors could take. However, this general flexibility should not mean that this collection is haphazard or without focus. On the contrary, we do start with some assumptions about families: for example, that they can be cradles of intense, sometimes even irrational emotions. We also start from the assumption that the family institution, especially in its "traditional" form, is an arena for differential power and influence. So, as editors, we have to admit that our orientation is more in line with interactionist and feminist theories about the family than functionalist ones. For example, we start from an acute awareness of how class, race, gender, age, sexual orientation, and the historical and ideological milieux of the family dynamics will colour the experience of conflict. We are also keenly aware of the possibility that, according to the historical context, the ideological milieu, and the gendered relationship of the players, some aspects of the conflict may be subdued and other aspects may be magnified. Nevertheless, the narration and most of the interpretation of the stories belong to the individual authors. We did not prescribe any format, we did not define any role, and we did not require any particular theoretical position from the contributors. We only asked the authors to provide a truthful narrative of a family conflict, as they saw it (see the call for chapters in the Appendix). As editors and as authors, we are aware of the fact that the same stories might have been told quite differently if another family member were narrating them. However, this possibility does not detract from the importance of the current stories. Instead, it underscores the complexity of family interactions and the possibility of differential views and experiences. This complexity also helps us to understand why people often get caught up in family conflicts in the first place. We totally acknowledge and respect the particular view of our authors; at the same time, we acknowledge that their views are just one of many possible ways of seeing the narrated events.

We also let our authors define what *they* perceive the boundaries of their families to be, rather than defining for them what their family should look like. As the readers will soon find out, the historical, spatial, and geographic boundaries of the families in the narratives are quite varied. Some span continents, others cross provincial or city boundaries. Also, who is included and who is excluded from the narratives vary. In some narratives, conflict among the currently living members of families is addressed; in others, people who have passed away continue to exert a strong influence on how the conflict unfolds. In some narratives, the conflicting members live in close proximity; in others, they live oceans apart. In each case, we see the conflict through our authors' eyes and through their words, but, as readers, we have the right to develop our own alternate explanations. The narratives in this book explore subjective meanings, not objective truths.

The Methods and Their Ethical Implications

In July of 2008, we sent out a call for chapters (Appendix) to colleagues we knew from many years of involvement in the International Sociological Association and/or the Canadian Sociological and Anthropological Association. Because this book is about serious forms of family conflict, and because academicians are asked to write about their own families, we chose to invite contributors whom we knew personally and ones who knew the seriousness of our work. Our original desire was to gather 12 narratives, but we could get only 10. We did not refuse any submission; instead, we worked with contributors when they needed clarification about what this book was about. Editorial changes were suggested for each chapter, and in the case of some chapters, this was done more than once. However, we made sure that the editing did not compromise the content of the stories being told.

Ethics

We believe that no sociological inquiry is possible without an honest discussion about ethics. As established sociologists with long research and publication track records, and as editors of this collection, we are keenly aware of the ethical dilemmas in addressing conflict in family relations. We acknowledge that numerous ethical dilemmas may have confronted the authors because each author is closely related to the conflict he or she has written about (Ellis, 2004). We know this dilemma first-hand, because we are also the authors of the first two chapters. Yet, we take comfort in knowing that none of the narratives were gathered for "research" purposes. Our authors were allowed to tell what they wanted to tell.

In narrating family conflicts, how much each author divulges, how many others the conflict in question involves, whether the author sought some kind of permission from others before making his or her narrative public, and the extent to which the author attempts to protect the identities of others in the story all have ethical undertones. We did suggest to the authors that their contributions could be published anonymously (Appendix). We also suggested that they could use pseudonyms for the family members in their stories. Beyond these basic reminders, our authors were the ones who chose different strategies to deal with the ethical implications of their own narratives. For example, in Chapter 1, the author uses pseudonyms from Greek mythology to refer to the members of her family. Her family lives in Turkey, which has a population of more than 75 million, so she is quite comfortable sharing her story with Western readers, who are extremely unlikely to meet the people in her narrative. The known identity of the author is her own choice. The author of Chapter 3 has chosen to use middle names for his family members. In Chapter 9, the author has chosen to refer to the members of her family only through relational terms (middle brother, baby brother, etc.). Moreover, it was also her wish to publish her narrative anonymously. The author of Chapter 7 has taken a similar tack and has referred to his family members by their positions (father, sister, brother, etc.). It is also interesting that the same author has chosen to use a completely different name to represent a version of himself who has accepted his sexual orientation (gay) while disguising his sexual identity within his family relations. In Chapter 8, the author uses her current name for the chapter, and she talks about her harrowing experiences of father–daughter incest. Yet, in real life, she has chosen to change her name and has basically cut off all but absolutely minimal contact with her mother. In Chapter 5, the siblings are referred to by pseudonyms, whereas only relational terms are used for the parents. In Chapter 10, the story is about a distant relative who lived part of her adult life as the mistress of a well-to-do married man. The author uses the first name of the central figure, who has long passed away. All the authors in this book, in their own way, have set their own boundaries of anonymity and confidentiality in response to the ethical implications of the narrative. What is crystal clear is that all of the authors have used a respectful language for the individuals in their narratives, despite the adversarial positions they may hold. As editors, we thank our contributors for their sensitivity. We also ask our readers to read these narratives with the utmost respect for the authors, known or anonymous, who have shared their family conflicts with them. Having written similar stories ourselves (Chapters 1 and 2), we know how difficult this process was and is.

In the narratives, the readers need to be cognizant of each author's locatedness and emotional involvement within the conflictual event(s) the story presents. How much of the author's narrative is reflective of the complexity of the events and how much of it is based on the standpoint of the author are worthy of contemplation. We have no doubt that the stories would have been somewhat different if someone other than the current authors had told them. As editors, we have made no attempt to check facts, corroborate events, or incorporate other people's views or judgments about the narratives. Each chapter simply captures a narrative of family turmoil from a single, unique perspective—the author's. We hope that all these courageous efforts will produce new insights for the authors, as well as provide food for thought for the readers, academic or otherwise.

In Chapter 1 (A. Sev'er), we meet an originally close and loving family which becomes fragmented after the sudden death of a baby girl. According to the narrator (the aunt of the baby girl), the bereaved mother's relationship with her own mother, her sister, and her husband irreversibly changed after this tragic loss. The ripples of the tragedy also extended to other relationships. For example, both the mother and the aunt (the author) divorced soon after the tragedy. Both the mother and the grandmother had unusually high expectations from the granddaughter that followed. Possibly with the exception of the grandmother, each member of the family picked up the pieces and moved on with his or her life. However, the family as a whole was not able to recover from the original loss, blame, and segmentation they experienced.

In Chapter 2 (J. Trost), we meet another family, this time in Sweden, that is grappling with a tragic loss. After giving birth to a baby boy, a young mother becomes clinically depressed. The narrator in this case is the uncle of the young mother. Rather than seeking medical attention, the young woman increasingly isolates herself from her husband and her baby, and eventually she commits suicide. In the grip of her profound loss, the grandmother (the author's sister) finds her own salvation in completely rejecting her son-in-law and her grandson. Moreover, the ensuing conflict spreads to other immediate and extended family members, who increasingly find themselves on opposing sides of a widening family fissure. The narrator puts some emotional distance between himself and the tragic suicide in his narration. Rather than analyzing the family conflict as *he* has experienced it, he "symbolically" invites three conventional sociologists to carry out the analysis for him.

In Chapter 3 (S. Ungar), we are introduced to a family that is incrementally losing one of their adult sons to the mental ravages of bipolar disorder. The narrator is the brother who lives at a distance but nevertheless shares his family's pain and bewilderment. The story captures what mental illness is, how it progresses, and how it may still be a source of stigma for the families involved. In this case, we read about the parents' (especially the mother's) continuous sacrifices, literally until the end of their lives, to provide some sense of normalcy for their son. The parents themselves experience increasing isolation, their lives revolving around the declining mental health of their son. Love, guilt, responsibility, shame, and hope weave a unique tapestry in this family's strained relationships, and eventually, external groups bring some relief and comfort despite the decline in mental health.

In Chapter 4 (T. Kepe), the powerful narrative transports us to a different continent (Africa). There, we again find a family struggling with deteriorating mental health—in this case, that of an elder grandmother. The narrator is the grandson who now works and lives in Canada. For an extended period of time in his childhood, the author was raised by his grandmother, and he still has very complex and affectionate feelings for her. He also has complex, and at times, contradictory feelings toward his biological mother. In this case, the readers become privy to a cultural clash between a Canadianized grandson/son and the very different norms and values of his South African family. The provision and quality of the care the grandmother receives is contentious. The grandmother's eventual death resolves some of the ongoing tensions, but the emotional distances created during the last few years of her life do not allow a restful place for the family skeletons.

Chapter 5 (B. Lashewicz) is also about the declining physical and mental health of an aging mother. In this case, the narrator is an academic who has closely worked with one of the sons, who is providing most of the day-to-day care of the mother. The readers see most of the events through this particular son's eyes, because he has insisted that the other siblings not be contacted by the author. In this case, most of the tension is between the brothers and the sisters, who happen to have divergent views about what is best for their mother. Although they all seem to have the best interests of the mother in mind, it is doubtful that some of the ongoing friction and controlling behaviours benefit the mother.

In Chapter 6 (H. Kamya), we are faced with an almost miraculous ascendance of a refugee originally from Uganda (the author). He eventually succeeds in getting a Ph.D. from Harvard and establishing an enviable academic career for himself. Along the way, he meets a mentor who profoundly helps him in his new life. Despite his many blessings in the United States, he also has to live with the fact that many of his family and friends were slaughtered in Uganda, and those who have survived are still facing battles with AIDS. In this moving narrative, readers will find the conquest of good over bad, light over dark, and an individual's struggle to better himself against all odds.

However, the personal triumphs are shadowed by the pain of what has been left behind.

Chapter 7 (K. H. Wong) is again about an individual man's struggle (the author), but this time the struggle is about trying to come to terms with his own sexual orientation. The struggle is exacerbated because he is from a traditional Chinese family, which insists upon a heterosexual identity, a heterosexual marriage, and fatherhood for their son. The long-term conflict, especially between the father and the author, has created many skeletons in this family's relationships. The presence of verbal and physical abuse toward the son has created deep wounds and burned many emotional bridges. Yet, in this story, the conflict within the self is at least as great as the conflict with the father; as readers, we see the author's almost superhuman effort to come to terms with both.

Chapter 8 (S. Transken) is about father–daughter incest. The author courageously explores the scars left by her long-term incestuous violation by her biological father. In her story, not only do readers come face to face with the evil of the sexual abuse of a child, they also "hear" the silences of the mother and siblings. To her credit, the author has survived the abuse through her own resilience and creativity; however, the toll that the father's exploitation has taken on this woman and on the whole family is insurmountable. In this case, it is exceptionally fortunate that long-term victimization and suffering has not ended in bitterness and giving up. Instead, the author has found her solace in helping others, by becoming an educator, writer, and poet.

Chapter 9 (Anonymous) is about a relatively large rural family. The parents toil to provide a decent life for their four children, and to a large degree, they succeed. Yet the struggle to provide the necessities apparently has precluded there being much affection, closeness, and mutual happy times between the parents and their children. Moreover, the narrator, who is the only female child among brothers, claims that there were both gender- and age-based inequalities in the upbringing of the siblings. However, the most hurtful conflict transpired not between the parents and their (now adult) children but between the youngest brother and the rest of the siblings. In this case, the culprit is seen as the sister-in-law, who has played the historical family tensions to create new fractures. Rather than questioning the controlling, domineering, and even threatening behaviour of his wife, the youngest brother's strategy has been rejection of his own siblings.

In Chapter 10 (C. Krekula), we are transported back to an earlier time, and we come face to face with another narrative that has highly gendered implications. The location is rural Sweden, and the narrator is a distant niece writing about a great-aunt. It seems that this family has had what they considered to be an ominous skeleton in their closet, known about by many but talked about by few. Through bits and pieces of information gleaned from pursed lips and lowered voices, the author eventually puts the pieces of the puzzle together and brings light into a dark closet. As it turns out, the great aunt was a long-term mistress to a well-to-do married man. He had fathered not only a number of children within his legal marriage but also four children with his mistress. The narrative is about the status of the mistress as opposed to that of the wife, and the status of the out-of-wedlock children as opposed to that of their "legitimate" brothers and sisters. As the story explores how society constructs social roles and how the society privileges some roles over others, readers gain insight into how different are the privileges bestowed on these functionally similar but morally differentiated roles. Moreover, the differential privileges mirror the highly gendered order of the time.

In sum, after trying to decipher some of the relevant theoretical, methodological, and ethical debates about family conflict, and after providing snapshots of each of the chapters, we now invite our readers to read each of the narratives for themselves. We invite our senior or graduate students; fellow academicians in sociology, social work, psychology, social anthropology, and other social sciences fields; and all other intelligent readers to read these stories with an open mind but also a critical one. We invite our readers to consider how the stories might have been different or similar if someone else from the same family had told them, and why. We want our readers to think how culture, age, class, and gender variables are intertwined in these narratives. We want our readers to be cognizant about the time and the place in which the family interactions in the narratives take place. Most importantly, we want our readers to find aspects which transcend the individuality and the uniqueness of the stories. Are there common denominators that help us to think about family conflict in more general terms? If so, what are they? Do any of these stories generate new insights about understanding new or old conflicts and frictions in our own family lives? We want our readers to compare and contrast the narrative method with more traditional methods used in social research. Can we reduce the insights in these stories to "numbers" and "percentages"? Why or why not?

Notes

1 *Mommie Dearest* (1978) is a daughter's narrative that spells out the cold, cruel, and abusive parenting style of one of the great film stars of yesteryear, Joan Crawford.

2 Of course, we are not talking about extremes where brain injuries or debilitating diseases like dementia or Alzheimer's reduce or erase the normal functioning of the brain. Even in those cases, there are many choices being made, but the rational self may not be the one who is making them.

3 It is through this shift in approach and reconfiguration of focus that sociology of the family has started to enrich its social vision. Perhaps one of the clearest examples of this much needed expansion was the new focus on gendered forms of violence—most specifically, the study of men's violence against women in intimate relationships (Dobash & Dobash, 1979; Sev'er, 1999, 2002).

References

Ambert, A. M. (2005). *Changing families: Relationships in context.* Toronto: Pearson.

Armstrong, P., & Armstrong, H. (1982). *The double ghetto.* Toronto: McClelland & Stewart.

Babbie, E. (1986). *The practice of social research* (4th ed.). Belmont, CA: Wadsworth.

Baker, M. (2006). *Restructuring family policies: Convergences and divergences.* Toronto: University of Toronto Press.

Bales, R. F. (1953). The equilibrium problem in small groups. In T. Parsons, R. F. Bales, & E. A. Shils (Eds.), *Working papers in the theory of action.* New York: Free Press.

Bales, R. F., Strodtbeck, F. L., Mills, T. M., & Roseborough, M. E. (1951). Channels of communication in small groups. *American Sociological Review, 16,* 461–468.

Berg, B. L. (1989). *Qualitative research methods for the social sciences.* Boston: Allyn & Bacon.

Bernard, J. (1972). *The future of marriage.* New York: Batman.

Böll, H. (1966). "Murke's collected silences." In L. Vennewitz (Tr.), *18 stories.* New York: McGraw-Hill.

Coser, L. (1956). *The functions of conflict.* New York: Free Press.

Denzin, N. (1997). *Interpretive ethnography: Ethnographic practices for the 21st century.* Thousand Oaks, CA.: Sage.

Denzin, N. (2000). Introduction: The discipline and practice of qualitative research. In N. Denzin & Y. Lincoln (Eds.), *Handbook of qualitative research* (2nd ed., pp. 1–28). Thousand Oaks, CA.: Sage.

Deutsch, M. (1973). *The resolution of conflict.* New Haven, CT: Yale University Press.

Dobash, R. E., & Dobash, R. P. (1979). *Violence against wives: A case against patriarchy.* New York: Routledge.

Durkheim, E. (1933). *The division of labour in society.* New York: Free Press.

Durkheim, E. (1951). *Suicide.* New York: Free Press.

Eichler, M. (1997a). *Family shifts: Families, policies, and gender equality.* Toronto: Oxford.

Eichler, M. (1997b). Feminist methodology. *Current Sociology, 45*(2), 9–36.

Eidelson, R. J., & Eidelson, J. I. (2003). Dangerous ideas: Five beliefs that propel people toward conflict. *American Psychologist, 58*, 182–192.

Ellis, C. (2004). *The ethnographic I.* New York: Altamira.

Folger, J. P., Poole, M. S., & Stutman, R. K. (2009). *Working through conflict.* Boston: Allyn & Bacon.

Ford, R. (1994). Conflict and bargaining. In M. Foschi & E. J. Lawler (Eds.), *Group processes: Sociological analysis* (pp. 231–256). Chicago: Nelson Hall.

Fox, B., & Luxton, M. (2001). Conceptualizing family. In B. Fox (Ed.), *Family patterns and gender relations.* Toronto: Oxford.

Freud, S. (1951). *Introductory lectures on psychoanalysis.* New York: Free Press.

Friedan, B. (1963). *The feminine mystique.* New York: Dell.

Frye, M. (2000). Oppression. In A. Minas (Ed.), *Gender basics* (2nd ed., pp. 10–16). Toronto: Wadsworth.

Goetting, A. (1986). The six stations of remarriage: Developmental tasks of remarriage after divorce. In A. S. Skolnick & J. H. Skolnick (Eds.), *Family in transition* (5th ed., pp. 351–365). Boston: Little, Brown.

Goffman, E. (1959). *The presentation of self in everyday life.* New York: Doubleday.

Goffman, E. (1961). *Asylums: Essays on the social situation of mental patients and other inmates.* Garden City, NY: Doubleday.

Goffman, E. (1963). *Stigma: Notes on management of spoiled identity.* Englewood Cliffs, NJ: Prentice-Hall.

Goffman, E. (1967). *Interaction ritual: Essays on face-to-face behavior.* New York: Aldine.

Lofland, J., & Lofland, L. H. (1995). *Analyzing social settings* (3rd ed.). Belmont, CA: Wadsworth.

Lorber, J. A., & Farrell, S.A. (Eds.). (1991). *The social construction of gender.* Newbury Park, CA: Sage.

Luxton, M. (1980). *More than a labour of love: Three generations of women's work in the home.* Toronto: Women's Press.

Mandell, N. (2010). *Feminist issues* (5th ed.). Toronto: Pearson.

Marx, K. (1978). In R. C. Tucker (Ed.), *The Marx–Engels reader.* New York: Norton.

Mead, G. H. (1934). *Mind, self, and society.* Chicago: University of Chicago Press.

Michaels, A. (1998). *Fugitive pieces.* New York: Vintage.

Murdock, G. P. (1949). *Social structure.* New York: Macmillan.

Nelson, A. (2010). *Gender in Canada* (4th ed.). Toronto: Pearson.

Nixon, H. L. (1979). *The small group.* Englewood Cliffs, NJ: Prentice-Hall.

Parsons, T. (1968). *The social system.* New York: Free Press.

Parsons, T., & Bales, R. F. (1960). *Family socialization and interaction.* Glencoe, IL: Free Press.

Parsons, T., & Shils, E. A. (1962). *Toward a general theory of action.* Cambridge, MA: Harvard University Press.

Perdue, W. D. (1986). *Sociological theory*. Palo Alto, CA: Mayfield.

Pruitt, D. G., & Rubin, J. Z. (1986). *Social conflict: Escalation, stalemate, and settlement*. New York: Random House.

Reed-Danahay, D. (1997). *Auto/ethnography: Rewriting the self and the social*. Oxford: Berg.

Rorty, R. (1993). *Contingency, irony, and solidarity*. Cambridge: Cambridge University Press.

Schettini, B., & Aiello, A. (2004). Autonarration in the group: From personal history to collective, cultural and social history. Psychology Faculty, Second University of Naples. Retrieved from http://www.formazione.unimib.it/v2/DATA/hot/600/schettiniaiello-autonarration in the group.pdf

Sev'er, A. (1999). Exploring the continuum: Increased violence of men and boys against women and girls. *Atlantis, 24*(1).

Sev'er, A. (2002). *Fleeing the house of horrors: Women who have left abusive partners*. Toronto: University of Toronto Press.

Sev'er, A. (2010a). All in the family: Violence against women, children and the aged. D. Cheal (Ed.), *Canadian families today* (2nd ed.). Toronto: Oxford.

Sev'er, A. (2010b). Marriage go-around: Divorce and re-marriage in Canada. N. Mandell & A. Duffy (Eds.), *Canadian families: Diversity, conflict, and change* (4th ed.). Toronto: Nelson.

Simmel, G. (1923). *Soziologie: Untersuchungen über die Formen der Vergesellschaftung*. Leipzig: Duncker & Humblot. (Original work published 1908).

Simmel, G. (1950). *Sociology of Georg Simmel* (K. H. Wolff, Trans.). Glencoe, IL: Free Press.

Simmel, G. (1971). *On individuality and social forms*. (D. N. Levine, Ed.) Chicago: University of Chicago Press.

Smith, D. (1974). Women's perspective as a radical critique of sociology. *Sociological Quarterly, 44*, 7–13.

Statistics Canada. (2001). *2001 census dictionary*. Cat. 92-378-XIE. Retrieved from http://www12.statcan.ca/English/census01/products/reference/dict/index.htm

Statistics Canada. (2006). Census family. *2006 census dictionary*. Cat. 92-566-XWE. Retrieved from http://www12.statcan.gc.ca/census-recensement/2006/ref/dict/fam004-eng.cfm

Stephens, W. (1963). *The family in cross-cultural perspectives*. New York: Holt, Rinehart & Winston.

Strauss, A. L. 1977. *George Herbert Mead on social psychology*. Chicago: University of Chicago Press. (Original work published 1956).

Tedeschi, J. T., Bonoma, T. V., & Schlenker, B. R. (1972). Influence, decision, and compliance. In J. T. Tedeschi (Ed.), *The social influence processes* (pp. 346–418). Chicago: Aldine.

Trost, J. (1988). Conceptualizing the family. *International Sociology, 3*, 301–308.

Whyte, W. F. (1943). *Street corner society*. Chicago: University of Chicago Press.

[1]

A SUDDEN DEATH AND THE LONG-TERM FRAGMENTATION OF A FAMILY

AYSAN SEV'ER

Through the many years of qualitative research I have conducted, I have heard many stories about other people's families. Some were very intense and difficult to hear, even though I hardly knew the players. Knowing how important they had been to the narrators of those intimate details made them especially challenging to write about. Therefore, I always tried to be as accurate, conscientious, and as honest as I could be when I incorporated their stories into my research papers. I tried to give a balanced voice to the voiceless and give some context to what appeared to be blind actions, always trying to preserve the integrity of the story and the dignity of the storyteller. Although those research efforts have been difficult, to say the least, those difficulties pale in comparison to writing a very vexing narrative about my own family.

It is extremely taxing to narrate something so powerful and intertwined, a tale in which I was not only an observer but a day-to-day participant. The events I am about to disclose have been so agonizing for all concerned that they have remained an "unspoken truth" for close to four decades. It is also challenging to recall all the harrowing details in order to capture the true magnitude of the events, because some dimensions stand out in the mind's eye more clearly than others. I also have to acknowledge that, although the facts will remain constant, the interpretation of the events would differ were another member of my family to write this narrative. This holds true for all narratives. Therefore, I have to admit up front that the interpretation of the events I present reflects my own locatedness in the story. I can only vouch for the accuracy of the facts.

Now I will try my best to narrate the unfolding of the tragic case, the aftermath of which altered numerous lives. Since the story is reminiscent of a Greek tragedy, I chose meaningful pseudonyms for the members of my family from Greek myths and tragedies. I encourage the reader to read the footnotes for the pseudonyms. Moreover, I truly believe that the ancient Greeks understood, possibly better than others, the relentlessness of conflict that can arise within and between family members. If it were not for Cronos, who ate all his newborn children so they would not topple his dynasty, and if it were not for Zeus, who killed Cronos (his father) and propagated the Olympian gods by marrying his sister (Hera), we would not have Greek mythology. If it were not for the love/power games of the Olympian Gods and some love/power-thirsty mortals (Helena, Hector, Paris, Agamemnon), we would not have the stories of the Trojan War or the Iliad. So, the exceptionally insightful ancient Greeks have long forewarned family sociologists like us where to concentrate our analytical gaze: conflict. The few names I borrow from the Greek myths are well suited, I believe, to represent the characters in the tragedy of my own family. I will not use a pseudonym for myself.

The Background

In 1966, my father, the truly dedicated, wise, and loving patriarch of our family, died of a heart attack at the age of 55. My mother, whom I will call Agape,[1] was only 44 at the time. My older sister (Demeter)[2] was in her mid-twenties and newly married to a young man (Atlas).[3] They were the love of each other's lives. I had just started my first year at Istanbul University, and my life was as carefree as a life can ever be.

In my view, my father's early departure was the first disaster that pulled the rug out from under my family's relatively well-established, yet often taken for granted, balance on life. My father's early death also led to unpredictable—and, as it turns out, irreversible—developments. Some of these developments helped to deal with the short-term disarray. However, over time, many members of my family, including myself, would have liked to take back some major decisions—though none of us had the power or the resolve to turn back the hands of the clock.

As the younger of my parents' two daughters, I was and am very much a part of this story. Moreover, the series of events and the artifacts of the events I am about to relate have dramatically affected many aspects of my own life. The above notwithstanding, however, this story is not about me. In a way, I just

happened to be the unfortunate bystander within its tumultuous development, a lonely rock standing in the way of a raging river that had jumped its
banks. To continue the rock analogy, sometimes I tumbled with the currents,
sometimes I was able to slow down the churning, but at other times, knowingly or unknowingly, I contributed to its negative force. Without further ado,
here is my narrative.

My mother (Agape) attended my father's funeral in a heavily sedated state,
while I said my goodbyes with many tears. Demeter made all the arrangements. A couple of weeks—or was it a couple of months?—after the funeral,
Demeter and her husband (Atlas) moved into what used to be my parents' (and
my) home. The reason given at the time—and probably, with the best of intentions—was that it was so they could help out Agape after her intense shock and
her irreplaceable loss. It was true that Agape was in no shape to run a house
or parent a daughter who was just turning into a young woman (me). In the
traditional society we lived in at the time (mid-1960s Turkey), the view was
that every household needed a man, and although my father's shoes were
much too large to fill, my sister's husband was the best available surrogate.
Given the mores of Turkish society, unmarried "girls" of any age[4] needed
parental figures in their lives, and since my father was gone and Agape was in
no condition to step up to the plate, Demeter took it upon herself to assume
the in loco parentis role.

Looking back on the events of 1966, at least from my perspective, there
might have been a latent, and much more pragmatic, dimension to Demeter's (and indirectly, Atlas's) move into my parental home. I think the recently
wedded couple saw an advantage in moving into an already established house.
The move gave them the opportunity to rent out for a nice income the flat they
had recently acquired. Although they both worked at well-paying jobs, no one
could deny that their taste for travel, expensive jewellery, good clothes, active
social engagements, and so on, received a further boost from the new living
arrangement. As a young "girl," I also cherished the fact that we all pulled
together under the same roof and continued to be a close family, despite the
fact that we had just lost its stabilizing core. Besides, both Demeter and Atlas
were very generous with their time and often included me in their interesting
social lives.

Within a couple of years, I got married and moved out. Within the same
period of time, what used to be my parents' home was in the process of becoming more and more the "hearth of Demeter" (pun intended). For example,
the furniture changed style and colour soon after the move-in, and the meal

times shifted to accommodate Demeter's and Atlas's hectic lifestyles. Arrangements to visit the home, even if it was to visit Agape, had to comply with Demeter's schedule and availability. Even the visits by Agape's personal friends got regulated. Nevertheless, no one, certainly not Agape, seemed to mind these mild restrictions. If anything, Agape considered herself blessed for her continuing family life after her own husband had "abandoned" her. Having been a single child, Agape had grown up to be childlike, often depending[5] on others to make major decisions for her. Thus, the void that was created by my father's death was incrementally filled by Demeter as her role ascended from eldest daughter to the new matriarch.

The Irreplaceable Loss

What was not on the table at the time of our father's death, but became apparent later, was that Demeter and Atlas were trying to have a child. This was exceptionally good news for all and rejuvenated feelings of happiness and hope for the future, where these emotions were hard to come by after my father's untimely demise. However, for some time their attempts were unsuccessful. The charged atmosphere of expectation made every passing month (and year) a roller coaster—soaring anticipation followed by a fall.

Eventually, it happened: Demeter announced that she was pregnant, and all of us were filled with indescribable joy. It took every single day of a little less than nine months (the birth was slightly premature) to get prepared: paint the baby's room, sew new curtains, decorate the nursery with the best furniture and other baby frills that money could buy, and so on. As the elated aunt-to-be, I bought an Elizabethan baby carriage that cost me more than a full month's salary. I did not mind. This was the first good news, the first blessing my family was to receive since my father's departure. My own wedding ceremony, which had taken place two years after the funeral and about two years before the announcement of Demeter's pregnancy, had been a muted event. This baby's arrival was the real thing!

The delivery was problematic and required a C-section. Thus, baby Aurora[6] came slightly early, but she was absolutely beautiful. Demeter was the queen, and Aurora was the princess in all our lives, and we seemed to leave behind all the dark clouds and rise up to a place of exceptional elation. Agape was truly happy and content after the period of emptiness she had endured. Holding Aurora in her arms, helping Demeter with the breastfeeding sessions, even changing the baby's diapers seemed to be the most joyful events for Agape. As a first-time aunt, I also felt ecstatic, and I started to visit the baby every day, sometimes twice a day, in the morning and at night. Suddenly, my family had found a new core, and the core was Aurora.

Of course, there were a few clouds, but we were too wrapped up in our collective happiness to register them. For example, the doctor who delivered Aurora had told us about the fact that she was slightly premature. We were also cognizant that Aurora's little ears and her little nails were still not fully developed. We were not aware at the time that her little lungs might also have been premature. But Aurora was beautiful, good natured, easy to feed, and gaining weight; so the hospital sent her home. With Demeter and Agape taking the lead, we all received this newcomer into the deepest, most precious parts of our hearts and our lives. None of us, certainly not Demeter or Agape, ever doubted that our little Aurora would blossom into the princess she was destined to become.

Alas, Aurora lived only three weeks. Thus, and by no fault of her own, she first gave my family the greatest joy of our lives and then catapulted us into the deepest of all agonies. To the best of my recollection, this is how Aurora slipped out of our lives: after a hearty feeding and much adoration, Agape had gingerly placed Aurora in her Elizabethan carriage, and in less than 30 minutes, when Demeter checked on her daughter, she was still warm, but gone.

Crib death,[7] they called it, a term that had no place in our family's vocabulary until then and has had no place in our language ever since. Besides, Aurora died in her carriage, not in her crib. Labelling aside, this was a flash of pain of unimaginable proportions. Every blanket, every toy, every spoon and bottle that had been lovingly bought or prepared for little Aurora suddenly became a sight of excruciating torture. The mobile that hung over her crib, which I had crafted out of colorful ribbons to represent exotic birds, tore our hearts as if it had suddenly transformed into a revolving blade. That spring day in 1970, our family, which had collectively recovered from the loss of our father, suffered a wound that still festers.

Grasped in the vice of her agony, Demeter took the bundle that used to be Aurora to the emergency ward of the nearest hospital. In their absence, and struck by an unbearable grief, Agape swallowed every medication in the house to end her own life. Ironically, among the pills she swallowed were Aurora's baby vitamins. Atlas, who was alerted to the unfolding tragedy by the hospital staff, arrived home to find his wife and baby gone and Agape unconscious. He then brought Agape to the same hospital where Demeter and her precious Aurora had gone. Only after so much had already gone wrong did Atlas arrive at my home, with the most ashen complexion I had ever seen on a human face, to bring me a "diluted" version of the grim news. He took me to the hospital, apparently to keep watch over my possibly dying mother, while he himself watched over his deeply wounded wife.

The human mind is capable of hanging on to bizarre images! At the time not yet privy to all the tragic details of the change in our lives but sensing that something was drastically wrong, I remember the oddest details. For example, I remember that I was wearing a scarlet red formal suit, and that I felt uneasy, sick to my stomach, and totally out of place at the hospital. It seemed that everyone in the crowded emergency ward, even those who had their own serious health problems, knew what had happened to us. They knew who I was, as I sat holding my mother's ice-cold hands and staring at her bluish-gray face. I was glowing like a huge stop sign in my scarlet red suit! I remember my mother's parched lips whispering a heart-wrenching, "What a pity, what a pity," over and over, through her drug-induced daze. I remember pleading with her not to leave us at the time we needed her most. I guess it was I who needed her the most, since I felt so alone, so young and helpless.

Agape's suicide attempt was serious, and the fact that she pulled through was a miracle. They had to pump her stomach and repeatedly flush out her system through numerous IVs simultaneously dripping into her veins. Although her life was saved, Agape never emotionally recovered. Neither did Demeter. The fact that Agape was the last person who had placed baby Aurora in her bed turned out to be the guilt chain that yanked these two, as well as the rest of us, through decades of unresolved anguish.

The Short-Term Aftermath

After Aurora's much-too-short life had ended, a life which first brought light and then took it away from our lives, nothing seemed to go right. Words that referred to children, pictures, images, or toys became triggers of intense pain, most particularly for Demeter. We not only learned to self-censor our language, but each one of us became experts at censoring friends, neighbours, workmates, even maids, who might erroneously utter a painful word. We stopped socializing with those who seemed too happy; we even felt guilty for fleeting moments of joy that any one of us experienced. We learned to walk on eggs, either when Agape was around or when Demeter was within earshot. In rare moments when they were together, the interactions turned into a ghostly dance of censored words. There were days when Demeter would not get out of bed; there were days when she would not join visiting guests who had come to give their condolences, although Turkish customs of hospitality were ingrained in all of us. On other days, at least on the surface, things appeared to be all right, until an unexpected trigger would start a new cycle of despair.

Life was equally difficult for Agape, whose body was still recovering from the self-administered poisons and whose mind was overwhelmed by self-inflicted blame. In order to compensate for the "unforgivable sin" she attached to herself—that of a grandmother who had somehow caused the death of her grandchild—Agape imploded. She lost her will to live, and she lost whatever agency she had over her own life. Thus, Demeter became the burning light, and Agape became the moth that turns round and round and round, with not much purpose or effect.

In the following months, things remained bad; the emptiness Aurora had left in our lives was profound, and the sadness of Demeter and Agape agonizing. Moreover, I was immature and young, and I was having a most difficult time dealing with the double loss of my beloved father and my precious niece. I needed a change from the internal loneliness! As it turns out, what I ended up doing helped no one and only made things worse: I got pregnant. Although I wanted this child more than anything else in the world, the first five months of my pregnancy were far from celebratory. Agape's cold reception of the news and the tears that Demeter fought hard to keep back are still etched into my memory. Although they both managed to mutter a few courteous words, the chilling message was loud and clear: I should not have gotten pregnant while my sister was still caught up in the throes of mourning. From the announcement on, my pregnancy became totally invisible. No one said anything directly about it; no one asked how I really felt. Moreover, no one engaged in any preparations for my child, and no one congratulated me or my husband. In another way, my pregnancy was like a mountain, silently shadowing and overwhelming all conversations and interactions. Looking back, I think this period also set in motion my eventual disengagement from my own marriage, since my husband was emotionally far removed from my own suppressed turmoil. It was clear that my child, regardless of who she/he may be, was not going to be the panacea for my family's loss. The initial cold climate surrounding my pregnancy also had a negative effect on my emotional health.

The last four months of my pregnancy were a little more bearable, although not much more "visible" or more acknowledged. Fortunately, Demeter also got pregnant, and that news immediately took on pivotal importance. The delivery of my daughter was exceptionally long and difficult, and to their credit, my mother and sister kept vigil just outside the delivery room. My husband had gone out for lunch. Thus, Electra[8] joined a mother who loved her more than anything else in the world, but she also joined a family that was already fragmented and unable to receive her as the gift she truly was.

Looking back at the old, yellowing photos, I am astonished to see how few pictures I have of my pregnancy and to see that in most of these pictures I am alone, without my sister and mother. What is also astonishing is that there is not a single picture of Electra with her grandmother from the first few months of her life, and only a handful after the arrival of Demeter's second daughter (Selene).[9] When Electra was a year old, my husband and I immigrated to Canada. Although immigration had its own serious challenges and costs, the move also released us, albeit only partially, from the grind of a very sad past.

The Long-Term Aftermath

My insights about the long-term effects of Aurora's loss on my family are harder to substantiate, because they materialized during the safe distance of my new life in Canada. Nevertheless, I am still convinced that my family never truly recovered from the loss of Aurora, whom we all intensely loved. Although Selene's birth soothed some of the rawness of Aurora's loss, Demeter and Agape still live in an atmosphere of continuous tension that exacerbates each other's pain. Yet, although these two women have trouble living with one another, neither has considered the option of living without the other for the last four decades. I think the intensity of their mutual pain has chained them to one another.

The role in which Selene was placed is also complex: she has always been very privileged, but sometimes over-controlled. Through no fault of her own, and whether she likes it or not, her life has been shadowed by a sister she never met. Moreover, Selene has had to deal with the overabundance of love that has tightly—she might say much too tightly—enveloped her since before the day she was born. Having experienced a tremendous loss, neither Demeter nor Agape was able to offer Selene an easygoing, gently protective sense of belonging. Instead, Selene had to live under two pairs of eyes that were always focused on her and never blinked. In an abstract way, she was expected to fill the gap her sister had left behind and be the panacea for the wound Aurora's loss had caused. Although Selene turned out to be an amazing young woman who is bright, outgoing, successful, and cheerful, she also has some deep-rooted resentment of suffocating forms of love. As soon as she could, and despite intense pressure from her mother and grandmother, Selene managed to move to the United States and make New York her permanent home. It is my contention that, despite the initial difficulties, the vast geographic distance she placed between herself and her overprotective family eventually saved Selene, Demeter, and Agape from a more apocalyptic confrontation. However, for Demeter and for Agape, Selene's permanent departure will always be viewed as a betrayal of their "endless love" and "sacrifice" for her.

My own relationship with Selene has always been amicable, despite the fact that I moved to Canada before she celebrated her first birthday. Since her move to the United States, we have gotten much closer. I truly cherish her humour, her exuberant energy, and her self-determination. I think she appreciates the guidance and love I am able to offer without too many strings and pressures. Selene also has a close relationship with Atlas and a close attachment to Agape. The love between Selene and Demeter is undeniable, but it is often tainted by Selene's struggles for her independence and Demeter's demand for close proximity and loyalty.

As far as the intense love and enviable friendship between Demeter and Atlas is concerned, that regrettably ended a short time after Selene's arrival. Although both were deeply affected by the loss of their infant daughter, Atlas wanted to move forward, celebrate life, and enjoy his new daughter without the omnipresent shadow of the past. In sharp contrast, Demeter wanted to hang on to her memories, repeatedly rehash her pain, and continuously grieve for her lost daughter, and she expected Atlas to grieve along with her. Their different coping mechanisms and needs no longer allowed a nurturing space for each other. Instead, their contrasting strategies pushed them apart. Although they remain friends to this day, their marriage crumbled. Demeter has never married again, dedicating her whole life to Selene's needs, wants, and well-being. Atlas has entered and exited from a number of other marriages and fathered two other children from two consecutive wives. To his credit, his relationship with Selene is close, warm, and non-judgmental.

As for my own marriage, it ended a few years after our immigration to Canada. Although my husband was a decent man, with no bad habits and only very minor shortcomings, we were truly the wrong match for each other. His absence from this emotional narrative is not an oversight but is indicative of his overall absence from any and all emotional dimensions of my life. We separated upon my request and have not been able to remain friends. Like Selene, Electra also became a beautiful woman with an exceptional mind and an incredible career. Unfortunately, my relationship with my beloved and only daughter has been deeply etched with problems. Electra always complained about too much love and control over her life, and possibly she was right. Having lost my niece in the blink of an eye, I may have turned into the controlling mother my daughter resented. So, Electra chooses to have no meaningful contact with Agape, Demeter, Selene, or myself. As cliché as it sounds, the saying "we hurt the ones we love the most" certainly rings true within my family.

Among all this fragmentation, I find Agape's life to be the saddest of all. Although she sacrificed whatever she had—her time, energy, independence, home, and income, as well as her old friends—she never found peace, and she never forgave herself. Despite her sacrifices, tension between Agape and Demeter is a daily occurrence. There came a point when nothing, absolutely nothing, consoled Agape, with the exception of Selene's proximity and presence. She was crushed when Selene permanently moved to the United States. Although the sharp edges of this crucial decision have been slightly chiselled across time, Agape's singular object of obsession is still Selene. However, despite all the admirable qualities of the love with which she has showered Selene, her obsession has been contentious and her continual self-blame exasperating. As an attempt at self-redemption, Agape transferred the title of her home into Selene's name, virtually renouncing her other granddaughter (Electra) and her other daughter (me). As for Demeter, she was already the reigning matriarch of Agape's house, and remains so after the deed transferred from her mother to her daughter.

So, What Went So Wrong?

Why did this family of smart, loving, well-meaning, and reasonable people become so fragmented? What went wrong? The short answer in this case is that everything that could have gone wrong did. I believe that all families, regardless of who their members are, where they live, or which stratification they come from, at one time or another are bound to face intense crisis. What differentiates one family from another are the cultural and social matrices in which they live, how the individuals deal with crisis, and whether they are able to leave the crisis behind and move on. All other possibly wonderful aspects aside, families are products of their social conditions. They are also deep pools of interpersonal emotion. Some families draw nourishment from that deep pool in times of crisis, and some families drown in the pool because it gets murky and turbulent. In the case of my family's fragmentation, the process was long-term, slow, and gnawing in its destructive effects. In the beginning, the love we shared was able to sustain us during the crisis of my father's unexpected death. However, the intensity of that love (and loss) also demanded its own "slaves" and "masters." Some of our problems were interpersonal, but others had their roots in the social milieu and in the structural constraints.

First and foremost, Aurora's demise was closely related to the efficacy—or lack of it—of the health care system available in Istanbul at the time (1970). Although Demeter and Atlas were able to afford the best available care for their infant daughter, even that care was insufficient to protect a premature child. We never knew what crib death was, had no access to baby monitors, and were never warned about the low but insidious correlation between prematurity and crib death incidents. We were never alerted to the possible dangers of quick weight gain in premature babies; in our unawareness, we rejoiced in baby Aurora's appetite. Besides, the hospital could have—should have—kept our vulnerable baby for longer observation. The point is that our family crisis took place within a structural matrix of weaknesses.

The lack of accurate information about the disaster that struck our family, and the lack of knowledge about the shortcomings of the medical system at the time, led to a never-ending cycle of blame: Agape blaming herself for placing Aurora in her carriage on that particular day; Demeter, for allowing Agape to do it rather than doing it herself; me, for getting pregnant without waiting for Demeter to have a second turn; Atlas, for not being capable of sharing Demeter's grief; my husband, for being emotionally absent. The grip of these cycles of blame was so powerful that even when we did accumulate information about the unpredictability of crib deaths, we were not able to transcend the pattern of *personalized* blame. In Agape's case, eternal self-blame has consumed the rest of her life, and it has even tainted the relationships that might have given her some relief and comfort (for example, lack of closeness with Electra and with me).

There is also a strongly gendered dimension to this tragedy. Although socialization of men and women is differentiated in most cultures (Brettell & Sargent, 2001; Gilligan, 1982; Marshall, 2000; Nelson & Robinson, 2002; Renzetti & Curran, 1999; Wood, 2003; Zinn, Hondagneu-Sotelo, & Messner, 2000), traditional Turkish culture makes a virtue of these differentiations (Kadioğlu, 1994; Kandiyoti, 1987). I doubt that Atlas's (and my husband's) perceived lack of emotion during and after the crisis, and Agape's, Demeter's, and my own emotional devastation, were totally random occurrences. Given the cultural context, they are also hard to write off as individual differences. They were and are casualties of a strongly patriarchal system. In Turkish socialization patterns, men are taught to be tough and unyielding (much more so than in Western cultures). In sharp contrast, the affective and emotional sacrifice women are capable of is deemed to be their greatest virtue. Moreover, self-sacrifice is closely tied to motherhood (Arat, 1996; Koçtürk, 1992). This reification of motherhood was crucial in Agape's generation, but it has also remained exceptionally strong ever since. Thus, regardless of the cause, if and when something goes wrong in that revered domain of motherhood, the sense of failure is intense, and it is *personalized*. This is a double-edged sword, since women personalize their failures, especially in terms of their children, but do not—or are not allowed to—personalize their successes. The latter is considered the outcome of their "nature." In the 1970s, attribution theories about women's precarious position in relation to success and failure showed how devastating this double bind might be for North American women (Horner, 1972). Although attribution theories have fallen out of vogue in social psychological literature, the convoluted and personalized ways in which women define failure still haunts Turkish women, especially women from Agape's generation. As a friend once commented, "We [Turkish women] all have Ph.D.'s in self-imposed guilt."

Another dimension that may be hard for Western readers to grasp is the venerated role of sacrifice and suffering, especially for mothers and wives (Ey Türk Analari, 2007; Turkish War, 2006). Of course, the importance of sacrifice and suffering has also been imperative in other cultures. As I outlined in the footnotes, Greek tragedies epitomize women's sacrifice. In the Christian tradition (i.e., in the suffering of Christ for the sins of others), we also glimpse a similar notion; however, the concept I am trying to reveal here is quite different, since over 99 percent of the Turkish population is Muslim, not Christian. Furthermore, in the Turkish tradition, the demand for emotional sacrifice from the self (or from others), is strictly gendered (Toktaş, 2002). It is also based on women's social roles and position (motherhood). In the rich Turkish literature of epic tales, folk stories, poems, songs, films, and so on, one of the most frequently occurring themes is the sacrifice women have made, especially as mothers (Turkish War, 2006). Through the countless wars that accompanied Turkish presence in the Anatolian peninsula (a span of about 1,400 years), women who sent their sons to the combat and never saw them come back have been exalted. Women are also exalted for acts such as feeding their husbands and children first (in that order) while going without food themselves, or giving birth to more sons, even when they may be in poor health (Sev'er, 2005: Sev'er & Bağli, 2006). Suffering and sacrifice in general, and self-sacrifice in particular, are not only expected, they are culturally approved of and praised. Women publicly wear their symbolic badges of suffering, and they receive recognition, even reverence, for having so suffered. What I am suggesting here is not a simple case of the rewards/costs/calculations that can be explained away through the Western concept of social exchange theory (Homans, 1961; Thibaut & Kelley, 1959). On the contrary, there are no "exchanges" and no "rational choices" here, only the tenacity of meticulously absorbed, strongly internalized gender patterns. Finding some form of legitimacy in the self through manifestations of gendered suffering is fuelled by a cultural psyche into which women are drawn and from which they have difficulty breaking away (Koçtürk, 1992; Sev'er & Bağli, 2006; Sev'er & Erkan, 2004; Sev'er & Yurdakul, 2001). In my family, this cycle of suffering and sacrifice was very much evident in the coping strategies of both Agape and Demeter. Yet, despite the value the culture places on the process, the suffering/sacrifice role also does a colossal injustice to women. Deep down, women may feel that trying to heal themselves or transcend a crisis, especially one that involves children, conflicts with how "selflessly" they ought to behave. In a way, the continuation of suffering, as a culturally approved and encouraged state of being, becomes more desirable than getting well and moving on.

In this narrative, there are also interactive components that await analysis. In my family's case, one of the greatest points of failure has been our inability to communicate our own grief and to understand the grief of another if the latter's manifestation did not resemble our own. The members of my family became experts at silencing our emotions, locking ourselves into rooms, shying away from friends, trying to eliminate or at least reduce triggers that might hurt Demeter or Agape. We were not able to talk openly about our loss or draw comfort from being united in our love. Even after close to four decades, in the home Demeter shares with Agape there are locked drawers that have remained untouched since the passing of Aurora. To this day, we turn off the TV when the subject is the death of a child. Moreover, both the depth of pain and the "legitimacy" of experiencing that pain have been hierarchized: the level of Demeter's pain trumps everybody else's feelings of grief. True as this may be, this ranking of pain has also been a tool of silencing others who were also deeply hurt. Taking Atlas as an example, the legitimacy of his pain and his right to express his emotions in the way he saw fit were marginalized. Cancian (1990) calls a similar process "the feminization of love." In this case, it was "the feminization of pain." In my judgment, the one who suffered the most from the course of events was Agape.

Last but not least, the weakness that afflicted my family was our inability to move on as a family. It is true that each one of us, on an individual level, not only managed, but thrived. Some of us, such as Electra, Selene, and me, ended up with advanced degrees and highly regarded professional lives. We were also able to sustain meaningful friendships, but not necessarily strong family bonds. Some, like Atlas, sought—and possibly found—fulfillment in a series of marriages and two other children. Atlas also managed to maintain a very close relationship with his daughter. Even Demeter worked for a while, as a successful business woman. However, and very sadly, our individual successes arose from the ashes of our family fragmentation. Somehow, our family is still transfixed by the day of our loss of Aurora, each member in her or his own way. Mostly Agape, but to some degree the rest of the family as well, lost the ability to celebrate other blessings that could have reunited our lives—with the single exception of Selene's birth. Mostly Agape, but in varying degrees both Demeter and I, as well, felt a tinge of disloyalty if and when our intense yearning for love found a different target, with the exception of our daughters. For example, neither Demeter nor I had the courage to have any more children. Our daughters, Selene and Electra, are well past their mid-thirties, but so far, they have chosen to remain childless. My family has always kept an enviable front stage for the world to see (Goffman, 1959). However, backstage, our relationship is more fuelled by regrets and blame than by the sheer joy and celebration of our togetherness. Although we discuss almost anything of mild concern, we have remained deafeningly silent on what matters the most: our feelings of loss and our dysfunctional ways of dealing with it. In Fritz Perls's Gestalt theory (1969), this process is likened to carrying a garbage bag of unresolved feelings and emotions on one's back. Perls suggested that, unless the items in the garbage bag are removed, examined, and disposed of, the bag will swell up and eventually crush the person who is carrying it. The members of my family, despite all good intentions, choose to walk under overstuffed garbage bags. Regrettably, but not surprisingly, the fear of loss continually trumps the potential for joy within less possessive forms of love.

Notes

1   In ancient Greek tragedies, the name Agape appears numerous times, each time as the name of a woman who represents a totally unconditional, absorbing, and self-sacrificing love, regardless of the presence or absence of lovable qualities in the object of her love. Early Christianity borrowed this Greek term and used it to denote a selfless love and dedication for the Lord. In more recent sociological interpretations (Lee, 1976), agape is considered to be a problematic love-style. Such extreme giving of the self may hollow out the giver—and suffocate the receiver—of such love.

2   In Greek mythology, Demeter is the goddess of agriculture, plants, and vegetation. She is one of the Olympians and is the sister of Zeus. She is the mother of Persephone, a beautiful, young, vibrant woman who is abducted by the hideous Hades (the god of the underworld). Demeter's anguish is so intense and her mourning so powerful that all the vegetation on earth dies. Seeing the total destruction, Hades agrees to a compromise: he allows Persephone to return to her mother in spring (and the plants rejuvenate in celebration of their reunion) but demands that she spend part of each year with him in the underworld (when Demeter mourns, and vegetation dies—the winter months).

3   Greek mythology starts with the mortal conflict between the Titans (led by Cronos) and the Olympian gods. Eventually, the Olympians win the battle, when Zeus (the leader of the Olympians) kills Cronos (his father). Atlas, one of the defeated Titans, was condemned by the victorious Zeus to bear the weight of the heavens upon his shoulder.

4   In Turkey, women of all ages are called girls until the time of their marriage. As a matter of fact, it is considered a slight to refer to girls as women before they are married, since the term girl also connotes purity and virginity.

5   In North America, some developmental studies indicate that single children are more independent and more assertive than children who have siblings. In Turkey, all other aspects being relatively equal, single children are a lot more closely watched and are socialized to be very dependent on their parents and other adults.

6   In Roman mythology, Aurora is analogous to the Greek goddess Eos, who is the daughter of two Titans, Hyperion and Theia. She is the sister of Helios (the sun) and Selene (the moon) and the mother of the four winds (north, south, east, and west). Aurora is beautiful, gracious, and colourful, and she represents the dawn. In the Greek version, she is depicted as pulling the gleaming chariot of Apollo (the sun god) across the sky. The chariot is pulled by winged horses. In the Roman version, Aurora is depicted as having her own colourful wings (the colours of dawn). Ironically, although Aurora brings all the colours and light to the earth (and thus into our lives), as she moves from the east to the west across the sky, she also takes the light away; when her journey is finished, she leaves darkness behind.

7   The actual term is SIDS, or sudden infant death syndrome. I found out about this syndrome only after I moved to Canada and searched the North American literature on the topic.

8   In some versions of Greek tragedies, Electra is a mortal: the daughter of Agamemnon and Clytemnestra. Agamemnon is one of the major heroes in the Trojan War, and a foremost character in the great epic-writer Homer's *Iliad* (and the *Odyssey*). He is one of the few heroes who actually survives the Trojan War and returns to Argos (Mycenae, in Homer), with a beautiful captive in tow (Cassandra). However, his wife, Clytemnestra, has also been busy and has found herself a new love during Agamemnon's 10-year absence. Eventually, the two of them destroy Agamemnon. Electra never forgives her mother for

that betrayal, and with the help of her brother (Orestes) she avenges Agamemnon's death. In other versions of the Greek myths, Electra is actually a minor goddess, one of the seven daughters of the Titans Atlas and Pleione.

9   In Greek mythology, Selene is Aurora's sister, and one of the three children of the Titans Hyperion and Theia. Selene represents the moon and is associated with the ethereal, pearly shimmer of lunar light. The Latin version of Selene is Luna.

References

Arat, N. (1996). *Türkiyede Kadin Olmak* [To be a woman in Turkey]. Istanbul: Say.

Brettell, C. B., & Sargent, C. F. (2001). *Gender in cross-cultural perspectives* (3rd ed.). Upper Saddle River, NJ: Prentice Hall.

Cancian, F. M. (1990). The feminization of love. In C. Carlson (Ed.), *Perspectives on the family: History, class, and feminism* (pp. 171–185). Belmont, CA: Wadsworth.

Ey Türk Analari [Salute to Turkish mothers]. (2007, March 16). Retrieved from http://www.2de1.net/paylasmak.istedikleriniz/50043-ey.turk.analari.and.8230.html

Gilligan, C. (1982). *In a different voice.* Cambridge, MA: Harvard University Press.

Goffman, E. (1959). *The presentation of self in everyday life.* Garden City, NY: Double-day.

Homans, G. C. (1961). *Social behavior: Its elementary forms.* New York: Harcourt & Brace.

Horner, M. S. (1972). Toward an understanding of achievement-related conflicts in women. *Journal of Social Issues, 28,* 157–175.

Kadioğlu, A. (1994). Women's subordination in Turkey: Is Islam really the villain? *Middle East Journal, 48,* 645–660.

Kandiyoti, D. (1987). Emancipated but unliberated? Reflections on the Turkish case. *Feminist Studies, 13,* 317–338.

Koçtürk, T. (1992). *A matter of honour.* London: Zed.

Lee, J. A. (1976). *The colours of love: An exploration of the ways of loving.* Don Mills, ON: New Press.

Marshall, B. L. (2000). *Configuring gender.* Toronto: Broadview Press.

Nelson, A., & Robinson, B.W. (2002). *Gender in Canada.* Toronto: Prentice.

Perls, F. S. (1969). *Gestalt therapy verbatim.* Moab, UT: Bantam.

Renzetti, C. M., & Curran, D. J. (1999). *Women, men, and society* (4th ed.). Boston: Allyn & Bacon.

Sev'er, A. (2005). In the name of the fathers: Honour killings and some examples from southeastern Turkey. *Atlantis, 30*(1), 129–145.

Sev'er, A., & Bağli, M. (2006). In who's interest? Levirat and sororat marriages in rural Turkey. *Hawwa, 4*(2–3), 274–299.

Sev'er, A., & Erkan, R. (2004). The dark faces of poverty, patriarchal oppression, and social change: Female suicides in Batman, Turkey. *Women & International Development Journal, 282,* 1–24.

Sev'er, A., & Yurdakul, G. (2001). Culture of honour, culture of change: A feminist analysis of honour killings in rural Turkey. *Violence Against Women Journal, 7*(9), 966–1000.

Thibaut, J. W., & Kelley, H. H. (1959). *The social psychology of groups.* New York: Wiley.

Toktaş, S. (2002). Engendered emotion: Gender awareness of Turkish women mirrored through regrets in the course of life. *Women's Studies International Forum, 25*(4), 423–431.

Turkish War of Independence 1922: Vatan Size Minnettar [The country is in your debt]. (2006, March 10). Retrieved from http://www.dailymotion.com/related/5436261/video/x1j9h_turkish-war-of-independence-1922_life

Wood, J. T. (2003). *Gendered lives: Communication, gender, and culture* (5th ed.). South Melbourne, Australia: Thomson.

Zinn, M. B., Hondagneu-Sotelo, P., & Messner, M. A. (2000). *Gender through the prism of difference* (2nd ed.). Boston: Allyn & Bacon.

[2]

GRANDMOTHER AND GRANDSON

JAN TROST

Background

Natalie is the grandmother in this story. She grew up in a Catholic family in Protestant Sweden. She had an older brother, Bert, and when she was three years old, her mother gave birth to another son, Edwin, followed three years later by a third son, Jan.

Natalie grew up admired by her father, who was a local artist, and protected by her brothers. She was well behaved, and she went to church every Sunday, as did the other members of her family. Her brothers were forced to go to church, but Natalie did it quite willingly. At 15, Natalie got arthritis and had to quit school. She was also struck by psoriasis, so severely that she had to stay in a special-care facility for several years. At 19, she was in better health and could attend a vocational school for a year. She eventually got a job.

She met a few men, but nothing serious—from her perspective, not necessarily the men's perspective. She would never have dreamt of having sex with anyone before marriage. As a good Catholic, being a virgin at marriage was very important to her. She attended church regularly and became a favourite of the priests. Suddenly, at 21, she met a man named Irving, who wanted to be an artist. In real life, he worked at a factory. He had graduated from high school with very good grades. After some time, Natalie convinced him to attend Uppsala University, some 60 miles away, in order to study French and English. So he did. Natalie also convinced him to convert to Catholicism,

51

and he did that, too. Eventually, they got married, and Natalie also moved to Uppsala as a housewife. Irving borrowed money to support his new bride.

Alfhild was born when Natalie and Irving already had a son, Theodore, who was 18 months old. When Alfhild was just two years old, Irving came home one day and announced to Natalie that he had met another woman and fallen in love with her. In fact, he had never talked to this woman, but he was in love with her, and he wanted a divorce. So, they got a divorce. Natalie went home to her parents, found an apartment in the same city, and settled in her parents' neighbourhood. They were very supportive of her.

Natalie stayed at home with her children for a while, but she had to find a job to take care of them and herself. She saw no other possibility than work; her cherished life as a housewife was over. Because the Catholic Church did not accept divorce, and because she was a devout Catholic, she would never be able to remarry and become a housewife again. That kind of life was totally lost for her. It was for this reason that she expected Alfhild to marry a dependable and stable person. To Natalie, a dependable person meant a physician or a banker. Such a husband would allow Alfhild to achieve what Natalie could never achieve again: being a full-time housewife and mother.

Alfhild grew up in the shadow of her older brother, Theodore. Natalie had already decided that Theodore was intelligent and destined to be successful. Whatever he did was good in his mother's eyes. Alfhild, on the other hand, was "just a girl."

Alfhild always had problems with her digestive system. She went to school, but she was not a brilliant student—according to her mother, contrary to her brother's brilliance. Eventually, Alfhild finished high school with acceptable grades, but not good ones. She had attended a vocational high school. After finishing high school, she got an office job, invoicing customers and handling customer inquiries about invoices.

Natalie had no problems with her son, Theodore, who went to college and studied economics and statistics. But she was concerned about Alfhild. Alfhild was expected to get married and become a housewife. These were the dreams Natalie had had for herself, which she had first achieved but then lost.

How could Alfhild, who worked in the office of a small company in a fairly small city, find a physician or a banker to marry? Alfhild also realized that she could hardly find a mate who would be acceptable to her mother. So, she went to bars and went dancing with her friends. They were all looking for a nice man and hoping to find one, the way many young women at that time did.

The First Part of the Story

When she was 22 years old, Alfhild met a man some years older than herself. He was neither a physician nor a banker, but he was quite charming and nice. He had no formal education but worked as a deep-sea diver in the city harbour. He earned a good deal of money, so he could be generous at the bars. Alfhild fell in love with him, and he with her.

Alfhild did not dare tell her mother about her boyfriend for several months. When she did, Natalie resented the news and told her daughter to end the relationship. Alfhild held her ground, but very politely. Eventually, Natalie agreed to be introduced to the young man, Arnold. She invited him for coffee one Sunday afternoon, after Natalie and Alfhild had been to church (where Natalie prayed for Alfhild to realize that this man was not the right one for her). An important aspect of this story is that Natalie was not only deeply religious herself, but she also tried to create similar convictions in her daughter.

Arnold turned out to be a shy man, and not a very good-looking one! Because Alfhild was of legal age, Natalie could do nothing but advise her daughter to forget the whole idea. Yet, her efforts were in vain. The relationship continued despite Natalie's opposition and attempts to convince her daughter of what a bad idea the liaison was.

After some months, the couple decided to get engaged. Natalie argued that Arnold was not a good man at all and that he would probably not be able to support Alfhild and all the children they would have. Because in Natalie's eyes Alfhild was a true believer, and because Catholics are not permitted to use contraceptives, Natalie assumed that Alfhild would have many children. Moreover, Natalie was convinced that Alfhild would be a virgin bride when she got married—as Natalie herself had been.

Natalie tried to get support from her son, Theodore, and her brothers, Bert, Edwin, and Jan, to break-up her daughter's engagement. Theodore did what he could, but the sole effect of his efforts was that he and Arnold became, if not enemies, at least hardly friendly toward each other. Alfhild was disappointed about Theodore's and Natalie's double standard: after all, he was living with a woman out of wedlock, and Natalie had no objections to that arrangement because Theodore was a man. Two of Natalie's brothers, Bert and Jan, said they thought Arnold was a very nice and skilful person and that the marriage had every chance of being as successful as most other marriages. Edwin, on the other hand, supported Natalie fully and found many things about Arnold that aggravated him. He also told Natalie about all the bad things he had discovered. Edwin's support made Natalie even more certain that she was right. Among this state of conflict, Alfhild and Arnold got married, and soon afterward, Alfhild became pregnant. Martin, a good-looking and seemingly very healthy baby boy was born.

However, soon after the delivery, Alfhild started experiencing a postpartum psychosis. She was deeply depressed, but like many depressed people, she did not realize she was depressed. Alfhild simply attributed the causes of all her problems to her son and her husband. She telephoned her uncles and told her friends about all the bad things in her life. However, not a single person was able to understand the real problem. She became even more depressed and felt that no one understood her situation—nothing was wrong with her, but things were wrong with everyone and everything else. The family failed to understand her!

There was one person who did not blame Alfhild: her mother, Natalie. Instead, she fuelled Alfhild's anger toward her husband. So Alfhild moved away from her husband and baby, and she went to live with her mother. In Natalie's home, they prayed to God for all the evil people to be saved and for Alfhild to become stronger so she could tolerate the people around her. They went to church to pray. They prayed everywhere and all the time.

One day, Natalie decided that she and Alfhild should go to a Catholic monastery that offered a retreat for people in need of time for relaxation and prayers. Natalie took Alfhild on a train ride, and they travelled more than 300 miles away from Alfhild's baby and husband. No one knew where they had gone or how long they would be away. Afterward, people were told that the two had been at a retreat for two weeks.

Occasionally, Alfhild went back to her home to pick up some clothes. One day, when Martin was four months old, she again went to her home when no one was there. Her husband was out for a walk with Martin and their dog. When he returned home, he found his wife hanging from the door—dead. He called emergency, and a physician and police officer arrived. They decided that this was a clear case of suicide. Arnold called Natalie and informed her of the situation. She first went to see her deceased daughter, and later she called her son, her brothers, and the priest at her church.

To Natalie, suicide was a mortal sin; therefore, her daughter could not have committed such an act. Not her daughter, Alfhild! Impossible! Evidently, it was not an accident, either: someone must have killed Alfhild. Who was the murderer? In her mind, there was only one person who could have done it: Arnold! For Natalie, the conclusion was easily reached. In the evening, Theodore went to visit his mother, and they discussed the terrible incident. It was also clear to him that his sister could not have committed suicide; thus, he fully agreed with his mother. They did not accept the judgment of the police. They called Natalie's brother Edwin, and he also agreed with them that Alfhild must have been murdered. Theodore called the police and demanded a re-investigation. The next day, the police conducted a new investigation and came to the same conclusion: this was a clear case of suicide, not murder.

Natalie, her son, and her brother reluctantly accepted the conclusion. However, they decided that even if Arnold had not murdered his wife physically, he had done so morally, through his behaviour. Thus, Arnold was defined as having morally murdered his wife, Alfhild. In Natalie's eyes, a moral murder was also a murder, and the person responsible for it was a murderer.

The funeral took place some weeks later. Natalie had convinced the priest that her daughter had died at the hands of a murderer. Alfhild's funeral was held in the church, and she lay in a white coffin. Thus, Alfhild was presented as an innocent child who was a virgin at marriage but who was later murdered. She had not committed suicide!

At the time of the funeral, Arnold was at the local hospital's psychiatric clinic with his son, Martin. Natalie did not allow him to attend his own wife's funeral. Only one of Natalie's brothers, Jan (Martin's great-uncle), visited them at the hospital on the day of the funeral.

Arnold remained in the couple's home town, where Natalie lived, for about half a year. During this time, Arnold and Natalie had no contact whatsoever. Natalie did not care for the baby or bother with his father. After a time, Arnold moved to another town with his son. About a year after the tragedy, Arnold married a divorced woman who had a son the same age as Martin. After a year, the new wife gave birth to a boy. The new family of five is still together.

The Second Part of the Story

An association interested in artists from the area decided to commemorate the 100th anniversary of the birth of Natalie's father. There was to be a major exhibition of her father's works of art at the local museum, open for viewing for about a month. Natalie and her brothers decided that all family members should gather for a big dinner party at the largest restaurant in town to celebrate the memory of their father and mother. Arrangements were made, and the restaurant was informed as to the number of invited guests from each side of the family.

One of Natalie's brothers, Jan—the one who had visited Arnold at the hospital at the time of the funeral—called Martin and his father to invite them to the celebration. Jan thought that if cousins, grandchildren, and in-laws were invited as members of the family, then Arnold and Martin should be there, too. Arnold refused immediately, saying that he did not want to see his mother-in-law, who had always disregarded her grandchild. But he also allowed Martin to decide for himself, as he had just turned 18. After some thought, Martin decided to attend the dinner party. Jan called his older brother Bert, and asked him if he would support Jan if something undesirable were to happen. He realized that he had planted a bomb, so to speak, with a high risk of causing a violent explosion.

The day before the dinner party, Jan called his sister and informed her that Martin would be joining them for dinner. At first she was very upset, but eventually agreed that Martin, too, was "technically" a member of the family.

On the day of the celebration, Arnold brought Martin to town. As it turned out, Martin had previously called the hospital and had asked for photocopies of all medical records relating to his mother's death. Because he was Alfhild's only child and of legal age, the hospital complied with his request. Thus, Martin gained access to all his mother's records. He read them before going to the exhibition, where he met his Uncle Jan. They walked around the exhibition and then went to the cafeteria where Natalie, Theodore, Edwin, and other relatives and friends were having a late lunch. Jan introduced Martin to these people and to some other relatives who were around, relatives Martin had never met or seen before.

The atmosphere in the cafeteria had been jovial before Martin and Jan came in, but it immediately deteriorated. Although everyone tried to behave cordially, there was a lot of tension. Soon, people left the cafeteria to go home and dress for the dinner party. Martin, Jan, and a few others went back to their hotels.

In the evening, all regathered and had a drink. They mingled as they waited for others to arrive. Martin had brought a very good friend whom he considered a family member. Her name was Zara. The party consisted of about 35 people of various ages. Some knew each other very well, while others had only heard about some of the family members. The seating arrangement was informal, so Natalie sat down at one end of the table. She also brought her son, her daughter-in-law, and their two children with her, so that they would form a kind of shield around her. However, Jan intervened and suggested that Natalie make room for Martin to sit next to her. After all, he was her first grandchild, and they had not seen each other for more than 18 years. Hesitatingly she agreed, realizing that the suggestion was difficult to decline. One of the relatives sitting next to Natalie changed seats so Martin could sit next to his grandmother.

They started talking, and Martin asked questions about his mother's pregnancy, his own birth, and his mother's death. At first, everything went well; Martin asked questions and Natalie answered. But after a while, Martin asked his grandmother why her description of what happened was different from what the medical records indicated. Was Natalie lying, or had the physicians recorded something other than what actually happened? Until that point, Natalie was not aware that Martin had just read all the medical records. Thus, she was not at all prepared for these types of questions and comparisons. After about 10 minutes, the "interrogation," as she interpreted the situation, became too much for Natalie. She told Martin to leave the table. She also told him that she never wanted to see him again.

Martin was shocked, and he immediately left the table. The atmosphere at the dinner party became chaotic. Jan and Bert left the table and joined Martin and Zara in the vestibule of the restaurant. Others came out, too, and small groups began to gather in the vestibule as well as in the main dining room. Everyone was upset, some because of Martin's "interrogation," and some because Natalie had driven away her oldest grandchild, whom they saw as a long-lost family member.

The party was over. Natalie, together with her son and her brother Edwin, told Jan and Bert that they were no longer considered as family members. She said that, from that point on, they "did not exist." This judgment is worse than persona non grata, because such persons at least are deemed to exist. Although 10 years have passed since the great exhibition and dinner party, no contact has ever been established between the factions.

How Can We Understand the Grandmother?

I have decided to shift the responsibility for discussing interpretations of the behaviour of Natalie to three colleagues whom I have met only mentally and intellectually through the sociological literature. In fact, these scholars were dead before I was born. These eminent colleagues are Jane Addams, Charles Horton Cooley, and Georg Simmel. Let me first introduce them very briefly.

Jane Addams was born in 1860 and lived her adult life in Chicago, where she established and ran Hull House from 1889 until her death in 1935. To some, she is known for the Nobel Peace Prize she received in 1931. For the purposes of this chapter, her work with the poor in Chicago and elsewhere is of importance, as are her publications, a number of books and articles. Some of her publications can be found in the list at the end of this chapter. She was an early social worker and sociologist, and she can be defined as a symbolic interactionist, like Simmel and Cooley.

Georg Simmel was born in Berlin in 1858 and lived and worked as a social philosopher mainly in Berlin, where he never held a tenured position. Only in 1914 was he tenured as a professor in Strasbourg (which at that time was part of Germany). He died of liver cancer in 1918. He also published a great deal, and some samples are listed below. Although he never knew anything about symbolic interactionism (a term coined in 1936 by Herbert Blumer), his work has influenced many of the old interactionists as well as current views of interactionism.

Charles Horton Cooley was a professor of sociology at the University of Michigan at Ann Arbor during his active professional life. He was born in 1864 and died in 1929. He became known throughout the Western world early in his career, and he published many interesting books and articles, some of which are listed below.

For a moment, let us imagine that these three scholars meet at a café where I have invited them for a cup of coffee and cake, to discuss the story of Natalie, Martin, and the others. I take the liberty of using their first names.

JANE: Because I'm the only woman here, I will start. This is indeed a terrible story. And yet, I have heard worse stories throughout my work.

As you know, when I was young, both my father and I felt I should enter into the service of God and the Church. That is why I began studying at a theological seminary. But soon I realized that that was not my cup of tea (by the way, this is an excellent cake our host is serving us! Thanks, Jan). There was too much hypocrisy there, and people were not at all ready to serve human beings who were suffering from poverty and related problems. As I said in *Twenty Years at Hull-House* (Addams, 1910), there was too much "canned theology," which is like any other canned product: not fresh and not prepared by oneself, something ready-made for which one has no responsibility. However, being as well behaved as I was socialized to be, I finished my studies there.

Georg: Excuse me, but I have to interrupt you and just say that I understand you completely. I've seen enough of that kind of people. As you may know, my parents were born Jewish, and although both converted to Christianity, I'm still looked upon by many as a Jew. Lack of reflection and insight combined with stereotypes were and still are all too common.

Jane: I'm glad you interrupted, Georg—by the way, I didn't know that about your background. This woman, Natalie, had a religious background, and then her husband came home and told her he wanted a divorce. For her, divorce was probably something sinful and simply socially unbearable—and as our story-teller, Jan, says, she saw divorce as full of shame in the context of her religious community. Evidently, she had to struggle with a social stigma, as Goffman (1963) would theorize. In Natalie's case, the stigma seemed to be in her own mind, independent of what the surrounding social group said—her perception of her own reality was what mattered to her. Many people who are some-what religious become even more religious when something terrible happens to them. We should also remember that when all this took place, divorces were rare and seen as shameful in the part of the world where Natalie lived. So, she transformed into an "ultra-Christian."

Furthermore, she evidently felt that women's role in society was to be housewives and mothers, as was common at that time. Although many con-temporary young people would not agree with this view, Natalie was a child of her own time, as we all are. She thought that her daughter did not have to be trained for a good job as her son should be: after all, her son had to sup-port a family. Instead, her daughter should just find a nice man—and a nice man has to have high social status and make sufficient money. Natalie did not want her daughter to marry a man like her own husband. Her husband had never completed a formal education and was not able to support her and their children adequately. It is quite understandable that she wanted her daughter to marry an educated and established man. Therefore, Arnold was certainly not a good choice for Alfhild, at least in Natalie's opinion.

Charles: I agree completely, Jane. And furthermore, I would like to look at Natalie's "looking-glass self" (Cooley, 1902). She saw herself in her mir-ror as a person who had failed in her mission to become a housewife and mother. She should have selected a "better" man, and she was very con-cerned about her daughter's well-being. But what worries me more is her rejection of the grandchild. It seems as if, already from the beginning of the child's life, maybe even during the pregnancy, she had defined him solely as an inconvenience.

GEORG: Yes, people would say she was extremely egotistical and concerned only about herself. Maybe she was this way even as a child. But one can also look at this from another perspective. My work on jealousy (Simmel, 1908/1923, pp. 210–212) might be relevant here. What I mean is that Natalie was not at all interested in Alfhild's well-being but only in her own well-being, both socially and materially. In my view, being jealous means defining a person's relationship to "me" as my "property." When someone else—for example, Arnold, and then Martin—came along, they threatened her exclusive ownership of Alfhild's relation to Natalie.

Using her own understanding of God, Natalie tried to use prayer as a means of maintaining her control of Alfhild's relationship. She could only do so by using God and by actively and physically excluding Arnold and Martin from her surroundings and from Alfhild's. She was kind of trapped in her own snare when she herself was caught off guard by the disappearance of her daughter.

A third way of seeing her behaviour is to say that she created a social reality; to her, of course, it was "real" and not simply a social reality, as we call it. By excluding her son-in-law, she constructed a reality that fit her, and when it was "objectively" proven that Alfhild's death was a suicide, she constructed the reality of Arnold as a "moral murderer." She even made up that expression, to degrade Arnold and to reinforce her own righteousness. In this strategy, her own problems with Alfhild's death and suicide were not solved, but her way of addressing the problem (suicide) was to redefine it out of existence. She shifted the burden of the problem over to her son-in-law and excluded him and her grandson from her family circle. Although this was unfortunate, it was quite rational from her perspective, I would say.

JANE: I feel pity for Natalie. And I just wonder what would have happened if Alfhild had not had a postpartum psychosis with a deep depression, for that seems to have been the case. We could also speculate that Natalie caused Alfhild's depression by constantly showing her dislike of Alfhild's husband—she evidently never accepted the relationship between Alfhild and Arnold. It seems she did not even tolerate it. What would Natalie have done if everything had been okay with Alfhild? I don't know, but I can speculate that she would have done something drastic in any case.

CHARLES: Jane, according to your analysis, Natalie used her power to control Alfhild. I recall what you wrote in 1912 about how young girls often enter into prostitution. There, you say that young girls are lured into prostitution by resourceful men, who use their financial power to keep the girls subservient. In Alfhild's case, there is no prostitution and no money, but Natalie seems to have been very resourceful in luring Alfhild into her net using God and prayers. In a way, Alfhild was promised a good outcome through the support of God and Natalie.

I would also, if I may, continue on with my looking-glass self-concept. You all know that I am not particularly fond of that metaphor, but since it has been on everyone's lips, I will stick to it. Natalie looked in the mirror, and what did she see? A few minutes ago, I said that she recognized she had failed in her mission as a wife and as a mother. But she also saw another picture in the mirror: she saw a responsible mother trying to make sure her poor daughter stayed on the right track and thus lived happily in the spirit of God. In a way, she was trying to save her own motherhood through saving her daughter from an "unacceptable" marriage.

GEORG: That is an interesting analysis, Charles. One could also apply to the situation my ideas about small groups and the power struggle within them. As I said in *Soziologie* (Simmel 1908/1923), the triad is the most vulnerable small group in existence, in the sense that it easily splits up into a coalition of two members and an isolated (or actively excluded) third person.

First we had the dyad of Natalie and Alfhild (Natalie's son, Theodore, had left and was, in this respect, out of the game). Then Arnold entered the scene. He established a dyad with Alfhild, who now belonged to two dyads—one with Natalie, her mother, and one with Arnold, her fiancé and later her husband. Natalie tried to create a triad with them by pretending to accept (not only tolerate) Arnold. Just when he felt accepted (or at least tolerated) as a son-in-law and a father, Natalie actively formed a coalition with Alfhild against Arnold. Most likely, she feared that she would be isolated now that Alfhild had a child and a husband she loved (a new triad). Given her hunger to belong to a family, it would have been a catastrophe for Natalie to be left alone. The sad outcome was that eventually there was only one dyad—the father and son. Natalie was left in isolation, but she still tried to form a coalition with her son and her brothers against the dyad of Arnold and Martin.

JANE: Okay then, let us delve further into what happened at the family dinner party. Let us review what you two say about the fact that Jan called Natalie and told her about Martin coming to the party. Was this a good strategy on his part, or should he have done otherwise?

GEORG: As a German, I prefer order. I think he should have told his sister about his intentions long before he even called Arnold and Martin. The last-minute information about inviting Martin was too blunt and irreversible, given the fragility of this family's boundaries. After all, Natalie was 68 years old and set in her ways; she should not have been presented with such a controversial piece of information in so abrupt a manner. My spontaneous reaction is to say that Jan should have discussed the issue with Natalie before inviting Martin. The secret invitation might be seen as a provocation and a way of punishing Natalie rather than as a way of supporting Martin. We do not know what motives Jan really had: by that, I mean that he might have intended to help Martin, and he might not have cared at all for Natalie. He in effect punished her by not being more reflective about the possible side effects of his secret invitation of Martin. Perhaps he was aware of some risks but failed to foresee others.

CHARLES: I don't see this the way you do, my dear colleague. I might be a bit more informal in my views: after all, Natalie's grandson was part of the family. If my assumption is correct, the other family members were not forced to inform everyone else about who they would invite to the family dinner party. Why do we insist that Jan should have informed his sister? Sometimes it is better to take things for granted. And if I am right, Jan was afraid that Natalie would try to sabotage Martin's presence in one way or another if she had sufficient time to do so. Jan knew that his sister was very strong and manipulative. Now, we could say that Jan was also manipulative for the sake of something good: Martin would be allowed to become a family member again.

JANE: I agree with you, Georg, and you, too, Charles. However, since Natalie was so strong willed in her rejection of her grandson, I think she should not have been informed earlier. Furthermore, I would like to take a look at her behaviour during the dinner party, when Martin was seated next to her. First, she wanted to be surrounded by her son, daughter-in-law, and other grandchildren; she wanted to be "protected" by them and avoid others who could disturb her circle. However, and to her surprise, she was confronted with the grandchild she had never cared for nor even cared about. She must have been nervous, and she was probably totally unprepared for what the conversation with him would lead to: an interrogation of her perceptions and a questioning of her trustworthiness and judgment.

What could Natalie do? Admit that she was wrong and that she was either lying or had forgotten the truth? Neither could she claim that the physicians' notes in the medical records were false or misinterpretations of the truth. She was trapped; she could no longer insist that she was right and everyone else was wrong. She had to find a way out. Had all this happened a century or two before, she could have fainted and solved the embarrassing situation that way. But not at the end of the 20th century. She had no way out other than to drive back the intruder. If you hide yourself by burying your head in the sand like an ostrich, you can pretend you are invisible. That is what Natalie did, by refusing to look at the reality, and by not looking at herself in a less distorted mirror.

Natalie had "known" for 18 years that Arnold had killed his wife—her daughter—at least "morally." This knowledge could not suddenly be reversed, and she was not at all prepared for Martin's interrogation.

GEORG: Yes, Jane, you are right. The coalition she again formed with her son and her brother Edwin was the only reasonable action she could take from her perspective. This was also done to clearly show herself and the others that she was right and that her brothers Bert and especially Jan were wrong. She had to maintain her contention that they were supporting a murderer—a terrible man—and his son, her disgraceful grandson who has also shown that he was an awful person.

CHARLES: Now she had proof that the ex-son-in-law was not only a terrible man and a murderer but also a bad father. After all, he had raised such a disrespectful young man. Natalie could not accept the possibility that she bore some responsibility for her daughter's depression and death. If she had accepted that responsibility, she would also have had to admit to herself that she had behaved dreadfully toward her daughter, her grandson, and her son-in-law. Such an admission would have been impossible for her to bear.

JANE: What a tragedy! It was very nice to see you two once again, and I hope our paths will cross soon. Thank you, Charles and Georg.

References

Addams, J. (1910). *Twenty years at Hull-House*. New York: Buccaneer Books.

Cooley, C. H. (1902). *Human nature and the social order*. New York: Scribner's.

Goffman, E. (1963). *Stigma*. Englewood Cliffs, NJ: Prentice Hall.

Simmel, G. (1908/1923). *Soziologie: Untersuchungen über die Formen der Vergesellschaftung*. Leipzig: Verlag von Duncker & Humblot.

Suggested Reading

Addams, J. (1902). *Democracy and social ethics*. New York: Macmillan.

Addams, J. (1912). *A new conscience and an ancient evil*. New York: Macmillan.

Blumer, H. (1969). *Symbolic interactionism: Perspective and method*. Berkeley: University of California Press.

Cooley, C. H. (1909). *Social organization*. New York: Scribner's.

Cooley, C. H. (1917). Introduction. In. M. Richmond (Ed.), *Social diagnosis*. New York: Free Press.

Cooley, C. H. (1918). *Social process*. New York: Scribner's.

Simmel, G. (1906). *Die Religion*. Frankfurt am Main: Rütten & Loening.

[3]
RUPTURE AND REPAIR
The Cascading Effects of Mental Illness on a Family of Innocents

SHELDON UNGAR[1]

Introduction

This chapter traces how the emergence, development, diagnosis, treatment, and stabilization of my brother's bipolar affective disorder created varying degrees and forms of family strife for more than 30 years. It shows that when our parents assumed responsibility for my brother (rather than abandoning or institutionalizing him), the disorder became the central determinant of family dynamics and impinged on almost every decision they made. Initially, the most disruptive issue arose over the baffling matter of blame. Subsequent conflicts arose from divergent goals, new religious orientations that emerged as a response to the disorder, and the threat of being submerged by the needs of others. Given these changes over time, it is significant that the progression of his case closely parallels the typical career of bipolar disorder as described by psychologists. Certainly my brother's history poses clear problems for sociological theories that hold that mental illness is a myth and largely a consequence of the labelling of socially unacceptable behaviour by others. Indeed, my family—and I believe this is commonplace—initially strove to ignore, deny, or neutralize his unsettling behaviours. When this proved impossible in the face of his startling manic episodes, further conflicts arose over how to manage the situation, especially as Mark (I will use middle names in this narrative) turned to religion. While the latter was the main source of familial conflict, it also proved to be essential in Mark's effort to reclaim something of a normal life.

Theory and Methods

I had already left home by the time my brother Mark had his first episode. The 500 kilometres separating me from my family meant that I assumed different roles than I would have had I been on the scene. Metaphorically at least, I served in a priestly capacity as they confided their trials and pains to me. Distance also rendered me a natural adjudicator, an insider-outsider who could ostensibly assess their situation and offer advice. At the worst of times, I returned home and became an active participant. But where I knew I would soon leave and return to my normal life, my mother (Rose), father (Meyer), and brother were confined together in what often seemed to be an unremitting hell. For me, any acute distress was normally confined to the Sunday morning phone conversation with my parents. From Meyer's first words I knew whether it had been an especially difficult week or not. Prying out details of what had transpired from either parent was never easy and underscores one of the central themes of this account: silence. Both Meyer and Rose were aware of the stigma ostensibly attached to mental illness. Hence they conspired to cover it up as much as possible and for many years lived almost a mute existence when it came to Mark and his mental problems.

Silence and stigma blend well with the second sociological theme threaded throughout this account: impression management. In interacting with others, people inevitably give or give off information that others will use to evaluate and respond to them. Clearly, it is advantageous for individuals to present themselves in ways that are, at minimum, adequate. Goffman's (1959) dramaturgical approach to social interaction asserts that individuals seek to guide and control the reactions of others by strategically exaggerating their positive characteristics and downplaying their negative ones. His research with the mentally ill, however, reveals that they have difficulty sustaining positive or idealized self-presentations, and, over the long run, they inadvertently leak information that discredits their identity (Goffman, 1961). The social reaction processes that can result in an individual being labelled mentally ill are usually initiated when that person displays behaviours that are sufficiently strange that they disturb significant others and compel them to seek outside help. In families that undergo such a transformative process, it is common to feel a collective sense of embarrassment and guilt, creating a need to manage impressions about the cause, nature, and consequences of the problem. Family members typically engage in teamwork to maintain a veil of silence and conceal unsettling events and dark secrets from others in general, even other family members.

Managing impressions is only a start. Managing the problem itself is a much greater challenge, and blunders here can be far more harmful than lapses in the presentation of a suitable familial face to outsiders. Ultimately, Mark and our parents evolved somewhat tolerable ways of coping with his mental illness. This was the upshot of a haphazard process that owed a great deal to his resilience and tenacity, their steadfast and resolute commitment to him, and ultimately the contributions of his orthodox religious community. In other words, it took the confluence of the individual (Mark never succumbed to his bipolar condition), the immediate family (they sacrificed a great deal for him), and the social support offered by a real community to allow Mark to prevail over his illness.

In recounting this, I must admit to being a somewhat unreliable narrator. Beyond the distance and my attendant dependency on what my family members would reveal to me, none of us initially realized that Mark had a serious mental illness and hence did not pay adequate attention to unfolding events, as we supposed that the problem would simply go away as he matured. Whatever the peculiarities of my own somewhat scattered recollections, there is an overriding propensity to remember the most extreme and unusual things, so it is most certainly the case that a balanced account of what transpired over 30 years is *not* presented here. I also have no privileged access to Mark's mind, and this report focuses far more on familial impacts than on his internal states or experiences.[2]

Personality Disorders and Misplaced Blame

There were no signs of disturbance in Mark's early years. Indeed, the first indication that something was awry occurred when he was 18. At the time, he was attending McGill University and had a group of close friends and a girlfriend. According to Meyer, Mark woke them one night and was extremely agitated and mumbled bizarre ideas. He calmed down in a few hours and recovered sufficiently by morning to attend classes. In the next few years he experienced a number of similar episodes, characterized by frantic excitability and overwrought anxiety. These events were sufficiently intermittent and self-limiting that they could be concealed from others and discounted or explained away. Considerable energy and ingenuity accrued to the latter. For example, Mark had recently tried marijuana, and his bizarre behaviour was initially attributed to the drug. Meyer went so far as to search out articles (this in pre-Internet days) suggesting that marijuana could produce temporary psychotic states. When Mark's girlfriend broke off their relationship soon after the first episode, subsequent occurrences were blamed on his resulting depression, and she was quickly transmuted from a wonderful girl who was ideal for him into a malign influence responsible for many of the ills that befell him. That she may have stopped seeing him because he started to manifest strange behaviours was never considered, or at least never vocalized. Except in the immediate aftermath of an episode, talk about his condition was verboten.

Mark's accomplishments did offer some grounds for hope. He maintained a semblance of normality in his daily life and went on to complete his B.A., followed by his M.B.A. These successes and all the hopes they embodied were offset by mounting setbacks that eventually became too obvious to ignore. His friendship network slowly disintegrated, and he was unable to establish another relationship with a woman. Despite his degrees, he was unable to maintain a job in the business field and ended up taking lesser jobs.[3] Behind these failings were subtle and not so subtle changes in his behaviour. His psychotic episodes became more frequent and intense, and he often seemed more distracted and fretful and too often impulsive. It was increasingly difficult to simply interact with him, and there was little doubt that he was often distressed.[4] Clearly his failings at work and in interpersonal relationships reflected his deteriorating state of mind. Above all, the feelings of futility and turmoil that impinged on the other family members, both individually and collectively, could no longer be disregarded or shrouded in silence. There was still little overt conflict, as the tensions and anxieties were turned inward. Family life was rendered worse when Mark, after living on his own for a time, moved back home. Our parents were gradually withdrawing from friends and activities as their world seemed to crash down on them. They shunned friends so as to avoid the horror of them witnessing any of Mark's disorderly behaviour.

They now had to do the unthinkable. Great shame and bewilderment attended their decision to seek professional psychological help. This was beyond anything previously envisioned, as families were supposed to function like silos and manage problems on their own. Madness bore an exceptional form of stigma, implying the possibility of both a hereditary taint and failed parenting (Goffman, 1963). But the seven or so years had exacted their toll, and my brother would now spend several years visiting psychologists. Unfortunately, therapy did not ameliorate his psychological problems, though it did serve to aggravate the family situation and bring conflict to the fore through the issue of blame. Based on their conversations with Mark, assorted psychologists diagnosed neurosis and, more specifically, personality disorders. Just what these personality problems entailed was never made clear, at least to our satisfaction. However, in an inversion of the usual attribution of blame in families, they pointed the finger at our father, Meyer, claiming that he was cold and distant and failed to provide the assurances required by someone like my brother. For what it is worth, my relationship with Meyer was neither cold nor distant.

Mark had always been much closer to Rose than Meyer, but once the psychologists ascribed most of the responsibility to Meyer, my brother and father became progressively more estranged and the discord between them palpable. Mark now seized on every opportunity to remind us of his sense of grievance, as he shaped his identity in the family around it. He blamed Meyer completely for his condition, and any conversation between them verged on acrimony. Although the ill feelings became somewhat mutual, Mark was much quicker to exhibit anger, make hurtful comments, and threaten to leave or "go to court." Meyer was more stoical. He often became exasperated, but he almost always maintained his composure. Between the two of them stood Rose. She was trapped in an unenviable role conflict, listening to and trying to understand and soothe my brother while at the same time endeavouring to support and placate Meyer. One strategy she used to maintain harmony was to keep them separated whenever possible. To this end, she encouraged Meyer to spend time away from home, especially when my brother was irritable.

Manic Episodes and the Role of Psychiatry

If home life was not quite unbearable, the worst was yet to come. My brother began to display explosive rage (officially termed "irritability"), combined with incoherent thoughts and agitated speech. An alarmed call by my parents brought me to Montreal where my brother and parents reside. Soon after I arrived we received a call from U.S. Customs informing us that Mark had been refused entry to the United States and sent back. Violating regulations, they supplied the name and rental location of the taxi he had hired and advised us to meet the taxi there. We did, and with great difficulty persuaded Mark to come home in the car with us. He insisted that he sit alone in the backseat. On the way, Meyer complained of severe chest pains and lay down in the backseat with my brother, who continued to be suspicious and jumpy. For my part, I was overwhelmed by the rush of events, as Meyer had not warned me that he was going to fake a heart attack to justify going to the hospital. On arrival at the hospital, Meyer revived and we used brute force and intimidation to convey Mark to the emergency department. For some reason, perhaps a sense of relief, he quieted down and became quite tractable while waiting there.

The story of Mark's day was incredible. He had taken a taxi to Dorval airport with the aim of flying to Israel. His plans were subverted, however, by his bizarre self-presentation. He had no passport, no funds beyond a credit card, no luggage, no winter coat on a cold February day, and he was wearing shoes without socks. When refused a ticket, he took the second taxi mentioned above and insisted on being driven to New York City so he could get a flight there. The taxi driver, who from our brief conversation obviously recognized that my brother was out of control, used an open credit card receipt to cover the cost of the trip. He charged $500 for the drive to the U.S. border and back.

This was Mark's first full-blown manic episode. He was also seen for the first time by a psychiatrist, a man who looked uncannily like Freud. During the part of the interview I participated in, Mark carried off the bravado performance of someone more or less normal. However, this was also my initial contact with one of his doctors, and while I do not recall the details, I was able to provide a systematic account of his recent history that helped confirm a diagnosis of manic depression (subsequently renamed bipolar disorder). I possessed only a superficial understanding of this psychosis at the time; however, I recollect that Mark's favourite singer was Jimi Hendrix. He particularly liked the tune "Manic Depression."

As a sociologist, I had read and actually taught theory that criticized the disease model of mental illness. Thomas Scheff (1966), the foremost proponent of this sociological approach, seeks to take the problem *out* of the individual and understand it instead in the context of social roles and role-playing. Scheff (1966) argues that, as a result of labelling by significant others, the "deviant" or "sick" role becomes stabilized. He suggests that the kinds of rule breaking (or discrepant self-presentations, to use Goffman's term) that are normally seen as indicative of mental problems are quite common and usually transitory. What we call a mental disorder is often a result of social reactions to such rule breaking that cast persons into the role of the mentally ill. It is the ongoing reactions of others that stabilize the strange behaviours that otherwise might disappear on their own. Once the person is well ensconced in the role, it becomes sticky and exceedingly difficult to escape.

While this labelling approach seemed plausible to me in the early stages of Mark's illness, his manic episode disabused me of this belief. His aborted day of flight could not be overlooked or tolerated as just somewhat unusual behaviour.[5] There were clear risks and costs involved, and these would worsen in subsequent manic episodes. In assessing the status of my brother's condition, it is essential to recognize that neither he nor our parents had any knowledge of manic depression, and hence it is very unlikely that his behaviours were a result of the actualization of stereotypes transmitted by social expectations and driven by interactional processes. My brother was not, as sociologists of deviance often hold, enacting a social role made available to him through commonly shared and well-demarcated scripts. Given their common ignorance of the condition, it seems most likely that his behaviour was driven by a state of psychological mania. These issues, of course, are of more than academic interest to a family managing a child with a psychiatric condition.

Mental illness has been more vulnerable to sociological encroachment than other illnesses because, unlike cancer or heart failure, where the "biological markers" of disease are fairly clear, parallel biological markers have not been pinpointed for psychoses (Shorter, 2008). In recent years, however, researchers have begun to identify the genes (there appear to be a number) seemingly involved in creating a predisposition for bipolar disorder. While brain imaging is still in its infancy, it provides suggestive evidence that there are differences of size, shape, and function distinguishing those with bipolar disorder from the general population.

In retrospect, it is apparent that Mark's case of bipolar disorder closely fits the classic psychological model of this condition (Goodwin & Jamison, 2007). The onset is usually in the late teens, and then it typically takes about 10 years for the condition to be confidently diagnosed. Bipolar disorder is characterized by periods of excitability or mania alternating with periods of depression. For some, as with my brother, the manic episodes are far more extreme than the depressive moods. According to the *Diagnostic and Statistical Manual of Mental Disorders* (DSM) (2004), *mania* is a distinct period of an abnormally elevated (i.e., euphoric) or irritable mood, accompanied by at least three out of seven other symptoms (four symptoms, if the mood is irritable rather than elevated). Those seven symptoms are captured with the mnemonic DIGFAST: distractibility, indiscretion ("excessive involvement in pleasurable activities" in DSM), grandiosity, flight of ideas, activity increase, sleep deficit ("decreased need for sleep"), and talkativeness ("pressured speech").

After this initial manic episode, my brother had several additional episodes in the next few years despite the use of antipsychotic drugs. This is consistent with psychological "kindling" theory, which holds that once a critical threshold is crossed (whether for mania or epileptic seizures or other psychological disturbances), it alters the brain in ways that increase the probability of further events (Monroe and Harkness, 2005). Having an initial manic episode means that there is about a 90 percent chance of undergoing another. Mark's next episode entailed his driving to Quebec City and calling my parents from there to taunt them. During that night he called several times and, consistent with a sharp increase in his activity level, checked in to about half a dozen hotels. This continued for two days before he flew back to Montreal. My father and I then had to venture to Quebec City to hunt for his car.

Finding Religion

These events were lacerating ordeals for my parents and dealt pathological blows to family relations. In the course of his manias, Mark hallucinated that Meyer was a Mafia kingpin specializing in extortion and murder. Such a distorted conception of his father undoubtedly reflects the deep animosity he held toward him. Through these same manias Mark also found religion. Unfortunately perhaps, though for a variety of plausible reasons, Mark's religious conversion was initially accorded about as much credence as his Mafia delusion. Although his religious community would prove to be crucial in the end, for many years it was a source of great strife among family members.

I know that Meyer was an atheist and believe that Rose, who rarely spoke of such matters, was probably one as well. Hence they did not receive his initial forays into Orthodox Judaism with much understanding, especially since his befuddled attempt to fly to Israel was the first clear indicator of this new orientation. Effectively, they took religion to be a manifestation of his madness, as well as a misguided way of trying to cope. They perceived him as extremely vulnerable to outside influences, and they were not enthusiastic about his intention of giving 10 percent of his earnings as a religious tithing when his "earnings" were no more than what they gave him. They believed that the religious community was seeking to take advantage of his condition, especially since my brother invoked religion in refusing to take any of the funding he was entitled to from the Quebec government. Mark's insistent claim that "God will provide" became a rare running joke, as it elevated Meyer well beyond the rank of mobster. Familial conflict pertaining to this issue, as well as many other aspects of their existence, was exacerbated by Mark's having joined the Chabad-Lubavitch, an ultra-orthodox branch of Judaism. Nothing in Meyer's and Rose's past prepared them for the exacting demands of fundamentalist Judaism.

Becoming religious was a protracted, involved, and challenging process. Mark was compelled to change his dress, his associates, his daily routines (he was to daven—recite prayers—mornings and nights), his diet (strictly kosher), his dating behaviour (meeting religious women through matchmakers), and so on. He was obsessed by the need to follow every religious rite and rule, and utterly terrified of sinning. Getting along in this life, including staying healthy and having a family, as well as the assurance of eternal life seemed to turn on the avoidance of a single sin. (Ironically, when he was seeking rabbinical approval for things he wished to do, he would consult various rabbis until he found obliging advice. Both Meyer and I sometimes mocked him for what we regarded as his scheming use of religion.)

Not only did Mark endlessly pontificate about religion with the exasperating certainty of a new convert, but he strove to recruit Meyer and Rose and even me when I was present or spoke to him on the phone. While his proselytizing resulted in tension and anger, he additionally, as a true believer, felt free to harangue us for our sinful lives. This was extremely upsetting for Rose, especially since Meyer and Mark frequently argued and sometimes got into shouting matches that fell just short of blows. I argued less, falling back on the expedient of telling Mark, "Lay off with your superstitions." When his religious tirades became insufferable, I would sometimes purposively engage in blasphemous talk. In this context, it is hardly surprising that whenever Mark came by, Rose would do her utmost to induce him to leave as soon as possible—and then fret about whether he was all right. She wanted him to visit in order to feed him proper meals and be company in his loneliness, but the longer he stayed, the greater the chance of disputes that all too often became personal and nasty.

Perhaps the most pernicious effect of his illness was the constant fear of another manic episode. This ultimately prevented Meyer and Rose from living a normal life. As Alphonse Daudet, a "literary syphilitic" who endured excruciating pain for close to three decades, observed, "Suffering is nothing. It's all a matter of preventing those you love from suffering" (Daudet, 2002, p. x). Where Mark demonstrated remarkable resilience, he was also consumed by his own subjectivity and instead of maintaining silence relentlessly divulged his thoughts, pains, and uncertainties. When he was around, conversation always focused on his interests or needs. He was too self-absorbed to recognize the realities of others, and he never seemed to consider how his demands and complaints affected them. Mark told Rose everything—his fears and anxieties, his sense of failure and inadequacy (especially in comparison with his brother), the difficulties he encountered with Meyer and me, his religious and personal need to marry, his difficulties with women, his sexual frustrations, and so on. The unveiling of some aspect of his soul was practically a daily event, and it was utterly draining for Rose. It was a few years after his initial manic episode that she began to suffer from irritable bowel syndrome. He completely disregarded my repeated requests to stop laying so much on her and to seek another outlet, including a therapist. Tellingly, we all remained mum about the question of whether Mark's actions were sickening Rose.

Accommodating Mark touched on all aspects of my parent's lives. Once he grew to be strictly kosher, meals became an ordeal. Everything he ate was subject to stringent scrutiny, and hell was to be paid if anything did not meet his dietary standards for Kashruth. One shelf in the fridge and one shelf in the pantry, both enveloped in tinfoil, were reserved for his comestibles. Needless to say, anyone who misplaced an item felt his wrath. He ate on paper plates and used plastics utensils, and if the oven was needed to prepare his meal, tinfoil was used to maintain the requisite barrier. Typically, he ate on his own, though I am not sure whether this was done to meet his dietary stipulations or was just a further severance to maintain peace. Keeping kosher in a way that satisfied Mark was challenging but achievable. Dealing with his persistent condemnations for our eating "trefa" (non-kosher) was unbearable. For the many years it took for him to be comfortable in his religious standing, hardly a meal at which he was present passed without at least a momentary upset.

Social Deaths

The tragedy of King Lear is that he demanded too much love from his daughters. Rose's tragedy was that she revealed too much love for Mark. My brother unquestionably needed and loved his mother, but he was also capable of using her bottomless love to his advantage. A clear illustration of this was the many times he borrowed money from Meyer for personal ends or business and then went to Rose to have the loan declared a gift. I doubt she ever refused him, despite the fact that it enraged her husband. The latter would seethe at this perceived betrayal, but he never, at least publicly, disputed her decision.

Our parents were children of the Depression and needed substantial savings to feel secure. But since Rose wanted Mark to live as normal a life as possible and not be deprived of anything, she saved such inordinate sums that she deprived Meyer and herself of the lifestyle enjoyed by their friends. The members of their community, as the children of recent immigrants, had grown up around Montreal's "Main Street" (made famous by Mordecai Richler). As they escaped their Depression roots, they moved en masse to the west end of the city. Many became sufficiently well off that they were able to purchase condos in Florida, where they spent their winters together. Meyer had always planned to join his friends down there, but it never happened. Rose refused to spend the money and maintained that it would be a waste because she was unwilling to leave Mark alone for more than two or three weeks. And while they made a number of trips down there over the years, not being there for the winter, where friends congregated much more frequently than they did in Montreal, served to isolate them within the group. A further wedge was driven between Rose and her friends as they claimed that she skipped engagements far too often due to being too indulgent of Mark. To a very real extent, Meyer and Rose suffered a social death. Their exclusion troubled Meyer far more than it did Rose.

Here again, as with labelling, we encounter a further problem for sociological theory (though clearly it is impossible to generalize from a single example). Goffman (1963) contends that mental illness is a highly discreditable condition that is broadly stigmatized by others. Certainly my parents initially believed this to be the case and thus maintained as far as possible a veil of silence around Mark. But over the long run it was impossible to conceal his mental illness, and it became common knowledge among relatives and friends. Except for the Uncle Rusty incident described below, my parents did not experience any embarrassing comments or reactions from their friends or relatives. They were not blamed for his condition, nor were they made to feel any sense of moral deficiency. To their often-stated surprise, people not only were understanding but pressed my parents to be less indulgent of Mark and get on with their own lives. A number expressed the view that he would do better if he was given more responsibility for himself rather than being, in sociological terms, cast in the sick role. Events described at the end of this chapter suggest they may have been right. But Rose would not relent. Ultimately, it was not an issue of stigma but of the overly protective Jewish mother—a stereotype that is often more than just fiction.

In light of this, the absence of any overt conflict between Rose and Meyer was perhaps the most surprising aspect of their lives. Living in an ongoing situation where interpersonal conflict seemed unavoidable, they managed through a common (though varying) commitment to Mark and their mutual affection to maintain a sound marriage. This is the conclusion I must draw from the years of seeing and talking to them. If there were indeed private conflicts or bitter animosities between them, their capacity to collude in managing impressions transcends anything Goffman might have countenanced. With friends they hid a great deal for many years, but gradually and guardedly disclosed much of the reality. In the most trying of times, Rose's devastation was palpably visible, and this accounted for some of the difficulties she had with friends.

Mark experienced a far more devastating social death. Besides losing his friends and rarely forming close personal relationships with his co-religionists, he suffered most from the inability to find a wife. Having large families has always been a strong aspiration among religious Jews, and this has become a great incumbency since the Holocaust. Orthodox Jews generally meet through the mediation of matchmakers, and Mark, in keeping with this practice, has visited matchmakers in a region that extends from Quebec City to Windsor and from Montreal through Boston, New York, and Washington. He has met thousands of women, all to no avail. In most instances, he does not progress beyond the first date. He has had a handful of relationships that lasted for weeks or months, but nothing came of them. Throughout his dogged efforts to find the right woman, Rose supported him financially and emotionally. Part of the reason she saved money so assiduously was to help support him should he marry. This produced extreme dissonance, as Meyer and I contended that he would not be able to cope as a father and could never afford a family. Even my wife and children felt slighted by the amount of money given to Mark, especially because we received a pittance. My parents spoke about our inheritance a number of times, though we recognized that it would be rapidly depleted should Mark marry. While Mark did not fritter money away, he was not frugal like our mother.

Rose observed a number of times that "women did not go for Mark." She sometimes seemed puzzled by this and would ask if he looked or acted strange. I was compelled to respond with a qualified yes, blaming his medications to spare her feelings. Antipsychotic drugs may have allowed him to live a somewhat normal life, but they have side effects that, contrary to the claims of the ubiquitous television ads for drugs, are neither rare nor minor. The drugs work, as can be seen in the close association between the times Mark stopped taking his medication and the onset of a manic episode. In one instructive case, a psychologist convinced him that he could stay under control without drugs. Mark slowly lowered his dosage under the ostensible care of this psychologist, and a relapse that resulted in his hospitalization immediately ensued. The drugs work, but it usually takes years to find the right combination and dosage. Careful monitoring is also required. At one point, perhaps four years into the drug regimen, my father found Mark unconscious in his apartment. The level of lithium in his blood had become toxic, and the attending physician said he was only hours from death.[6]

The side effects that manifested in Mark's case included weight gain, lethargy, a need to sleep excessively, shaking, facial tics, and sometimes slurred speech. Altogether, these do not form a winning combination, especially when coupled with his low-status occupations and little prospect of improvement. The reality of his handicapped self-presentation was chillingly revealed in an incident with Uncle Rusty, Meyer's brother. Rusty owned a small grocery store and hired Mark to work there. One Friday afternoon, he told Mark not to come in Monday as he was fired. This precipitated a manic episode, with traumatic effects on my parents. In the course of this episode Mark uttered various threats and more or less confined them to their home. Subsequent to my arrival he threatened me, and when I went outside he followed and proceeded to tear a thick limb off an apple tree, a demonstration of strength that appalled me. As for Uncle Rusty, he informed us that he was forced to fire Mark because his presence was disturbing some customers. Meyer's rejoinder that Mark might have worked on the stock rather than with customers drew a nebulous response. So did Meyer's objections to the way Mark was let go, particularly the absence of any warning. Rusty eventually lost the store and ended up on welfare. This time he did not approach Meyer for financial assistance, though Meyer had given him substantial help in the past. It was 15 years before they saw one another again. I believe they met only one more time before Rusty died. It took considerable cajoling to convince Meyer to attend Rusty's funeral.

Death and Restoration

For all their efforts, it should be apparent that our parents lacked the resources and capacity to help Mark cope on his own and live something akin to a normal life. Indeed, they could barely keep themselves together, as Rose suffered debilitating headaches for the last five years of her life. Although she was seen by a host of medical specialists, no organic source for her pain could be found. Medications that at one point included morphine failed to relieve her suffering. Meyer and I attributed the headaches to Mark's illness and his incessant demands on her. Significantly, Mark never countenanced any links between his troubles and her irritable bowel syndrome and later headaches. Rose did her utmost to enforce silence on this issue.

Meyer's and Rose's efforts were complemented by Mark's resilience. This combination of individual perseverance and unwavering family support allowed them to keep going through a series of manic episodes and other setbacks that continued for five or six years after he was diagnosed as bipolar and put on drugs. Strikingly, he has since gone more than 20 years without a recurrence. This extended period of relative good health and passable social functioning is better than the norm for persons with bipolar mood disorders (Goldberg & Harrow, 2004). Part of his stability undoubtedly stems from the psychiatrists getting the drugs right. More significant in this regard is his total integration into the Orthodox Jewish community he joined. To put it all together, effectual undertakings at every level—the individual, the familial, and the community—have been decisive in Mark's sustained stability.

Meyer and Rose never fully reconciled to Mark's religious calling. But when he moved out of their home for good sometime after he was relatively stabilized, family conflicts eased. Both they and he had more freedom, and brief visits benefited both parties. Mark could never cease proselytizing and thereby continued to engender anger and discomfort. Meyer also continued to find fault with the religious community. For many years Mark worked in the stockroom of a drugstore. After an extended family struggle, he decided to start his own business. In one venture he tried to sell mutual funds, but members of the Orthodox community did not invest with him (no Bernie Madoff here). Meyer was annoyed by this, and he and I had heated discussions about what one could realistically expect from Mark's community, especially since their usually large families meant they were financially strapped. Mark now operates a small enterprise that sells promotional items to companies. Members of his community have provided him office space and use of a secretary. He has also been given opportunities to sell products for some of them.

Mark's total existence revolves around his Orthodox community. In what is close to literally the case, he dwells in their village.[7] And they have more or less accepted him as a full-fledged member. Indeed, I have heard several of them refer to him as "special," and it was quite clear that they were not using the term in the way it can be patronizingly employed in politically correct discourse. His specialness has nothing to do with his mental history or with any special needs; instead, it is a combination of his standing as a convert to orthodoxy and their genuine affection for him as a person. I have been pleasantly surprised seeing him interact with members of his community. Sociologically, they have provided Mark with the social supports and solidarity that have made his long-term stability possible (Durkheim, 1897/1951).

That his community has had a remedial effect on Mark is best seen in his reaction to the deaths of our parents. As could be gleaned from the prior discussion, stressful events typically preceded his manic episodes. There seemed to be little reason to doubt that the death of our parents, particularly of Rose, would set off another episode. Yet, he was able to deal with the two deaths without a relapse. When Meyer, who went first, was dying, life went on more or less as usual. Mark dutifully visited and phoned, but he was not closely involved. The animosity that existed for decades was still manifest. Conversations continued to revolve around religion when Mark was present, and about two months before Meyer died, he responded to something Mark said as follows (his words are ingrained in my memory): "Mark, it sounds like you are just waiting for me to die so that you can collect your inheritance." Yet there were other signs of trust. Mark's inheritance was originally to be held in trust to make sure he couldn't squander it in the course of another manic outbreak.[8] However, when their condo was sold they gave Mark his share outright, and I, as executor, was told that I could do the same with the remainder of his inheritance.

Rose's death, eight months later, was very different. In her last illness, Mark visited her daily and made the long walk to the hospital on the morning she died (it was Saturday, so he was not permitted to drive). Though we knew her death was imminent, he had gone to the synagogue to pray that morning. It was the members of his community who told him to leave and be with his mother. He suffered tremendously both before and after her death, but he remained stable. I spoke at Meyer's funeral, but Mark, who has no experience in public speaking, spoke at Rose's. His first few sentences came out haltingly. It seemed he could not continue, as he was unable to articulate any words. But he eventually managed to give his talk, just as he has managed to cope in the year that has passed since her death. This was his finest moment, and it would be inconceivable without the social support provided by his community.

I had long wondered whether we would remain in contact after our parents were gone. As it turns out, he calls me weekly (to be fair, I have called him). Our conversations are a bit more superficial but less contentious than they used to be. The death of our parents, rather than crushing him, has seen him acquire some confidence and self-reliance. Indeed, he has done so well in the past year that it lends credence to the notion that Rose's constant ministrations had the unintended effect of casting him into a sick role. In effect, she sanctioned his deviance and exempted him to a great extent from the responsibilities of ordinary social roles (Mechanic, 1995). The loss of our parents more or less forced him to become more independent, and it turns out that he can function quite adequately on his own. He is not only keeping active but working harder at his business. For a time, he was terribly upset at the economic crises, fearing the loss of much of the inheritance he ultimately relies on as well the possible impact on his business. He has settled down, however, and he claims that his sales are steady and even increasing at times.

Perhaps this will help him in his ongoing quest for a wife. The perceived failure to form a marital union is certainly the greatest dysfunction of his religious life. There is a certain incongruity between the inordinate pressure to find a mate and the highly restricted pool of women deemed eligible. But this is a paradox that Mark can no longer grasp, so in the end he is precluded from fulfilling the most important role demands put on the Orthodox—marrying and propagating. While the latter has been rendered exceedingly unlikely because of his age, he has no idea how to improve his self-presentation to make himself minimally attractive to women, cannot learn this within his community, and will not listen to outsiders.

Notes

1 The author would like to thank Laura Mattila for helpful comments on several versions of this paper.

2 Michael Greenberg's *Hurry Down Sunshine* is probably the best account of the subjective experiences associated with bipolar disorder.

3 Even during his worst manic episodes, Mark could present a lucid and controlled front, at least for a brief time. He was sufficiently adroit that he managed to find jobs and disarm psychologists.

4 Looking back, I can only be bemused by my undergraduate self that fully accepted R. D. Laing's (1965) claim that mental illness was liberating. No joy can be found in my brother's case. And while some people diagnosed as bipolar have been extremely creative, including Schumann, Byron, and Van Gogh, they constitute so small a proportion of those identified as bipolar that their creativity may well be independent of their illness (cf. Jamison, 1993)

5 According to Goffman (1967, p. 141), "Psychotic behaviour is, in many instances, what might be called a situational impropriety." He terms psychiatric intervention a medical "misfortune."

6 I never raised this directly with Meyer, but intuited in various ways that he wondered whether we might not all have been better off had he not discovered Mark in time.

7 In light of religious restrictions about driving on the Sabbath, as well as the need to pray twice daily and to eat only strictly kosher food, most Orthodox Jews choose to live close together in bounded geographic areas.

8 To be clear, Mark has never earned enough money to support himself and has always required financial assistance. His inheritance, which our parents amassed by denying themselves, is critical to his future security.

References

American Psychiatric Association. (2004). *Diagnostic and statistical manual of mental disorders* (4th ed.). Arlington, VA: Author.

Daudet, A. (2002). *In the land of pain* (J. Barnes, Trans.). New York: Knopf.

Durkheim, E. (1951). *Suicide: A study in sociology* (G. Simpson, Ed.; J. Spaulding & G. Simpson, Trans.). New York: Free Press. (Original work published 1897).

Goffman, E. (1959). *The presentation of self in everyday life.* New York: Anchor.

Goffman, E. (1961). *Asylums: Essays on the social situation of mental patients and other inmates.* New York: Anchor.

Goffman, E. (1963). *Stigma: Notes on the management of spoiled identity.* Englewood Cliffs, NJ: Prentice-Hall.

Goffman, E. (1967). *Interaction ritual: Essays on face-to-face behavior.* New York: Anchor.

Goldberg, J., & Harrow, M. (2004). Consistency of remission and outcome in bipolar and unipolar mood disorders: A 10-year prospective follow-up. *Journal of Affective Disorders, 81,* 123–131.

Goodwin, F., & Jamison, J. (2007). *Manic-depressive illness: Bipolar disorders and recurrent depression* (2nd ed.). London: Oxford University Press.

Greenberg, M. (2008). *Hurry down sunshine.* New York: Other Press.

Jamison, K. (1993). *Touched by fire: Manic depressive illness and the artistic temperament.* New York: Free Press.

Laing, R. D. (1965). *The divided self: An existential study in sanity and madness.* Middlesex, England: Penguin.

Mechanic, D. (1995). Sociological dimensions of illness behavior. *Social Science and Medicine, 41,* 1207–1216.

Monroe, S., & Harkness, K. (2005). Life stress, the "kindling hypothesis" and the recurrence of depression: Considerations from a life stress perspective. *Psychological Review, 112,* 417–445.

Scheff, T. (1966). *Being mentally ill: A sociological theory.* Chicago: Aldine.

Shorter, E. (2008). *Before Prozac: The troubled history of mood disorders in psychiatry.* London: Oxford University Press.

[4]
"NOT MY HAPPY ENDING"
A Family Struggle to Define Roles
in a Challenging Time

THEMBELA KEPE

I need to declare from the beginning that I write as an African who grew up to adulthood in South Africa but who now lives in Canada. This is significant because, in this chapter, I write about a conflict in my family, yet I myself admit occasional failure to successfully negotiate clashes between my African and North American cultures. I have often found that when I am in South Africa for a visit, I get frustrated when I sense that my North American identity, albeit newly acquired, gets in the way when I interact with fellow Africans or analyze everyday situations. Similarly, when I am in Canada, I have created difficulties for myself by sometimes assuming that everyone around me understands the African ways of doing things or thinking. Sometimes this conflict, which I imagine is experienced by multitudes of other people in similar situations around the world, hurts to the core of my being. I declare this reality from the beginning, because my different cultures were important considerations in my decision to tell this story.

The African in me reminded me that the practice of storytelling has a higher purpose in my culture, in that all stories almost always have a lesson for somebody. But my African culture also dictates that one's seniors in the family or community are supposed to be treated with respect, which includes respectfully retreating when a confrontational situation seems imminent between oneself and them. On the other hand, the academic and North American influences in me have encouraged me to re-evaluate some aspects of my behaviour concerning certain cultural values, especially my right to be heard by senior family or community members. In my view, this is not all that bad, because even my South African culture has, without my influence, undergone changes of its own, for better or for worse. The story that I share here, therefore, is as much about an internal and emotional conflict among my own values as it is about conflict between members of my family.

In this story, and whether I like it or not, I am a major player. I believe that if I had never been born, or if I had kept my mouth shut concerning the main issue of concern, then there would not have been a conflict to write about. The other key players include my maternal grandmother, whom I will call Gogo; my mother, whom I will call Zizi; her sister, whom I will call Kazi; my two sisters, Zi and Lusu; and my cousin Mbana. The story spans an almost five-year period during which Gogo was suffering from dementia and other age-related mental illnesses. Different members of my family reacted differently toward Gogo's illness, and toward each other. Concerning how we understood her situation and how we treated her, most of us had very different positions. Gogo's situation and my family's behaviour are apparently not that uncommon, especially in South Africa. Extrapolations made toward the end of the 20th century indicated that by 2010, 6.8 percent and 2.8 percent of South Africans would be over the ages of 60 and 70, respectively (Kinsella & Ferreira, 1997). It is also common across cultures and nationalities that when there is a chronic physical or mental illness of the elderly, family members react differently to the situation, including significant emotional reactions that often lead to family conflicts (Hall, 1989). Despite these commonalities, however, Udvardy and Cattell (1992) argue that beliefs, definitions, and experiences of aging and the elderly are culturally distinct. My story, then, attempts to bring illumination to these commonalities and differences.

As I said earlier, it is unlikely that there would have been a conflict had I not taken a role that other family members thought I was not entitled to. I probably would not have taken the role that I took had it not been for the relationship I had with Gogo, as well as my different life experiences, including my higher education and Western influence. In this chapter, therefore, I first present some background material that can shed light on the events that unfolded from about 2000 to the middle of 2006.

The Context

The struggle with my identity within my family began around the time I was conceived and born. My mother grew up on a farm about 50 kilometres from the city of Grahamstown, South Africa. My mother and her parents were all farm workers. In the early 1960s, my mother left the farm to look for domestic work in the city. While there, she met my father, Gala, who also came from a farm, located about 20 kilometres from my mother's home. Apparently my grandparents were very strict people, so when my mother became pregnant out of wedlock, she was expelled from home. As it turns out, my father was also not pleased with the news, and he was unwilling to stick around to welcome my birth. Expelled from her home and forsaken by the father of her unborn child, Zizi (my mother) found refuge with relatives in the city. When I was born, Zizi's relatives in the city pleaded on her behalf that my grandparents take the child (me) so that she could work to support her new family. Gogo (my grandmother) and her husband agreed, and so began my new life on the farm.

I cannot remember much about the very early years of my life, but what I recall in glimpses is that Zizi was known to me as my aunt (rather than mother) and Gogo was my real mother. I recall vividly that my grandmother always referred to me as *mtan'am* (my child), and that I slept on the same mat next to her. Zizi rarely visited the farm, apparently due to her very tight work schedule as a domestic worker. Besides, there was only one bus per week (on Wednesdays) from the city, which had a stop about 10 kilometres from my mother's home. Thus, travelling to the farm was always a challenge. Even when Zizi visited from the city, neither she nor Gogo explained to me that I had this entire "mother thing" wrong. Instead, in my view, like any aunt who worked in the city, Zizi always brought with her gifts, including clothes for me. The only confusion I had was why I always had a birthday cake from Zizi when my other cousins on the farm never had one.

Then, one day, everything changed unexpectedly. Zizi came to collect me to live with her in Grahamstown. She lived in this one-room place with a man that I was later told was Gala (my father) and a little baby (my sister Zi). Later, I also found out that my father had come back from wherever he had disappeared to, and in 1969, he and my mother had gotten married. They had then decided that I should move in with them so that I could get a better education in the city. I did not enjoy these strange people at all. The place we lived in was far too small for four people. I was used to open spaces on the farm, not to the restrictions in the city, where I was told if I ever ventured outside, cars might kill me. I waited for Gogo to come for me, as I did not believe that these people were my parents. My reasoning was, "Where had they been all along?" Going to school was not a consolation either, because I simply missed my home on the farm. Fortunately, my mother and father took me back to the farm during school holidays.

Before I get into the divisive conflict in my family, I need to briefly talk about the years between my arrival in the city and the time I was about 14 years of age. These were the years in which I reacted very badly to just about everything that my city parents tried to teach me. It was also the time that I received the most punishment from my mother, more than any other child in our neighbourhood. In my culture, spanking—including using the front part of the shoe sole or twigs from a tree—was not restricted by any law, nor was it frowned upon by the community. For a stretch of about seven years until the age of 14, I stole just about anything I considered useful to me and to my friends, fought on the streets, ignored my chores at home, went to the movies without permission, tried smoking cigarettes and cannabis, sniffed benzene and gasoline to get high, joined a gang, and many more unacceptable activities. While dishing out punishment, Zizi would repeatedly threaten me, or maybe just to talk to herself, that she wanted to send me away to Tukayi (a home for delinquent boys). From what I had heard about Tukayi, boys who went there had a tough life, and they often came out worse. I could not fathom any parent wanting to send her child there. To this day, my mother recalls the times I used to respond to the beatings and threats of being sent to Tukayi by saying, "You are not my mother. I know you adopted me."

Ironically, even during these same years of bad behaviour, when I was back on the farm I reverted back to being a model child. I only occasionally got a spanking from my grandmother when I stayed with her during school holidays. The bottom line is that, although to many people my mother's marriage to my father might have sounded like a happy ending, to me it was the opposite. I was always full of suspicion, especially when I compared the treatment and punishment that I received from the two women/mothers. It was only in my mid-teens and young adulthood that I started to appreciate my mother as somebody who loved and cared for me. Still, this realization did not replace the feelings I had for Gogo.

The Problem with Aging Gogo

The aging of my grandmother, along with the mental illness she suffered in the process, caused deep divisions in my family. This new chapter in Gogo's life started slowly. In 1980, she and my grandfather left the farm after he was deemed too old to work. They lived for two years at another farm, with one of my uncles. Then, for about another five years, they lived on their own in Bantustans (reserves for Blacks during apartheid). While they were there, my grandfather passed away. At the suggestion of my mother and her sister, Kazi, Gogo moved to the city of Grahamstown so that she could be closer to her daughters, as her age was by then affecting many of her faculties. For the following eight years, Gogo lived in her own house in the city, with two of her other grandchildren. However, just around the time she turned 90, Zizi and Kazi decided to take turns keeping her in their homes, presumably until the day she died. Gogo was apparently not pleased with this development, often complaining that she did not feel free. She made regular requests, which were initially granted, to go and spend time in her own house. These visits would, however, only last for a day or so. From then on, she would not be allowed to spend time alone.

In 2000, while I was working in Cape Town, I began hearing reports from home that Gogo was being "difficult." Zizi would say, "Oh, Gogo is so stubborn now. She refuses to change clothes or she interferes in business that is not hers." I would also be told that "Oh, now she is here with me, because Kazi needs a break." Other times Zizi would say, "I have now sent Gogo to Kazi; I need a break, too!" When I visited Grahamstown, I would acknowledge the aging part, but I suppose I simply refused to see or find any fault with Gogo. To me, she was the same industrious person who always wanted to keep busy by working around the house. By 2002, the situation had escalated. Gogo was 96 years old, and Kazi and Zizi now used words such as "I am now tired of Gogo" or "She embarrasses us." If one listened to what they said about her, one would conclude that they simply blamed their misfortune on her nasty and annoying personality. Kazi and Zizi assumed that Gogo could change her behaviour at any time she chose but was declining to do so. I used to remain passive when I heard these comments and accusations, although I felt that I understood what was going on with Gogo's health and they did not. My problem was that I felt powerless to intervene over the phone. I could not explain to my mother what Gogo was suffering from and that the behaviour she was exhibiting is common to most people her age.

In September 2002, I got the opportunity to observe things more closely. I had just finished my doctoral degree, and my family, including Gogo, came to Cape Town to celebrate the occasion with me. I was obviously delighted that they decided to bring her along so that she could see where I lived. However, I was also mindful of the fact that the real reason they brought her along was that they did not trust anybody else to manage her the way they did. The second reason why they brought her along, as admitted by Zizi later, was that they wanted me to see how troublesome Gogo was. Zizi said something like, "We know you don't believe us when we tell you what Gogo does, so we want you to observe her over the next three days."

It was not long before, to Zizi and Kazi's gratification, I was called outside and shown that Gogo had taken my neatly folded clean laundry and hung it outside on some tree branches. Upon seeing this, I recalled how on the farm there were no clotheslines; laundry was hung on anything that stood up, including trees, garden fences, and so forth. My reaction was simply a feeling of amusement and sadness. But I could see that Zizi and Kazi wanted me to either get upset or admit that Gogo was out of control. My other response was to ensure that the door to my bedroom was locked when I was not there, and I advised other occupants in my house to keep an eye on their belongings. In a way, my reaction was a form of prevention, rather than blame or punishment of Gogo's actions. This discourse, of course, did not satisfy Zizi or Kazi, who expected me to join them in their view and condemnation of Gogo's actions.

Nobody Understands

The next stage in Gogo's aging and illness was extremely difficult. It was clear that she suffered from dementia, but she was not taken for a medical assessment for her ailing health. As a very strong and physically healthy person most of her life, she rarely visited doctors. The cost for a doctor's visit may have also been an issue, but I am not certain about this. There are three main aspects that made Gogo's last five years of life difficult for all of us, including causing a huge conflict that only the closest family members ever talked about or acknowledged. First, Gogo got worse in her "troublesomeness." Second, those who looked after her (mostly the two daughters), escalated their tactics of dealing with her. This included how they physically handled her to "encourage" her to do certain things, or to restrain or "discourage" her from doing certain other things. Third, and as a result of the previous two points, I could no longer keep my mouth shut. These three issues caused so much anger and resentment among my close relatives that the negative effects have lasted to this day. In the following segment, I will revisit these three points to show how they all tested the highest limits of tolerance for all those involved.

Consistent with somebody suffering from dementia, Gogo was in and out of sanity almost every day between 2002 and 2006. Evidently, people with dementia retain aspects from their long-term memory much more so than from their short-term memory. Thus, it appears that there were moments in which Gogo's memory went back to her time on the farm. In those moments, she would pretty much do things the way she had done them on the farm. For example, I was told that one day she was in the kitchen alone, and when somebody checked on her later, they found that she had gone outside and collected twigs from a bush in the backyard and made a fire on top of the gas stove. There was another day when she disappeared, resulting in the whole neighbourhood joining in to help in the search for her. As it turns out, she had simply gone to meet her husband, who, she claimed, must have been wondering about what was holding her up for so long. Gogo did not remember that her husband had been dead for over 20 years at the time. These episodes, including a recurring one that used to cause a lot of embarrassment to my family—whereby Gogo would peak through the locked gates and ask strangers who passed by to please open the gate for her as she was being held against her will—resulted in a rapid loss of patience by my mother, aunt, and sister Lusu. After all, they shared the total responsibility of looking after her. From what they told me, it is clear that none of them had experienced quite this version of aging (*ukwaluphala*) before. For the average person in my community, aging is mainly exhibited through diminishing physical attributes, such as poor eyesight, loss of hearing, slowness, and perhaps the occasional inability to control one's bladder. As far as the psychological aspects of aging were concerned, my family had only limited understanding. They thought the effects were limited to occasional forgetfulness of people and events. Full-blown dementia was something they had trouble understanding, let alone accepting as a fact of life. It is also possible that the mysterious and degenerative outcomes of dementia are little known in a society that has had a very low life expectancy for its impoverished people.

Gogo beat the odds in life expectancy, but unfortunately for her, she could not beat the negative outcomes of her advanced age. In affluent, welfare-based societies such as that found in Canada, the universal health care system, old-age pension, disability pensions, other retirement benefits, higher levels of education, homes for the aged, and so on, all combine to cushion some of the ravages of old age. In countries such as South Africa, where the indigenous peoples have been colonized, exploited, and kept poor and uneducated, responsibility for dealing with the ailments that come with aging is dumped on well-meaning but totally unprepared relatives. As my narrative shows, much human suffering is often the outcome.

So, how did my relatives react to Gogo's "antics"? Well, I can only talk authoritatively about those instances that I observed. More often than not, it would involve yelling at her, either to warn her or to repeat an instruction that she had already been given several times. I remember on many occasions when Gogo would be holding her plate or cup of tea but would not pay attention to how these were balanced in her hands or on her lap. The consequence would be a spill on the floor, or on many other occasions, a near-spill. Somebody would shout, "Gogo, look at you again. You are going to spill. How many times should we tell you that you need to hold the dishes firmly in your hand and pay attention throughout your eating!" In such cases, and if Gogo was still not responding, a member of the family would stand up and vigorously shift the cup or plate to the suggested position of safety.

There were times when I would observe Gogo refusing to go to bed, even when everybody else was prepared to call it a day. In such cases, she would just ignore calls for her to go to bed. My family would resort to pulling her by the arm in order to take her to bed. One day, I noticed that they had a new strategy of asking her to sit on a blanket on the floor, so that if she refused to go to bed, they could simply scoop her up by the blanket and drag her to bed. During most of these struggles, I sadly observed that Gogo did not enjoy any of this treatment. She would, unsuccessfully, try to hold on to the furniture. In all honesty, at no time did I witness any beating or physical force used upon Gogo that caused hurt or injury. I had read many newspaper reports and watched secretly recorded tapes of the abusive treatment that some elderly people suffered in old-age homes or even in the care of their relatives. I must admit that, in my observation, what my family was doing did not rank up there with those abusive acts. Nevertheless, Gogo's reaction, coupled with my understanding of her helplessness, of aging, and of mental illness convinced me that what my mother and aunt were doing was not the best they could do for her. Besides, I had also observed the pleasant treatment of the elderly in other cultures. I felt I had seen enough; I felt I had to intervene on Gogo's behalf.

I could no longer stand and watch Gogo's frail arms holding on to chairs while others pulled at her by any available limb to get her to bed. I wish I could forget her look in my direction and her words on several occasions, saying, "Look my child what they are doing to me (*jonga mntan'am into abayen-zayo kum*). They treat me like a child. These people are so cruel (*bakhohlakele*)." So, when a similar event happened during one of the nights that she refused to go to bed, I spoke up and told them to stop, as I could not stand to see her fear and anguish. They stopped, but they challenged me to get her to bed. I could sense the silent accusation and sarcasm in their challenge. I told them I would try, then proceeded to give Gogo a few minutes to calm down before I attempted to persuade her that she should go to bed. Within a minute or so, on that particular night, she stood up and went to bed. I am very much aware, and openly admit, that her docile agreement to go to bed without further fuss could have been a fluke. My family was also quick to remind me of such. Yet no one forgot the occasion, because this was the first time I really expressed my disapproval of how they treated Gogo, and because I showed them an alternate way. I knew that I was levelling an accusation against my mother, aunt, and sister. I also knew that I would hear from them about this for a long time to come. I was right!

I was told by my family members that I did not understand Gogo or the situations I was reacting to. On many occasions, my mother said to me, "You do not live here. You only observe portions of what Gogo is like. You have no idea what it is like to live the life we are living with her!" She proceeded to tell me that it was unfair of me to accuse them of being heavy-handed. These words hurt me, because I could sense that they went beyond explaining that I had limited experience with Gogo's illness. I felt they were loaded with additional meanings. My Western education, my years in Canada, and my apparently diminished respect for certain aspects of my cultural ethics (such as not challenging senior family members) were part of the statement my mother made. In a way, her words were a counter-accusation. Given that I had already stirred the pot, I proceeded to tell them that I thought they did not understand Gogo's illness either. I told them that no yelling at or pulling of Gogo by her limbs would make her remember from day to day what she was supposed to do or not to do. They needed to understand, I told them, that it was unlikely that things would get any better. Unfortunately, it appeared that my statements simply made the situation worse. Suddenly, I felt I was an embarrassment to my family for daring to challenge their judgment, especially given my distance from the situation. What was even harder was a sense I began to have of their message: "Back off." I think I was also given a similar message through my mother's other little statements: "This is our mother, not yours." Even though this was never verbally or openly communicated, I felt the weight of the message. It offended me to the core. In my world, Gogo *was* my mother, and it was obvious to me that she needed my protection. I knew that even in her compromised state Gogo did feel emotional pain. I observed that on occasions during her illness when she lost two of her sons and two grandsons. She remained quiet when they told her about the deaths, but, in her own time, she began to cry without telling anybody what she was feeling. These observations convinced me that my culture needs to find a better way of dealing with issues such as mental illness among the elderly. But the cultural barriers between me and my mother and aunt also prevented them from understanding why I was so bothered by their actions. After all, they thought they were doing what any well-meaning relative should do. They thought it was I who was out of line; it was I who needed to brush up on my cultural manners.

In the last year of her life, I saw Gogo twice. Both times, I was told by my mother that Gogo did not remember people anymore. But on both my visits from Canada, upon being asked if she knew who I was, Gogo would say "You think I am stupid. How can I not know Thembela." Then they would ask her whose child Thembela was, and she would answer, "Mine." This response thrilled me, but I also suspect that this clear recognition was not easy for people who were not always remembered by Gogo.

This sad chapter in Gogo's life ended in the middle of 2006, when she departed from this world. I am told that she had gone to the hospital because she was not having regular bowel movements. At the time, she was 100 years old and could no longer stay still. Even though her hospital bed had sides to keep her from falling out, the nurses had apparently left them down. She fell from her bed and broke her arm. She never recovered from that injury, and after a few weeks, she died. The last episode was typical of the life Gogo lived in her last five years in this world—that is, not being fully understood about her illness. As a result of the earlier misunderstandings and tensions, I have never really shared with my family about how I felt about Gogo's death. Neither did anybody care to ask me about how I felt. I was already living in Canada when she died and therefore was not able to attend her funeral. Sometimes, I feel that my absence was for the best. I feel I would have struggled to see my relatives crying or doing any other form of public grieving when I knew deep down that there was probably a huge element of relief that they felt.

I have now visited South Africa several times since her death, but the topic of Gogo is rarely raised. When there is any mention of her at all, it is usually in reference to points in time when all was good. I still feel some resentment for not being fully acknowledged as someone who had a say in how my "mother" (Gogo) was treated. I also feel that all of us are angry at how things unfolded between us (the accusations and counter-accusations), and, as a result, we are unable to deal with our grieving by recalling Gogo's last days publicly or out loud. Hidden in between our feelings are family secrets—how poorly Gogo was treated and how we accused each other. We eventually have come to a place where we can express love for each other—of course, outside of the bubble of our family secrets.

One thing that I did—and I still wonder if it was a wise thing to do—was to buy Gogo's house during my first trip there after her death. The beneficiaries had been my mother and her two sisters, and they needed the cash; I needed something to connect me to Gogo. What unfolded after the deal went through requires a whole other story. For now, it is sufficient to say that there are tenants occupying my house, and that I played no part in selecting them or approving their presence there. Even after three years, I have yet to see any sort of income from the rent. Because of the caution regarding discussing anything to do with Gogo, I have just left things to continue the way they are. I am the owner only insofar as my name is on the deed; otherwise Gogo's "children" are in charge. Only time will tell what kind of a role this house will continue to play in my life.

As an academic, I have tried to remove myself from the situation, albeit temporarily, and have attempted to analyze and see what went wrong in my family beyond the descriptive narrative I have given above. Perhaps, according to the African culture, nothing went wrong. Maybe the only thing that went wrong is me, through my own exposure to the norms and practices of other cultures. It may be difficult for Western readers of this narrative to fully appreciate the roots of the conflict I tried to describe. For example, it might not make sense to Western readers that my grandmother's illness was not fully understood or appropriately dealt with; they may also not understand why a grown-up man like me should feel restricted from expressing his opinions to other family members. However, there are serious cultural differences in how families can and do interact, and there are rules about who can say what to whom. In many part of Africa, younger people, regardless of their age, are expected to act with deference toward their elders. As Giddens (1997) reminds us, as social scientists, we should try as much as possible not to judge other cultures by comparing them to our own. Despite colonialism and other foreign influences on the Xhosa culture, to which I belong, there are no norms or values for dealing with dementia. To my knowledge, there is not even a corresponding Xhosa word for describing what my grandmother was going through. In my culture, this is all lumped under one word: aging (*ukwaluphala*). However, ironically, in my frustration with the situation, I was guilty of acting like the very thing I detest the most: an outsider who fails to understand the dynamics of my culture, passing judgment on my culture. It is ironic, but true, that in this conflict, I had become the outsider who passed judgment. I now realize that deep down I probably would have preferred to have my grandmother taken to a home for the elderly and taken care of. I was momentarily blinded to the fact that in my culture, sending one's parent away to live with total strangers when they grow old is close to a taboo. Makiwane and Kwizera (2006) argue that there is a cultural expectation that children will take their parents in, for good, until the last day. A well-known Canadian sociologist has also written extensively on the social aspects of ethnic identity (Isajiw, 1990). Isajiw talks about "obligatory identity" to refer to aspects that different ethnic groups consider a must in the preservation of intact cultural relations. If all or most members of the ethnic group are immigrants to another country, then the obligatory identities, over time, may change in unison, without causing too much of a conflict among family members. However, if certain members of the ethnic group leave and others stay put, strong differences in the understanding of rights and obligations may develop over time. The source of the conflict, at least in my eyes, was this change in the perception of obligations: I was expecting a medicalized, more interventionist type of care for Gogo, whereas her daughters' insisted on keeping her at home and relating to her as if everything was the same (with the exception of her increased "difficulty").

I also admit that much has changed in the country of my origin, especially in the wake of the devastation brought about by AIDS; there is a reversal of roles whereby the elderly often end up being the ones who take care of their adult children, as well as their grandchildren. Even if there were no cultural barriers to having Gogo go to a home for eldercare, research shows that, with the global pressure on health care systems affecting even industrialized countries, the provisions made for the elderly in a changing society such as South Africa would be limited (Bohman, Vasuthevan, van Wyk, and Ekman, 2007). In other words, even if they had tried, my family would have had a hard time finding a place for Gogo, especially one in a city of their choosing. In addition to this, Møller (1996) believes that harsh apartheid laws, among other things, weakened traditional intergenerational support systems, and that they may have, in fact, contributed to many conflicts between the generations of urban Blacks in South Africa.

It may also be hard for Western readers to understand why it was, and continues to be, difficult for me to confront my mother and my aunt about events concerning Gogo, especially as it pertains to the physical handling she received. I believe anthropologists such as Monica Hunter (1979) who have conducted detailed studies of South African cultures are correct to suggest that one's cultural identity partly relies on the individual's choice to embrace certain aspects of his or her culture. So, as I mentioned in the beginning, while there is sometimes internal conflict about which cultural aspects I should feel comfortable with or base my decisions on, I have no desire to outright reject huge chunks of what made me who I am in the first place. This is probably why I have not continued to talk about Gogo with my family. It allows some form of peace, albeit not a negotiated one. Additionally, by continuing to tread carefully around the past, I feel I am saving myself from being given further lessons on Xhosa culture. I may also be giving myself permission to disregard how much my own views and expectations may have changed. My hope is that neither I nor any of my remaining family members will have to go through what Gogo went through.

References

Bohman, D. M., Vasuthevan, S., van Wyk, N. C., & Ekman, S. (2007). "We clean our houses, prepare for weddings and go to funerals": Daily lives of elderly Africans in Majaneng, South Africa. *Journal of Cross-Cultural Gerontology, 22*(4), 323–337.

Giddens, A. (1997). *Sociology* (3rd ed.). Cambridge, MA: Polity Press.

Hall, B. L. (1989). The hospitalized elderly and intergenerational conflict. *Journal of Applied Gerontology, 8*(3), 294–306.

Hunter, M. (1979). *Reaction to conquest: Effects of contact with Europeans on the Pondo of South Africa.* Cape Town: David Phillip.

Isajiw, W. W. (1990). Ethnic identity retention. In R. Breton, W. Isajiw, W. Kalbach, & J. G. Reitz (Eds.), *Ethnic identity and equality: Varieties of experience in a Canadian city.* Toronto: University of Toronto Press.

Kinsella, K., & Ferreira, M. (1997). *Aging trends: South Africa* (International Brief). Washington, DC: Department of Commerce.

Makiwane, M., & Kwizera, S. A. (2006). An investigation of the quality of life of the elderly in South Africa, with specific reference to Mpumalanga. *Applied Research in Quality of Life, 1*(3–4), 297–313.

Møller, V. (1996). Intergenerational relations and time use in urban Black South African households. *Social Indicators Research, 37*(3), 303–332.

Udvardy, M., & Cattell, M. (1992). Gender, aging and power in sub-Saharan Africa: Challenges and puzzles. *Journal of Cross-Cultural Gerontology, 7*(4), 275–288.

[5]
MY SISTERS ARE THE PROBLEM

Sibling Struggles over Power and Identity in
Relation to Caring for an Aging Parent

BONNIE LASHEWICZ

Families are central to our views of how the care needs of an aging population are met, with adult children being the most likely group of relatives to provide instrumental and emotional assistance (Karantzas, Foddy, & Evans, 2003).
The terms *filial responsibility* and *filial obligation* have been applied to capture
the combination of love, duty, and desire to reciprocate for their upbringing
that motivates adult children to provide care to aging parents (Aronson, 1990;
Gans & Silverstein, 2006). And because they occupy the same location in the
family lineage, adult children have genealogically equivalent relationships to
parents and accompanying expectations for sharing parent care obligations
with each other (Finch & Mason, 1990; Globerman, 1995; Lashewicz, Manning, Hall, & Keating, 2007). Yet although obligation is shared, actual sibling
contributions to care are often diverse and uneven. Factors such as personality, gender, other family responsibilities, employment status, and proximity to
the care recipient influence the type and extent of caregiving involvement.
For example, comparatively less care is provided by siblings who live at a distance or are employed full-time (Ingersoll-Dayton, Neal, Ha, & Hammer,
2003). The influence of gender is evident in tendencies for brothers to become
helpers and co-providers while sisters are more likely to initiate care and
become care coordinators (Hequembourg & Brallier, 2005; Matthews, 2002).

Siblings are a distinctly equivalent group who take careful account of each
other's circumstances and care contributions. Tensions among siblings over
how care is shared have most often been reported as arising when some

siblings view others as contributing inadequately (Lashewicz et al., 2007). Contrasting with findings of tensions over some siblings not doing their share, a few research accounts identify sibling concerns with feeling excluded because others are maintaining control over parent care decisions (Cicirelli, 1995; George, 1986; Lashewicz & Keating, 2009). Paul's story, presented below, illustrates dynamics of sibling resentments that can occur when some siblings are perceived as dominating parent care decisions. Paul's story was collected as part of a study of how siblings share tasks and responsibilities for the care of their aging parents and whether they regard their sharing as fair. Paul is from a family of six siblings, and his account is one of opposing sibling styles and divided loyalties. Paul agreed to be interviewed on the condition that his siblings not be contacted; he was insistent on avoiding what he viewed as a risk of further "stirring things up." Thus Paul provided a privileged perspective, as his was the only sibling voice heard first-hand. Paul elaborated his representation of his siblings' points of view by sharing a collection of written correspondence between himself and four of his five siblings as they attempted to work through how their mother's care needs should be met.

Paul is the eldest of the six siblings and lives an hour away from his mother. He has a sister, Sarah, who is three years younger, and a brother, John, who is five years younger. Sarah also lives an hour from their mother, although in a different direction from Paul; John lives in another province. Another sister, Geraldine, is nine years younger than Paul and lives four hours away from their mother. Twin brothers, Barry and Nick, born when Paul was nearly 20 years old, complete this sibling group. Barry lives near John in another province, and Nick lives near Sarah, an hour from their mother.

In Paul's family, parent care needs had arisen nearly six years earlier when Paul's father was diagnosed with cancer. The cancer was aggressive, taking the life of Paul's father 10 months after being discovered. Paul's father's cancer treatment and accompanying care needs were intense, and it was mainly Paul's sisters, Sarah and Geraldine, who mobilized to support their mother and care for their father during his illness. For the last few months of the father's life, one or the other of Paul's sisters stayed at the parents' house. As their father's life ended, their mother's care needs came into clearer view. Their mother showed symptoms of dementia, which until then had been to a large extent covered by their father's provision of structure and guidance and by the subsequent concentration on their father's care needs.

Confronting Parent Care Needs: A Matter of Style

Paul recognizes the effort his sisters extended during their fathers' illness, both in helping their mother through this phase and in providing hands-on care to their father. Paul notes that, following this demanding time, Sarah and Geraldine were likely exhausted to the point of burnout. Although Paul is thankful for the care provided by his sisters, he does not agree with his sisters' caregiving styles. He views Sarah and Geraldine as quick to take charge and eager to impose their ideas. Paul points out that their father had been an opinionated man and believes his sisters take after their father. According to Paul, Sarah in particular feels the need to spell things out to others. Sarah had taken some nurses' aide training and considered herself the "medical expert" in the family. At the front of Paul's mind is an example of how Sarah's controlling style infringed on his own privacy. In the final days of his father's life, Paul went to his father's bedside to have a quiet conversation. Sarah followed Paul into the room and sat behind him while finishing her lunch; this experience left Paul sad and resentful that he did not have a private final conversation with his father.

Paul notes that given the forceful styles of both his sisters, their co-operation with each other in the care of their father was not representative of how they usually got along together. There had been a 13-year period when Sarah and Geraldine did not speak to each other, a falling out that had included prohibiting communication between their respective children. By comparison, Paul describes himself and one other brother, Barry, as mild, quiet, and taking after their mother. His other two brothers, John and Nick, are opinionated, outspoken, and, like Sarah and Geraldine, take after their father. Beginning early in life, Paul and Barry were inclined to go with the flow in the family, whereas John and Nick were more provocative and would often argue with their father. Paul draws a distinction between his two assertive brothers and his two comparably assertive sisters in terms of their propensity for holding grudges. Contrasting with the disagreement between his two sisters that led to a lengthy estrangement, Paul notes that, although there had often been disagreements between his opinionated brothers and among the four brothers in general, none of the brothers had ever gone a day without being on speaking terms with any of the others.

When it comes to caring for their mother, Paul makes the distinction that, whereas his sisters impose solutions according to their own beliefs, he and his brothers, particularly Barry, are inclined to observe and try to follow their mother's preferences and wishes. Paul's father believed Paul's quiet demeanour made Paul the right person to serve as his mother's executor and power of attorney; the importance Paul's father placed on style is reinforced by his designating Paul's quiet younger brother, Barry, to be the backup executor and power of attorney. Paul's less reserved brothers, John and Nick, are accepting and supportive of their father's decision and Paul's central role in their mother's later years.

Paul says that Sarah and Geraldine have acknowledged his responsibility and care for their mother. Yet, they qualify their recognition with claims that, although Paul may be doing what he thinks best, there are urgent needs to which he is not attending. The contrasting viewpoints and styles of the sisters versus the brothers have led to a pronounced divide in this family. Given that neither Sarah nor Geraldine was interviewed, however, the sisters' perspectives on the nature of the family divide are contained to excerpts relayed by Paul.

The Inception of the Divide: Dad's Final Weeks and Final Wishes

During the difficult time surrounding their father's illness, Paul notes that Dad's greatest concern was Mom. Their father had been a vigorous, youthful man, and there had been a sense in the family that he would likely outlive their mother. As his illness quickly progressed, their father was anxious to make plans so that their mother would have the support she needed. Their father was in some ways "old school," holding traditional views about gender roles in families. He took his four sons together to the bank to review his financial affairs. In designating Paul to serve as the executor and by giving him power of attorney for his wife, their father considered Paul's gentle style as well as his status as the firstborn son. Paul said his father did not discuss this decision with Sarah and Geraldine because he wished to avoid a confrontation, particularly at a time when his energy was depleted by his illness. Nor did Paul's father appoint Sarah, the older daughter, to be the executor or power of attorney because Paul's father knew Sarah would do things her own way, "come hell or high water, whether Mom liked it or not." Thus, as well as managing his mother's finances, Paul assumed the less typically male role of coordinating his mother's care.

What Mom Needs: Who Knows Best?

Friction between siblings over their mother's care needs began immediately following the death of their father. Paul assumed the power of attorney role. He believed in and shared his mother's special attachment to her home, a house her husband had built and subsequently shared with her for nearly 60 years. As his effort to support their mother's wish to remain in her house for as long as possible, Paul made monitoring telephone calls to her twice a day. Paul had heard from a neighbour who worked in long-term care that a main reason people are admitted to residential facilities is because of inadequate nutrition. Paul developed a system of providing meals to their mother where he prepared and packaged daily meals, which he delivered once or twice a week. One of his monitoring calls was in the evening to ask their mother what she was having for dinner, thus ensuring she was eating the meals he had prepared.

Sarah, allied with Geraldine, opposed this meal provision arrangement on a number of counts. Initially, the two sisters claimed that their mother needed to learn to do things for herself. Paul notes that his sisters think their mother was controlled by their father and, after his death, needed to stand on her own two feet. Geraldine claimed that caring for their father at the end of his life gave her and Sarah considerable insight into what their mother needed. Geraldine declared the expertise she and Sarah had gained in an email to her siblings where she began, "Let me tell you a little about Dad's last weeks." Geraldine noted that their father wanted her and Sarah nearby. At the same time, Geraldine described how their father objected when she or Sarah would intercept and question his nurses (first at home and later in hospital). Geraldine contended that she and Sarah had to get information directly from their father's nurses because their mother would block out things she did not want to hear and was thus not a reliable source of information.

Paul is frustrated by his sisters' assessment that their mother was failing to fully comprehend what was happening. In Paul's view, their mother was overwhelmed as her husband's health rapidly declined and her own early symptoms of dementia progressed. Paul considers his sisters' intervention with their father's health care providers and insistence that their mother "face facts" as lacking regard for the dignity of both parents. Specifically, Paul claims that their mother was struggling with many losses to the point of falling apart, yet his sisters were pushing her to do things for herself, including planning and preparing her own meals. Eventually, as their mother's dementia progressed and her needs became more pronounced, Sarah and Geraldine conceded that meal provision was appropriate, but they claimed the meals provided by Paul were not nutritious. Furthering the sisters' position that Paul's meals were not adequate, Sarah went on to arrange for a formal Meals on Wheels service, despite the fact that Paul continued to provide meals.

The lack of sibling agreement over their mother's dietary needs intensified into a more serious conflict over where their mother should live. Paul continued in his conviction that their mother wanted to be in her own house and should be supported in her wish to remain there for as long as possible. By contrast, Sarah and Geraldine were anxious for their mother to move to a residential facility. This subject was debated extensively among the siblings. In a group email, John expressed his belief that the sharing of care among the siblings was effective in enabling their mother to remain in her home. John summarized that Paul was providing meals, Sarah was taking their mother out each week, Nick was doing chores toward the upkeep of the house, and each of the siblings, including the three who lived at greater distances, occasionally had their mother stay with them for the weekend. John concluded that "if we all continue to do our bit, Mom can remain in her house."

While remaining active in the sibling group's support for their mother in her home, Sarah was the first to declare that their mother needed a new living arrangement. Sarah's claim was fuelled by an incident where their mother had refused to attend her day program by abruptly turning away the transit driver who had been scheduled to take her to the program. Sarah contended that their mother's resistance to the day program was a result of their mother being confused and disoriented. Sarah had an added sense of urgency about their mother's need for a new living arrangement, as Sarah worried about the potential for their mother to lock herself out of her house, especially troubling given the approach of colder weather. Sarah issued an email call to action to her siblings, claiming that their mother's needs were being neglected. She wrote, "I hate to see Mom treated like this. This is tantamount to elder abuse. Mom is unable to help herself and desperately needs our help. Time is critical. There is no time like the present! What are we waiting for?"

Paul remained convinced that the best place for their mother was in her own home. Paul attributed their mother's refusal to attend the day program to her disinterest in the program. Further, Paul's position on where their mother lived continued to include the idea that supporting her to remain in her home maintained a key part of their mother's identity as a physically active woman with a great love for walking. Their mother had, as long as Paul could remember, taken brisk one-hour walks every morning. In addition, their mother walked to purchase her groceries at the neighbourhood supermarket every second day. Acknowledging that their mother was forgetful, Paul had, to an extent, addressed the concern over the potential for her to lock herself out of her house by leaving a house key with the neighbour. This neighbour had lived in the house next door for Paul's entire life. He and Paul had grown up together, and the neighbour had given Paul an added assurance that the positioning of the kitchen windows enabled him to monitor whether Paul's mother was in her kitchen each morning and evening.

Several months after Sarah declared the urgent need for their mother to move to a residential facility, Paul also reached the conclusion that it was time their mother began planning to move. Unlike Sarah's decision, Paul's was not spurred by an incident in their mother's behaviour; rather, it was arrived at in response to their mother telling him that she thought it was time she moved to a supported living setting. Once Paul conveyed to his siblings his belief about their mother's readiness to move, the focus of disagreement between Paul and his sisters shifted from whether and when their mother should move to which facility would be best for her.

The formal planning began with their mother undergoing an assessment for long-term care placement, which was scheduled by Paul. By the time of the assessment, Barry's wife, Tammy, was staying with their mother; Tammy was in town as part of her program of training to become a home care aide. At their mother's request, Tammy accompanied her to her assessment appointment. Sarah also attended the assessment appointment, although she was not invited, and was deeply hurt to find Tammy there. Paul relates that, in scheduling the assessment, their mother had explicitly asked that Sarah not attend. Their mother worried that Sarah would tell cousins and aunts about the process, and their mother did not want details of her memory problems widely known. Their mother had frequently spoken to Paul of her distress over an incident where Sarah had not kept personal information private. At their mother's house, Sarah had met with someone who was hired to mow their mother's lawn; Sarah had called across the yard to the gentleman, as he was leaving, that he should call her if their mother forgot to pay him. Their mother was embarrassed by this incident and, in all, found Sarah's approaches to be demanding and insensitive. Paul notes that their mother had, on a number of occasions, asked him what she had to do to get Sarah "off my back." In Paul's opinion, Sarah let her own need to be in control take priority over others' need for privacy.

In the further interest of maintaining privacy about her health, their mother requested that her long-term care assessment results be sent to Paul and not shared among the sibling group. Almost immediately after the assessment had taken place, Geraldine became the spokesperson for herself and Sarah in asserting their right to see the results. Geraldine's requests were frequent, lengthy, and urgent sounding. She claimed that she was not getting information she deserved and needed. More specifically, Geraldine claimed, Paul was withholding information from her and Sarah yet sharing the information with their brothers. Paul was irritated by his sisters' accusations and reiterated that he was keeping the information between himself and their mother because this was what their mother requested. Paul also says that Geraldine has a double standard. She was quick to assert her own right to information, yet she kept information from others when it served her. For example, on occasions when Paul arrived at their mother's home to visit or drop off meals, he was surprised to find Geraldine visiting. Geraldine would respond to his surprise by referring to her visits as her "little secret."

Geraldine's distress over not receiving information was echoed by Sarah's criticism that Paul was mishandling the placement process and acting as if his was the only sibling opinion that counted. In one email, Sarah lamented that "when you have a 'dicktator' in the family, there isn't much anyone else can do." Paul indicates that there was a recurrent email communication pattern around their mother's status and care needs: Paul would regularly send a factual account of steps he had taken in managing their mother's care and Sarah would respond with a list of criticisms about what Paul had done. Paul's telephone communication with Sarah followed the same pattern: he would provide a brief update to Sarah but then be drawn into a lengthy debate and justification of his decisions.

Paul's brothers Nick and John had described similar patterns of communication with Sarah. Nick lives in the same community as Sarah. He relayed to Paul that one day when driving home, he noticed Sarah's vehicle coming up behind him. Nick turned off on a side road, acting as if he was going to a call (as part of his maintenance job), because if he had gone home as originally planned, he believed Sarah would have followed and engaged him in a lengthy debate about their mother's care. John, who lives in another province, expressed similar frustration with email communications. John had reached the point where he felt so aggravated by Sarah's lengthy reactions to Paul's email updates · that John no longer read the emails. Instead, John asked his wife to read the correspondence and provide him with a summary.

Overall, Paul felt harassed by communications from Sarah, yet he remained determined to do what his mother wanted him to do rather than what his sisters insisted on.

Talking Face-to-Face

In light of her unhappiness with what she regarded as Paul's control over decisions about where their mother would live and her ongoing belief that a new living arrangement was needed immediately, Sarah called a family meeting with her local brothers, Paul and Nick. Geraldine did not attend because their mother was in the middle of a two-week stay at Geraldine's home when the meeting was held. At the meeting, Sarah presented what she and Geraldine had investigated and determined to be the absolute best residential option for their mother. Sarah was in fact adamant that their mother should not return to her home after her visit at Geraldine's but should go directly to this facility. Sarah was not receptive to concerns raised by her brothers—for example, that at this facility, their mother would be the only woman in the four-unit wing. Further, Paul and Nick held that their mother should not move immediately, because, at that time, Tammy was again in town for training, completing a four-month field placement and staying with their mother. In response, Sarah accused her brothers of conspiring to find a different facility that would be inconvenient for Sarah to visit. The debate was heated, and Paul left after Sarah called him a name. Nick left in frustration shortly after Paul. In the meantime, Tammy had arrived at the house, having finished her field placement shift for the day. Sarah and Tammy continued to debate residential placement, with Tammy agreeing with Paul and Nick that Sarah and Geraldine's choice of placement was not ideal. Their discussion ended when Sarah became enraged enough to strike Tammy in the face. The next day, Tammy filed a police report about the assault.

Sarah too was, of course, dissatisfied with the family meeting. After responding to the police follow-up about the complaint filed by her sister in-law, Sarah proceeded to act on her belief that the residential placement she and Geraldine had found was best. Sarah relocated their mother to this residence without informing her brothers. Three days after the relocation, Sarah sent an email to her siblings explaining what she had done and that her mother was settled into the new living arrangement. When Paul went to see their mother at the new residence, their mother told him she wanted to go home, so Paul helped her pack and took her back to her house.

Severing Contact

Tensions between sisters and brothers had been building up in the weeks preceding the relocation and counter-relocation of their mother. John had interjected that although many nasty emails were being exchanged among the siblings, any communication was better than none. The tug-of-war over the best place for their mother to live was the point at which communications from sisters to brothers stopped entirely. Shortly before this communication shutdown, Sarah had lamented that Paul was the one with the power and that Geraldine's and her opinions did not count. Such, concluded Sarah, is the life of being "a female" in this family.

Paul had held his ground, insisting that steps were being taken to find a residential setting where their mother would be happy. Within the next two months, their mother made the transition to a facility that she and Paul agreed was suitable. In this setting, their mother took part in an array of social and recreational offerings and quickly came to be regarded as the most active person who lived there. Paul admits that the situation is not perfect; he gets called because sometimes his mother is anxious and wants to go home. At the same time, Paul is satisfied that, of the options available, this one best fits his mother's style and needs. Paul regrets the damaged relationships with his sisters yet concludes that he is as determined as ever not to let anyone run over Mom.

As an important part of a kinship group, siblings spend a lifetime establishing links with each other. They also spend a lifetime separating their identities. When parents enter their later years, identities and interaction styles of each of the siblings get reasserted in the face of rising parent care obligations (Lashewicz & Keating, 2009). Given the demanding nature of caregiving, it is commonsensical to expect siblings to be attentive to whether other siblings are meeting filial obligations. Paul's story directs attention to how filial obligations are negotiated and renegotiated in light of rights and obligations to influence parent care decisions and outcomes. Silverstein, Conroy, & Gans (2008, p. 73) note that studies of the division of caregiving labour often do not account for "interpersonal dynamics that underlie negotiations." Paul's account provides a window into the types of interpersonal issues that arise as siblings work through how parent care will be provided. Through his story, we get a glimpse of how gender and birth order may confound perceptions and expectations and may affect the apportioning of responsibilities among the siblings. It is quite telling that Sarah complained about "being a female in this family." From the sick father's "paternal" arrangements for his wife to the continuation of protection by the sons, there seems to be a gendered axis in this family, as is the case in many families. It is quite possible that women's legitimate concerns, per-haps including the claim by Sarah and Geraldine that their mother had been controlled by their father, may be interpreted as illegitimate, whereas men's con-cerns, such as Paul's belief that the house built by their father should be main-tained, might be seen as more legitimate.

At the same time, caregiving is a domain of family life where women's opinions have often prevailed. For example, Matthews (1995) found that both brothers and sisters tended to view caregiving tasks performed by sisters as more important than tasks performed by brothers. Scholars have long dis-cussed women in terms of their positions within families as kin keepers (Rosen-thal, 1985), who maintain connections and coordinate care in response to illness and advanced age. Perhaps the gender struggles in this family relate to Sarah and Geraldine feeling displaced from rightful positions of authority as care coordinators. The sisters seem to have taken pride in managing their father's care. When it came to the care for her mother, Sarah may have felt displaced not only by her care-coordinating brother but also by her sister-in-law's involvement as a substitute female perspective on care planning. Of course, there could be no justification for turning one's frustrations into a physical assault (as when Sarah hit Tammy in the face). Yet, it is possible that the frustrations in this family run deep, frustrations that may also be gen-dered.

In this story, the readers did not hear first-hand accounts from the siblings other than Paul. However, it is obvious that the coalitions are gendered—two sisters versus four brothers—and that the latter seem to have gotten their way. It is also quite obvious that both sides, despite the one-sided accusations of Paul, are intent upon getting their way in doing things (e.g., the relocation, and the re-relocation, of the mother). Although apparently each sibling seems to intensely care about his or her mother, the power plays and the gender dynam-ics in this family are more about the needs of the siblings than the needs of the mother.

References

Aronson, J. (1990). Old women's experiences of needing care: Choice or compulsion? *Canadian Journal on Aging, 9*(3), 234–247.

Cicirelli, V. G. (1995). *Sibling relationships across the life span*. New York: Plenum Press.

Finch, J., & Mason, J. (1990). Filial obligations and kin support for elderly people. *Age-ing & Society, 10*, 151–175.

Gans, D. S., & Silverstein, M. (2006). Norms of filial responsibility for aging parents across time and generations. *Journal of Marriage and Family, 68*(4), 961–976.

George, L. (1986). Caregiver burden: Conflict between norms of reciprocity and solidarity. In K. A. Pillemer & R. S. Wolf (Eds.), *Elder abuse: Conflict in the family* (pp. 67–92). Dover, MA: Auburn House.

Globerman, J. (1995). The unencumbered child: Family reputations and responsibilities in the care of relatives with Alzheimer's disease. *Family Processes, 34,* 87–99.

Hequembourg, A., & Brallier, S. (2005). Gendered stories of parental caregiving among siblings. *Journal of Aging Studies, 19*(1), 53–71.

Ingersoll-Dayton, B., Neal, M. B., Ha, J. H., & Hammer, L. B. (2003). Redressing inequity in parent care among siblings. *Journal of Marriage and Family, 65*(1), 201–213.

Karantzas, G. C., Foddy, M., & Evans, L. (2003). Obligatory and discretionary motives of intergenerational caregiving. *Australian Journal of Psychology, 55,* 49.

Lashewicz, B., & Keating, N. (2009). Tensions among siblings in parent care. *European Journal of Ageing, 6,* 127–135.

Lashewicz, B., Manning, G., Hall, M., & Keating, N. (2007). Equity matters: Doing fairness in the context of family caregiving. *Canadian Journal on Aging, 26*(suppl.1), 91–102.

Matthews, S. H. (1995). Gender and the division of filial responsibility between lone sisters and their brothers. *Journal of Gerontology, 50B*(5), S312–S320.

Matthews, S. H. (2002). Brothers and parent care: An explanation for sons' underrepresentation. In B. J. Kramer & E. H. Thompson, Jr. (Eds.), *Men as caregivers: Theory, research, and service implications* (pp. 234–249). New York: Springer.

Rosenthal, C. 1985. Kinkeeping in the familial division of labor. *Journal of Marriage and Family, 47*(4), 965–974.

Silverstein, M., Conroy, S., & Gans, D. (2008). Commitment to caring: Filial responsibility and the allocation of support by adult children to older mothers. In M. E. Szinovacz & A. Davey (Eds.), *Caregiving contexts: Cultural, familial and societal implications* (pp. 71–91). New York: Springer.

[6]
SITTING AT THE STEPS OF HOPE, LOVE, AND HOSPITALITY

HUGO KAMYA

Arriving in the United States over a quarter of a century ago, I was confronted by the challenges that face all new immigrants. How was I going to make it in a new country? How would my family react to the changes that were about to happen in me? Out here, who would be on my side? Was I giving up too much in return for so little? More importantly, how is it possible that I had escaped the violence in my homeland while most of my family could not?

Two wishes captivated me: university education and training in the use of computers. They are emblematic of what I have come to learn about myself, my family, and the world. They also serve as metaphors for hope, love, and hospitality in my life.

I knew that going back to school and obtaining desirable academic credentials would open the door to the world of my dreams. I had always loved school, but the political problems in my country of origin (Uganda) made it difficult for me and my peers to pursue an education. On many occasions we had to settle for something much less, such as hanging around on street corners. Due to violence and rampant disease, a number of my classmates did not even make it to their 21st birthday. So when I arrived in the United States, I was intent on a university education. I saw a degree as a ticket to lifelong freedom.

Before I received a letter of acceptance from Harvard Divinity School, I worked in a home for the mentally ill, where I was humbled to learn that what separated me from those men and women was far less than what united us. I had heard so much about Harvard, but I did not realize that this was going to be the beginning of a life transformed by love and God's grace. In many ways, I had always seen the hand of God in my life, but not to the extent that life at Harvard revealed to me.

On a nice spring day, I showed up at Harvard for an open house with no clue about how I was going to afford the financial costs of my education. I sat on the steps of Andover Hall, excited about the prospect of entering Harvard. I was also plagued by the fear and sadness that this may not work out in my lifetime. As I sat on the steps, I looked at the buds on the trees, which announced the arrival of spring and a new life from the dead of winter. In the fresh cool breeze of the coming season, I felt a certain pride that I had gotten as far as I had already done. I was happy that I was there—not just because it was Harvard, but because Harvard represented, for me, a university education I yearned for so much. My home country had not offered me or many of my peers such an opportunity.

As I sat on those steps, I thought about my life's journey and my immigrant experience in the United States. The events that forced me to leave my country also had constituted the first cultural conflict for me. I was leaving home. I was leaving my family. I was also not sure about what I was going into.

I was born in Uganda at a time when the country was under the political colonial patronage of Britain. Post-colonial Uganda witnessed tyrannical and brutal regimes that forced many to flee their homeland in search of safety. My family had been targeted by the government simply because my father belonged to one of the ethnic groups that had opposed the government policies. The brutal rule of Idi Amin sought out and destroyed everyone who was affiliated with any type of opposition. The intense fear of being caught, tortured, and possibly killed led me to flee to Kenya. I travelled at night, hitching rides from strangers and walking on foot as I crossed into Kenya with very few belongings. The journey across the border would not allow me to carry much luggage for fear of detection and the uncertainties that lay ahead.

I travelled in a minibus with at least 13 or 14 fellow travellers. None of us said a word to each other. Although it was clear we were all escaping Uganda, no one dared to mention our final destination or why we were travelling at all. I still vividly remember sitting nervously in that minibus, without daring even to make eye contact with another passenger. Everyone was suspect. No one could be trusted. As much as I wanted to connect with someone on that bumpy ride, I had to maintain a psychological distance to ensure that no one asked me questions or recognized my nervousness. Our distance from each other, despite being tightly squeezed in such a small vehicle, was a necessary protection for all of us.

At various roadblocks, soldiers would pull us out of the vehicle and yell at us in Swahili, a language none of us spoke but which many of us identified with intimidation and brutality. Our fate depended on the whims of the soldiers who manned the checkpoints. Some people were hauled out of the vehicle, interrogated, pushed around, and eventually released before the vehicle took off. Others were not as lucky. They were hit with the butts of rifles and threatened with the barrels pointed at their heads. The name on one's identification card often sealed one's fate. If you belonged to a tribe that was not in favour of the government, you were a prime suspect.

We were all trying to escape the fear, intimidation, and uncertainty that came with the ethnic wars. We also lived distrusting everyone else, including people who were supposed to be our neighbours. Sometimes we knew who our enemy was; sometimes we did not have a clue. Anyone could have been an enemy. Indeed, my life was engulfed with anger and fear as I lived under oppression, and the fear continued to accompany me in my effort to escape from it.

After reaching Kenya, I breathed a sigh of relief, but I was also immediately plunged into something new and unfamiliar. I could not speak Swahili, the commonly used language in Kenya. Besides, I was averse to learning the language that reminded me of the turmoil in Uganda. As a male, I again became a suspect in Kenya. People I encountered often wondered if I had been a collaborator with the brutal regime in Uganda. I could see the distrust in their eyes.

In those days, my survival was paramount. I had to make it, I needed to be strong, I needed to feel accepted. Deep down in their hearts, Ugandans believed that Kenyans hated them even as they opened their borders to them. As refugees, we thought that there was a catch to their generosity. We did not trust them, and I believe the feeling was mutual. I needed to balance a range of emotions to survive there. I could not present papers that qualified me for any work. Employers knew well what was going on in Uganda and why Ugandans did not have official documents, but they still felt the need to protect themselves from the "bad guys."

As I did menial jobs to survive, I lived with the hope that things would change in Uganda. I started attending school as soon as I could secure my academic records. I had to convince a lot of people that I was who I said I was. As the war raged in Uganda, it became harder to stay in Kenya. With more people escaping Uganda, Kenya put Ugandans under strict surveillance. One of their surveillance programs was the so-called Kipandilisho, a Swahili term for being documented. All Ugandans had to carry a large identity card that had to be stamped regularly to authenticate their legal status.

At some point, I knew I had to get away. During my absence, more of my family members had been targetted because of their political views; therefore, returning to Uganda was no longer an option for me. Kenya was going through its own political upheaval as more and more people lost jobs and the cost of living skyrocketed for the locals. Many blamed Ugandan refugees for their economic turmoil. In social sciences, this is known as "scapegoating."

Leaving Kenya and travelling to the United States brought with it mixed feelings. On the one hand, there was the excitement of coming to a place that was previously presented to me as one that embraced diversity. On the other, the move brought to the surface old images of marginalization and feelings of alienation. I needed to assert myself, to prove myself every step along the way. Many things I took for granted I would find in the United States, such as equality and freedom, did not materialize—at least, not in the beginning. I found myself in a place where I again had to explain who I was. In a way, I was reliving the trauma I thought I had left behind. The "othering" I experienced somewhat tainted the otherwise impeccable regard I had for my new home. I spoke a language that I thought was English, but my accent raised eyebrows. I met several people whose story was different from mine but who had also suffered from the effects of wars. Their foothold in the country was as tenuous as mine.

As I sat on the steps of Harvard, I noticed the ants that seemed to move aimlessly from one step to another. I thought about how minute their lives were; yet, however small, their lives likely mattered to them a lot. I wondered about what it feels like to be an ant. I wondered if there was any organization in their lives that, as just an onlooker, I failed to see. I imagined myself to be an ant and asked myself questions that—at least for a fleeting moment—gave me a sense of satisfaction about where I was located in my own life. Did ants care about the future or what was to come? How much did it matter if their course of activity was disrupted? Did passersby care about them? These questions led me into another journey of self-inquiry: did anyone here (in the United States) care about me? Did they care that I left my home and my family behind to come to this place? How did my own family members react to my departure from home? What day-to-day activities was I missing? What kind of a history was being written for them that I did not share anymore?

As I was lost in my own thoughts, a man, perhaps in his sixties, joined me on the steps. He asked me what I was doing there and where I had come from. I told him I had just arrived from Uganda and was working at L'Arche, a home for the mentally ill in Syracuse, New York.

"How do you like your work at L'Arche?" he asked. I told him about what the residents had actually taught me, and how much I was learning from them about the simplicity of life and the spirituality of care, love, and hospitality. Our conversation then turned to the books I was reading at the moment. They included some by a spiritual author named Henri Nouwen, whose commitment to hospitality, ministry, and woundedness had appealed to me a great deal. At some point, I stopped and asked the man why he was so interested in my interest in these books. He replied, "Well, I am Henri Nouwen." I took a step back and looked at him. I could not believe that here was the man whose books I had been reading for such a long time and for whom I had developed a deep sense of respect and admiration. He looked at me intently, but with kindness. He talked about his wish to work with L'Arche and respond to the invitation to hospitality. He believed that people with mental challenges invited us to look at our own woundedness. As he talked, I felt that he revealed a sharpness of mind, an openness of self, and a heart that was immensely generous.

As we sat on those steps conversing, he communicated a depth of presence I had not come across before. He said, "Young man, you look sad. What is going on?"

"I have been accepted at Harvard but cannot accept the offer because I cannot afford it."

"Is this something you really want?"

"Yes, it is … and I am also afraid this opportunity will never come my way again."

I looked away and waited for him to express his disappointment for me and move back to the conversation about his books or about L'Arche. Actually, meeting an author and talking with him about the very books I had been reading was exciting enough. It had already made my visit to Harvard and Cambridge worthwhile.

"Well," he said at this point, "I will give it to you." For a moment I could not believe what I was hearing. To meet an author I admire, and then to be told that he would sponsor my education—it was baffling, to say the least.

I thanked him and sat back to think about how the invisible hand of God was writing and rewriting my life through this man. This was the beginning of a long friendship that lasted until Henri's death in 1996. During the decade or so between our meeting and Henri's death, we lived quite different lives. He left Harvard and the academic world, went to Latin America, and returned to work at L'Arche. He practised his views on hospitality. I left L'Arche, went to Harvard, and joined the academic world. But we grew closer all the time. For me, this friendship became a spiritual connection and support. On those steps of Harvard, I had made a great friend and found a lifelong mentor.

In his letters to me, Henri asked about my coursework and my own connections to the mentally handicapped. For my part, I devoured more of his books and plunged further into the questions of meaning and purpose in life. I began to think about my life and what I had done to deserve this blessing when most of my friends had been killed back at home. When Henri walked into my life, I knew something larger than life had happened to me. It was an invitation to open the same hand to many others who also await love in their lives.

There was something else: I began to develop a higher level of appreciation for the world of mental illness. Back at home, one of my brothers was born with a hearing impairment. His disability had caused a lot of problems for other family members as they struggled to understand and cope with his condition. Instead of calling him by name, they simply called him "Deaf." Working in the home for the mentally ill helped me to come to terms with my own brother's disability.

My second dream was to learn how to use computers. I marvelled at what computers could do and what they represented in this day and age. When I arrived in the United States, I started to learn how to use computer technology in my work. At the university, I started writing my papers using computers. It was a big shift for me, because I had to learn to type and to use computers at the same time. My fascination with computers soon translated into examining what coming to the United States had opened up for me. My relationship to computers made me appreciate what I had in my life. I also began to see that the only way I could truly enjoy computers as gifts of technology would be to bring some back to my own country. So, over the years, I have made a commitment to give back to my country in ways that bring knowledge to people. Computers have come to represent "technologies of healing" to those who need them.

After being absent for a number of years, I went back to Uganda for the first time. I was surprised to see that there was a lot I still had in common with my country folk. I also noticed how much the country had been devastated by the war and the AIDS epidemic. Many of my friends had been killed during the war or had died in the aftermath of war. But HIV/AIDS is proving to be even more devastating. The pain and the suffering created by this epidemic hit home when my brother contracted HIV.

During my visit to Uganda, I wanted to reconnect with the people I had left behind. I went to the university to find out about some of my classmates. To my surprise, there were none left at the university. Many had died during the war, but many more had been killed by the AIDS epidemic. I was devastated by this discovery. As I sat on the steps of the administration building, I recalled the day I had first sat on the steps of Harvard. My thoughts travelled back to my brother, whom I had just seen upon returning to my country. I had come back with great trepidation, not knowing if I would find him alive or dead. As it turns out, he was barely alive.

My brother Henry lay in one corner of the living room in the little house I grew up in. I vividly remember walking into the house and seeing everything looking so familiar. Yet, there was something very different and ominous. His emaciated body said more about his suffering than I can ever put into words. He looked at me with piercing eyes. I looked back at his motionless body and sought to understand the things he was telling me without speaking. Many questions raced through my mind. Was he dying? How long would it take? What did he want to say to me and to those around him? Given his condition, how much could he ever say? Through what language was his body communicating? What meaning was the rest of the family members assigning to his condition? How did his illness define his reality? Was he living with HIV or dying with HIV? How could this scene reveal so much but at the same time disguise the obvious? Was there any hope, strength, or meaning left in his frail reality? What did my brother think about the fact that he was dying whereas I would continue living?

I recalled that my brother had once asked me to take care of his children. What did it all mean now that he was passing away? What had it meant then, when we were both young and in good health? What other stories of pain and resilience did his terminal condition speak about? Whose stories are intertwined with his story? How will his death contribute significance to the stories of the others that are yet to unfold?

I looked at my mother, who sat next to my dying brother. She told me she would not leave his side until the very end. I heard in her voice a sense of fear of the approaching death but also a determination to stay engaged with her son, something she had always done for all her children. I wondered where my father was, given the fact that my family was experiencing a major rupture. What messages were my brother's sons and daughters getting from seeing their father in his deathbed? How did my brother, as sick as he was, putting it all together for himself as a man, a father, a husband, and a brother? How did this picture speak about larger forces or stories within the family, how did it reflect on our culture? How do these narratives gain dominance over others that are momentarily marginalized? What stories of justice or injustice are captured in the dying moments of my brother? How does this picture speak about the obligations and responsibilities of richer nations in the face of the sheer deprivation of many under-resourced nations?

My mother's stoic strength has been an inspiration to me. She found a calling for herself, even amid the extreme helplessness we all felt while we watched my brother die. I also gained strength from her strength. So, along with a number of students, I went back to Uganda a few years later. We established a summer exchange program for students, and that program became a way to give back to my place of birth. In 2005 we started the Makula Fund for Children (MFC), an organization that provides tuition fees, breakfast, and medical care for children. *Makula* means "gift" in Luganda. MFC is dedicated to providing Uganda's orphans with a gift toward a positive future.

In the last few decades, up to two million children in Uganda have lost one or both parents to AIDS. In addition to their emotional turmoil, these children face a daily struggle to meet their own basic needs. Due to limited government support, children must find their own source of money for school fees, school supplies, and the required uniform. Without a basic education, these children's chance for a positive, self-sufficient future is severely limited. Obtaining food and basic medical care presents further challenges for these orphans and other vulnerable children in Uganda.

MFC's programming focuses on a daily breakfast club for an average of 50 children and fully paid annual school sponsorship for 140 children, as well as basic medical care. The work of the MFC has grown with each year of its operation. All children are engaged in periodic social activities for social support and encouragement. Children who have come of age and are declared fit are encouraged to develop income-generating activities so that their long-term self-sufficiency can be achieved. I have observed one young man who has started a brick-making project that raises funds for his brothers and sisters. A girl has joined two others in raising chickens to help all three lead an independent life.

In addition to recognizing the social and emotional needs of HIV/AIDS orphans and child-headed households supported by MFC, the staff provides general social support and counselling during breakfast-club times and through school and home visits. It has been an absolute joy to watch these children become self-sufficient. Not only has their self-esteem grown, but their sense of isolation has also been lifted. One important lesson I have gained from this experience is the significance of giving back. I have watched with admiration how children as young as five or six years old are being transformed and, in turn, are transforming others, including me.

One important story sticks out for me. On one of my many visits to the Makula Breakfast Club, I observed a depth of spirit and generosity that moved me. As breakfast was served, I noticed children whose eyes told a larger story than their malnourished bodies. They all looked on as a thick paste of porridge was served to them. They ate it hastily. For many, this was their only meal of the day. On this one occasion, some bread was also served to enhance the nutritional value of the porridge breakfast. While the hungry children devoured the bread, I noticed the excitement in their eyes. Some of them went back for seconds, even as others waited for their first turn. In one corner of the room, a small child sat and held on to his slice of bread. When the time came to go to school, this boy placed his slice of bread in his pocket. At some point, I asked him why he did not eat his bread. Shocked at being "found out," he said he was saving it for his brother, who could not come for breakfast that day.

I know that breakfast clubs are not related to computer technologies. They are, however, technologies of hope and healing, and the stories of these children have inspired me in pursuing a dream for their future. Their survival has now become my survival, and in a small scale, many people's survival in Uganda.

Looking back, my brother's dying of HIV/AIDS was not conflict free. For all my family members, important questions surfaced: Out of all the children of our family, how is it that I was the one who escaped the intolerable conditions? Why did the others stay back? What helped me to take the many risks I did? How is it that my brother survived the atrocities of war but succumbed to a cruel disease? Could I have helped them to escape these gruelling circumstances? Should I have also stayed? As we all sat next to my brother in the last moments of his life, the silence was pregnant with these unanswered questions.

My brother could not speak. My mother's grief and sorrow were so deep that she also was unable to speak.

As I think about the silence that engulfed all my family members at the moment of our despair, I wonder about the various silences and the part they play throughout our lives. In our family, silences served many purposes. There was the "prisoner's silence" that overcame us when my father was put into detention for protesting against the government. We could not speak, because we feared that whatever we said would backfire. We were not sure what would happen to us, or to our father. Much later, in my adult years, there was the "lover's silence," where my partner and I stared into each other's eyes, knowing that what bound us together was far greater than what pulled us apart. Then, there was the "baby's silence" and the innocence of life that surrounded such silence. And sometimes, it was a "sleeping person's silence" perhaps not unlike a dead person's silence, where the world would briefly come to a halt. In Uganda, death and uncertainty were looming parts of everyday life. And above all, there is the silence I keep. Most people are not interested in the harrowing experiences of my childhood, or the equally harrowing experience of my escape. Most of the time, I put such experiences in a mental closet.

Across time, some of these silences grew and engendered some additional family tensions. Since my brother's death, both my family and his family have had additional expectations of me. In a way, my moral responsibilities have doubled. I am the father to my own children as well as the surrogate for my brother. Rightly or wrongly, they see my life in the United States as a privilege, and many family members place their hopes on me. In a way, I am expected to pave the road, so more of them can achieve better lives and attain a higher standard of living. Since my brother's passing, many of our interactions revolve around what they could get from me. This one-sided expectation is more of a testament to the difficult conditions they live in; it is not because my family is either selfish or greedy. I do understand their predicament, although they may not be aware of the predicament I find myself in.

These increased expectations aside, the remaining members of my family and I are still struggling to redefine our relationships, which exist across an ocean. One major tension stems from the fact that, to a degree, we have all grown apart in significant ways. For example, one of my brothers became a Catholic priest. His decision to join the clergy may have been a direct response to our parents' message about the importance of giving back. However, his commitment to social justice issues has also led him to question some problems in the Catholic Church itself. It is also ironic that, in trying to give back to his family and country, he had to leave his country and his immediate family behind. Unlike my brother, one of my sisters chose to abandon her religious practices all together, to the ire of our parents. So although my family is a cradle of strongly held belief systems, the intensity of our belief systems has also occasionally been a source of disconnection and disunity.

Indeed, we came to occupy different locations—both geographically and emotionally—in this world. However, despite our quarrels and fights, we still have more that binds us together than what tears us apart. For my part, I came to the realization that I still need my family as much as they need me. On several occasions, my family has called me to help them quiet a situation, and I was happy to oblige. In a way, due to my higher educational attainment and my brother's absence, I have been bestowed with "elder" status. I struggle to uphold the high regard my family bestows upon me. Their high expectations are more than I bargained for.

My new life in the United States brought me yet another source of happiness, but also another source of tension and conflict. I have a mixed marriage, which has resulted in marvellous mixed-race children. Occasionally, I have wondered how much my children understand about my roots and the trials and tribulations that my Ugandan family has gone through. I still struggle with how much to reveal to them about my painful experiences without causing them undue emotional bruises. I have yet to share with them the tumultuous feelings I experienced while sitting at my dying brother's bedside. Fortunately, the visits back and forth to my country of origin have helped a little, since my children have accompanied me on some of those occasions. However, there are so many differences between the life they know and the life I have left behind. I fear that they may never be able to catch up on what I would eventually like them to know. I have wondered about the varying levels of physical, psychological, sociological, emotional, and spiritual/religious rootlessness my children must experience when they meet my family in Uganda. How do they make sense of my family, whose lives are so dramatically different from their own? One important point of tension is the alienation they must feel, as my Ugandan family members treat them as objects of curiosity. Sometimes, I feel that my children are overwhelmed by this attention. I also worry about my family's expectations of them to communicate fluently in their father's native language. Ultimately, a level of disappointment surrounds these unfulfilled expectations. This is a difficult aspect even for me. I know that I have struggled with my children's level of enthusiasm—or lack thereof—in learning my native language. Part of me hopes that they would choose to learn something that is so dear to me, something we can share, and something they can hold on to. While my younger daughter enjoys asking questions about my origins, my older daughter still struggles with what my Ugandan background means for her. As unlikely as it may be, I often wonder what would happen if my children went back to live with my family in Uganda. Would such a decision bring us all closer, or pull us further apart? Like the lives of many other immigrants and refugees, my own life is filled with many blessings, but there is also some emotional cost that comes from fragmentation.

Being in a mixed-race relationship and raising multicultural children, I have wondered a lot about the unfolding of my life. I have watched my children grow into teenagers. I have marvelled at the challenges and the opportunities that a mixed-race relationship brings. I see that all of these combine to turn into moments of education, for all of us. It is as if my life is a template for new technologies of loving and caring. As I sit on the steps of my current family home, I think about my family of origin and the social and cultural matrix I have been part of. I continue to ask myself important questions: Who am I? Who am I to become? One thing is reassuring for me: in going away from my family, voluntarily or involuntarily, I have again come home. Beside each family hurt in my heart, there is also a place for family pleasure and hope.

Sitting at the steps of hope, love, and hospitality is an invitation that I have been confronted with over and over. For me, it has meant a daily self-examination of what I bring to the work I do with families here and abroad. I believe that I must keep searching and asking questions of myself, especially when the questions far outnumber the answers.

[7]

A GAY ACTOR WITH MULTIPLE SCRIPTS

Impression Management Strategies to Comply
with Traditional Chinese Family Norms

KIN HO WONG

How we become who we are—how we incorporate the perceptions of others into how eventually we perceive ourselves—has formed the basis of inquiries of early as well as more recent sociologists: C. H. Cooley (1902), G. H. Mead (1964), and E. Goffman (1959, 1963), among others. What is important to note is the necessity of arriving at some workable balance between how we come to see ourselves and how others see and relate to us. Almost everyone has challenges in navigating the "different messages" he or she may receive during his or her early socialization. Moreover, the incongruity of the messages may be particularly significant, depending on one's status characteristics, such as race or gender. The different voices one needs to deal with might be especially incongruous if factors of ethnicity, social status differentiations, and so on, also come into play. Especially in traditional cultures, it may be exceptionally treacherous to formulate an integrated sense of self when one's sexual identity falls outside the "mandatory heterosexuality" norms. The following story traces my original role confusion, attempts at impression management, and deep fragmentation of myself as a gay Asian man, first living in China and then in Canada. My gender, race, and ethnicity all served to make my coming-out process a lengthy, and at times, difficult one (Fassinger, 1991), and managing a stigmatized identity was a primary developmental task that created guilt and secrecy (Radkowsky & Siegel, 1997). My story captures also the deep-rooted conflicts, alienation, and superficial cover-up efforts that have arisen in the process.

I was born in Hong Kong 39 years ago. Wong is my family name, and my Chinese name loosely translates into English as "rich mineral." My parents and grandparents carefully selected my name to symbolically mean a strong, successful individual. I must add that the complexities of the strokes used to write each Chinese character of my name foreshadowed how I collectively represent myself to my traditional Chinese family today. At a very young age—I think I was four or five years old—I mastered how to write my Chinese name. This task was a big challenge. The three characters consist of over 50 strokes, and each stroke has to be placed in a formal order to create the actual character. My parents coached me in calligraphic writing. I mastered that task and was praised for producing beautiful characters in writing. My parents even went so far as to believe that my beautiful calligraphy was a predictive trait of a future scholar. My behaviour as a child and as a young adult parallels the formality of Chinese calligraphic writing: I learned how to cultivate many role scripts that would comply with my traditional family's norms in order to create a front stage. Not to sound like a drama queen, but my life became very much like a performance on a stage because I have one trait (my sexual orientation) that needed rigorous impression management (Goffman, 1959; 1963).

To elaborate, in Hong Kong, admission into the best kindergarten school was very competitive. Moreover, the "brand name" of a particular school served as a foundation for future academic studies. Education is a strong traditional Chinese family value, and my first obligation was to fulfill my familial expectations by getting into this prestigious school. On the morning of registration, my mother set the stage by dressing me all in white: long tailored pants with a polo shirt and shoes. I had long, shiny, wavy black hair that contrasted nicely with my outfit. As my mother was prepping me for the entrance exams, I was also told how beautiful I looked. To this day, I recall how nervous I was walking into the principal's office. Little did I know that it was my first stage performance, and my first role was to look and act like a student.

When the principal saw me, he immediately said to my mother, "What a handsome young man!" I vaguely remember standing in front of the principal, who was seated in a big chair, and being asked to write my name in Chinese calligraphy. He watched intently as I meticulously spaced and properly ordered each stroke to construct the complex Chinese characters of my name. His response was the same as my family's: "You have beautiful character writing abilities." My well-groomed appearance and calligraphic abilities together represented the persona of an ideal student. Superficially, I looked the part. However, that success was short-lived. The principal proceeded to ask me some basic questions. He asked me to point left, right, north, south, east, and west. I failed this exercise. Afterward, I remember my mother saying how very fortunate we were to be accepted to the school. She also told me not to tell my father that I failed the exercises. She said there was no point in explaining my failures: just let my father believe I am an ideal scholar like I am supposed to be in his eyes. Upon reflection, I now wonder if that exercise foretold the lack of my role clarity within my family unit. It is amazing to realize just how early on I learned that the front stage does not have to match what happens behind the curtain (Goffman, 1959).

Behind the curtain are my father and his traditional expectations. He is a traditional family man who possesses very strong beliefs about how a family should be organized and what it should look like to the outside world. We are a family of five. I am the youngest, with one older sister and a brother. My father's beliefs are grounded in the Chinese cultural norms. I remember that, for most of my life, he regulated and controlled all of us by designing role scripts according to our birth order and gender-role expectations. When we deviated from the norms, his authoritarian approach (and reproach) would set us straight. My mother insured that the familial expectations were implemented by modifying any role deviation through socio-emotional encouragement. Together, my parents worked hard to construct and maintain our front faces to any onlookers. Backstage, our lives were sometimes surreal.

As the youngest son, with my sister being the oldest and my brother the middle child, we all felt pressure from our father's traditional expectations. My sister did not meet our father's expectations because he wanted a male child as the first-born. On many occasions, my father publicly told the story of how he was awakened from his afternoon nap with the news that my mother had given birth to a girl. His response was to go back to his nap. He always ends this story with the same declaration: "What good is it to have a girl?" I now know that my father was emotionally distancing himself from what he considered to be his paternal failure: producing a female first-born. Consequently, my sister worked toward fulfilling the first-born male role, despite her gender. She was the first of our family to graduate from a university, with a Bachelor of Commerce degree, and she presently works at an international financial firm, is married to a Chinese chartered accountant, and has two sons. My sister is also the one who advises my parents on all family financial matters. She performs all the functions of the eldest, first-born male in a traditional Chinese family. I believe that she also embraces that role. In contrast, my brother is athletic rather than intellectual, and he works as an auto mechanic. He is recently divorced, with no children—thus failing to carry on the family name. In my father's eyes, he has failed to meet his obligations as the first-born male. I wonder who is more disappointed, my brother, the non-professional, who did not have a role model and chose to not carry on the family name, or my father, who did not know how to be a role model because he himself grew up without a father. My parents often refer to my brother's job as a person who "lies under a car for a living." How my brother functions in our family unit is in constant conflict with my father's expectations. My parents constantly correct my brother's inconsistencies. A large portion of the family money has gone into the construction of a face-saving persona for my brother. For example, my parents co-signed a loan just so my brother could appear as a business owner rather than a car mechanic. Needless to say, my parents' return on their investment has been nil. My brother just refuses to comply with their role expectations for him.

Because of my brother's failure to save face for the family, a portion of his expected responsibilities was shifted to me. My mother stressed the importance of keeping up public appearances and expectations: one male child has to go to university, and everyone must be financially independent. Thus, my mother's role has been to strive to actualize my father's expectations. However, I possess one trait that is in direct contradiction of my father's familial expectations and that remains unspoken about in most Chinese and non-Chinese family conversations (Chan, 1994). The role my father has played in my life has been that of a disciplinarian. He disciplined me with beatings for one reason or another when I failed to meet his expectations. The beatings he unleashed on me were different compared to those my brother received. My beatings were always concentrated on my face. Very early on, I was told that I had a beautiful, somewhat Caucasian face. My eyes are big, with double-folded eyelids; I have long lashes; my cheekbones are high and well defined; and my nose is well proportioned. When I was a child, everyone commented on how beautiful I looked and that I resembled my mother and not my father. Some people would follow up with the comment that I looked like a doll—meaning girlish. I guess this explains why my father attempted to make me more masculine by toughening my facial features through beatings. One time, I remember he hit me so hard across my cheeks that I had to cover them with my small hands. I thought he would stop, but the final blow was aimed at the centre of my face, causing a bleeding nose. My mother later explained to me that the beatings were a traditional form of Chinese family discipline. Knowingly or unknowingly, she justified her husband's actions.

I remember that the worst beatings occurred on my birthdays. For example, on one of my birthdays, I wanted to light and blow out the candles on my own cake, but my brother wanted to do it, too. I raised such a fuss that my father beat me. On another birthday, I was lucky enough to have two big birthday cakes. I remember I wanted to have a piece from each cake, but my father stated that we should finish one first before cutting the other. Again, he beat me, because I was defiant. One time, as he was slapping me across the face, he shouted, "Who do you think you are? Do you think you are special? You are useless." His final comment before he walked away was "You are a faggot." I am the last-born, seven years and five years younger than my sister and brother, respectively. As a child, I wondered why my birthdays were not celebrated like those of other children. As an adult, I still don't dare to ask if I am the "accidental child." The combination of that uncertainty, my Caucasian features, and my sexual identity made me feel that my family was not completely accepting of who I was and am. Family acceptance is key to bridging the gap between the private and public selves in order to develop a strong identity (Tasker & McCann, 1999). Because of my family's non-acceptance, my self-development was challenged and thwarted.

My first experience in secondary socialization was not pleasant. A new school year began, and that year I was accepted into a highly regarded English-immersion elementary school. I was enrolled in that school because my parents had plans of emigrating from Hong Kong to Canada. During registration, my mother and I encountered a North American bias. The school would not let me enroll because I did not have an English name. My mother suggested that we could Americanize my Chinese name by phonetically translating it. The school administrator did not approve. My mother called my father so that they could decide on an English name. He said, "Just name him anything." My mother was not an English speaker, and in the '70s, she loved the Donny and Marie show. Hence, on that day I became Donny and not "just anything." Donny was a name that I would have to learn to spell and print. The Chinese character strokes I had learned and perfected were no longer necessary. This was the day I started to embrace my Euro-Asian identity.

My teachers were not fond of Donny: I looked different. One teacher asked me, in front of the entire class, "What is the use of having big beautiful eyes if you don't use them?" At that moment, I looked around the class and realized that all my classmates' eyes were slanted and very small. Later, I told my mother what had happened and asked her if I had ugly eyes. She told me I had beautiful eyes, but I realized that mine did not look the same as my brother's and sister's eyes. Neither did I look Caucasian. Yet, it was my appearance that my family emphasized. Strangers and teachers also commented on my looks. Gradually I realized that my double-folded eyes and long lashes were the reason for the attention and affection—my eyes looked Caucasian. Many people would hug and kiss me while they commented on my features, "He looks so American." As I grew up, I was no longer called by my Chinese name: everyone called me Donny. However, my brother and sister were still called by their Chinese names. Symbolically, this produced an in-group/out-group effect, and I did not feel close to my siblings. My father was proud of me for being beautiful—an "object" of affection. In public, when people commented on how beautiful I was, he would adore me. In private, he would often beat me up. I think my father beat me up because I did not meet his expectations of masculinity. I realized that when he called me a "faggot." What Asian father wants a gay son who does not look Chinese and who is called Donny?

My mother and father actively tried to conceal my sexual orientation from the public—and from me—through all types of strategic actions and sanctions. As I was growing up, my sexuality produced more of a role conflict in maintaining the front stage to onlookers. My parent's dramaturgical approach served as a preparatory stage where I would learn the skills needed to deflect any public scrutiny (Goffman, 1963). I recall that, as a young child, I did not comply with "appropriate" gender-role games. As a matter of fact, I don't recall passing through any "play stage" of my life. I would play with my mother's makeup rather than with toys. I did not wear it, but I sat at her makeup table and arranged her lipsticks, brushes, compacts, and perfumes in a pleasing way. My mother would come home and be surprised at how I had set out every item. She praised my "design abilities." She told me that when I grew up, I would become an architectural engineer. Additionally, she reframed my playtime as task management. When she would leave the house, she would instruct me to "clean" her makeup table. This repackaged information and constructed social reality served to slowly build an ideal persona for a son in my parents' minds (Berger & Luckmann, 1966).

My mother's ability to reframe a situation was excellent. Today, I believe that her abilities saved me from more beatings by my father. Just imagine what would have happened to me if, every day, I was found playing with my mother's makeup rather than "cleaning and organizing." Nevertheless, at the age of 16, I found myself working behind the cosmetics counter at a department store as a fragrance sales clerk. My parents rationalized my occupational choice to the extended family and friends by saying that the company hired me as a marketing strategy to attract female clients. They made comments such as, "He is a handsome young man; what woman would not buy from him?" In truth, I sold men's fragrances. This front allowed others to "understand" me on the basis of how my parents projected my sexual orientation. For me, their messages served to let me know that it was my appearance they appreciated, not me. At the age of 18, I worked as a model in fashion shows, earning a steady income. My parents rationalized that occupational interest as a phase and told me that I should not make a career in fashion or cosmetics; instead, I should go to university and become a businessman. The messages I got from my parents were clear. Although they never openly stated it, there was an aura of silence I felt and understood as saying, "Do not look feminine!" The traditional heterosexual expectations contradicted my core sense of self, and this had a large influence on my identity vis-à-vis my identity confusion stage (Cass, 1979).

The understanding I gained, which came from my family, was that I must construct a heterosexual, masculine persona. In the Chinese family, the youngest child is typecast as the spoiled one—one who does not really make anything out of his or her life. Given the fact that my family felt my brother had failed them, they focused on my performance to repair the family pride. Being gay and uneducated was out of the question. Erving Goffman (1959) uses the concept of "team work" to illustrate the work of a group of individuals, in my case my family members, who co-operate in performance, attempting to achieve the goals sanctioned by the group. Our team assembled in full force when they thought I was approaching my first romantic relationship with a boy; in actuality, however, I was going through a phase of identity comparison (Cass, 1979). One day, I reconnected with a junior-school classmate named Dean. We quickly became best friends and started doing many things together. I was different from Dean. He was very handsome, with blond hair and blue eyes; he was tall and muscular. We had some things in common, however; we both complained about our fathers, and we did not have girlfriends. We were inseparable. The major difference with Dean was that he liked girls and I did not. I did not understand my parents' negative reaction when it came to my friendship with Dean. I just felt these undefined feelings, because words about sexuality were never spoken out loud by my parents. Looking back, it is clear that I was experiencing role confusion within my family unit. As I recall, when my siblings' friends came by the house, my parents had friendly conversations with them. When Dean came to the house, they did not talk to him. After a while, I did not invite Dean over to my house, understanding that he was not welcome. As long as Dean did not come by, my parents could ignore his existence, and our friendship was never a part of family conversations. Because of my hidden role and my parents' reactions, I learned to compartmentalize my feelings, thus complying with my parental wishes. By that time, I was a master in maintaining a clear division between public and private performances. But the constant imposition of role distance also served to fragment my sense of self as the gap between my private and public self widened (Tasker & McCann, 1999).

Not having Dean around the house served only to keep him out of sight. For me, it meant that I had to keep Dean separate from my home life, unlike my brother's and sister's friends. I only made one mistake: one afternoon, I came home and greeted my mother who was cooking in the kitchen. My mother commented on how much she liked my new sweater. I told her the sweater was not mine, that I was actually wearing Dean's sweater. She accused me of flaunting Dean in her face and ordered me to take off the sweater before my father came home. I did so, but I did not understand why she was so upset or what I had done wrong. Upon reflection, I can see that I did have a crush on Dean. Some of those feelings were sexual in nature. I was confused and at that time could not sort out my feelings. I think Dean sensed it, too, and tried to talk to me about my ambiguous sexuality, but I did not clearly comprehend my own situation. Now, I realize that I have also compartmentalized my feelings toward him.

One day, the telephone rang, and my sister answered the phone. It was Dean on the phone, asking me to go out to the mall after dinner. I said yes. I remember my father's exact words: "Dean is only your friend and he wants to do things with you, because he has no one to do stuff with." The table was quiet, my father watching me, and then the performance started with my brother taking the lead. He said, "Dean is gay. Are you?" At 18, I knew that the word *gay* meant "faggot"—that was what my father had called me as a young child. Naturally, I said no, hoping the response would take the spotlight off me. But, in my mind, it triggered some feelings as to why I found some boys mysteriously appealing and had no feelings for girls. My brother continued to tease me about being gay. My mother asked if it was true. I could not answer her question; I did not know. I was not ready to accept the label of being gay, but I knew I was different from my peers because I was not dating and I did not find girls interesting. Moreover, I had more female friends than most boys of my age did, but I did not have a lot of male friends. My father said, "Don't be gay; gay people are useless!" My sister, whom I looked up to, remained silent. After dinner, when no one was around, I confronted my sister. We were both in the backstage, and from this perspective, I discovered I had an ally. I asked her why she did not defend me. My sister's official stance on this situation was simple. She said, "You don't need to defend yourself." This behind-the-scenes dialogue with my sister served as a haven, and it also fostered a close relationship between the two of us. Looking back, I think she was trying to tell me that she accepts me for who I am. In some Asian cultures, it is not uncommon for brothers to initially come out to the sisters (Bhugra, 1997). It is no coincidence that I later instinctively chose to first come out to my sister, at the age of 33.

At age 18, I did not understand why my family members were accusing me of being gay. I was not even able to articulate my sense of self to myself beyond being a son who was always told he was beautiful and would one day be a scholar. Additionally, I realized that some of my female friends also thought I was gay. It appears that everyone knew I was gay except me. I was either confused or in denial, and I now question how I could have been so clueless (Cass, 1979). Perhaps the muted but accusatory conversations with my family about my sexuality served to blot out that portion of myself—confining me to the typecast role of being a scholar. A few weeks after that dinner conversation, I no longer hung out with Dean. My ability to compartmentalize my life heightened. I became a loner, only surrounding myself with a few female friends. I hoped that by only associating with females, I would pass as a straight male to the audiences who scrutinized my behaviour. However, while misleading people to make myself appear "normal," I developed ambivalent and alienated feelings that in turn hindered my self-development. Because my parents were approving of my educational achievement, I avoided social settings. Rather, I focused on studying harder to get into university. When I was accepted to a university, my parents were relieved. It was then that I started to reflect on my sexuality and began to build my own tolerance toward being of a different sexual orientation. Was I gay?

My father posed the dating topic as a question: "Why don't you have a girlfriend?" Extended family members and family friends also made comments to test my social identity through questions such as "You are so handsome; how many girlfriends do you have?" or "I bet you have to fend off many girls!" or "A handsome man like you can pick and chose any Chinese girl; when are you going to settle down?" There was an aura of silence combined with a mysterious boundary when it came to exploring my sexuality (Chan, 1994; Morales, 1990), which was unusually difficult for me to understand.

The social prescriptions were simple: Be straight. Be attractive. Be smart. But was I? I was told I did not look Chinese, so what was my ethnicity? I was told I was going to be a scholar, but I was only a C-average student. Soon, I was not even told I was beautiful; thus, one of my positive "identities" was curtailed. The front stage and backstage of my life were more divergent now (D'Augelli, Patterson, & Ryan, 2001).

A partial haven appeared in the role of university student, and I embraced that role wholeheartedly. My status as a University of Toronto student relieved some of the family pressures and became my new identity. I was no longer deemed useless; instead, I was a symbol that saved face for my family because my brother was not a scholar. My relationship with my sister strengthened as she provided tutoring and emotional support for me through difficult and challenging assignments. However, my relationship with my brother became more distant. In a way, my brother's rebellion—to the point of getting into trouble with the law—served as a family distraction. He took on the "black sheep" status. For a while, he took the focus off my sexuality. My parents told my brother to be more like me. Once again, I became the object of my father's affection. He woke up very early in the mornings to drive me to the university. He made an effort to take me out to lunch when he was not busy with his friends. He even told me how good I looked, and that I would make some girl very happy one day. I remember he would hug and kiss me, too. Although it would appear that we became closer, however, I don't remember us having any meaningful conversations. My mother bragged about my acceptance into the university. From that point on, I realized the value of an education for my family's front stage (Goffman, 1959). Finally, I was feeling that I was doing something right in my parents' eyes. I did everything I could to keep their approval and immersed myself in the academic world.

In my second year at the university, I studied under an openly gay professor, and later he hired me as his teaching assistant. Although this professor served as a source of gay peer support, at this point in my life, I was only barely tolerant of my emerging self identity (Cass, 1979). My parents bragged enormously about my achievement. This professor helped me to cultivate my academic abilities until, one day, he asked me out on a date. I told him I did not want to date him. Basically, that was the end of our academic relationship. I had finally convinced myself that I was being recognized for my scholarly abilities, but that was obviously not the case. The experience left me feeling worthless and objectified all over again. But life took a different turn when another professor hired me. She helped me to overcome some of my insecurities. She taught me the value of hard work. As a mentor and positive ally, this professor is still in my life now, even after 20 years. I remember my parents saying how fortunate I was to be hired for a full-time position. During the four years of employment with this professor, I realized my potential, both academically and personally. During the same period, I started exploring my sexuality in the gay community and began entering a stage of greater self-acceptance (Cass, 1979). Moreover, using my teaching-assistant status, I gained employment in non-profit organizations doing HIV/AIDS prevention outreach and education work within the gay Asian community. My parents rationalized my involvement with gays as purely academic and as a career opportunity. They highlighted to their friends how caring I was and how noble it was to be working with our community. It gave me an outlet to be around people like myself. I acknowledged myself as being gay and actively sought out peer support for dating issues, employment, and social engagements (Cass, 1979).

As a university student and staff member, I actively embraced those roles, and my positive profile increased in my family unit. On the other hand, my parents still had to fend off social inquiries while bragging about my accomplishments. After all, I was about 24 years old and according to the Chinese norms, I should have been at least dating a girl seriously by now. At family gatherings, my parents' friends continued to ask me directly, "Where is your girlfriend?" However, my mother would always answer for me: "He works too hard!" or "He is too picky!" or "What is the rush?" or "I will find a girl who deserves my son." The ironic thing was that the more my parents said these things, the more they believed what they were telling other people. Until that point, some aspects of my life were harshly criticized and other areas were heavily encouraged and reinforced; my parents were actively shaping my life as part of their duty to prepare me for the scrutiny of extended family members and the world at large (Chan, 1994). The pressure got to me, and one day, I made arrangements with a good female friend. We decided that she would become my pseudo-girlfriend during family events. Elizabeth began showing up at family events to help me with my impression management (Goffman, 1959; 1963). It was strange. My father adored her and insisted that she come by the house more often—unlike Dean. My brother and sister looked at Elizabeth and me strangely. My mother disliked her; after all, my role as the last-born included serving as a companion for her. She may also have felt the effects of an empty nest now that all of her kids were grown up.

A university student with a "girlfriend" was a legitimate role in my parents' eyes, and they granted me a lot of freedom. I was allowed to stay out all hours of the night and even allowed to walk into the house in the morning without being questioned as to where I had been. I was allowed to go on vacations because it was assumed that I was going with Elizabeth. My parents' assumptions were wrong. I was spending my time on homosexual experimentation, where I connected with the homosexual subculture and its members (Cass, 1979). The dilemma was that I compartmentalized my experiences and was unable to synthesize my identities (Cass, 1979). I kept myself organized by creating a new persona, and I even created a new name for that persona. My gay self is called Jonathan Cassidy. It makes sense for me to have a non-Chinese last name; after all, I was told at an early age I did not "look" Chinese. I chose "Jonathan" as a first name because I believe there is an innocence to it. In a way, Jonathan gave me permission to play. Donny Wong was the university student, teaching assistant, and community worker. Jonathan Cassidy was the sexual being, free to explore his sexuality. I was Chinese at home, with a Euro-Asian persona in the gay community. The compartmentalization of my gay and Chinese selves allowed me to feel safe in moving from one sphere to another. It was my way of having one foot in the family closet and one foot in the gay community. I thought it was a way to get to know myself, but it only widened the gap between my public and private selves (Cass, 1979).

Whether the gay community welcomed me—or whether I did not welcome it—is a big question mark (Chan 1994). During my developmental years, I cultivated the skills of setting social boundaries so that people could not discover or expose my true sexual identity (Cass, 1979; Tasker & McCann, 1999; Radkowsky & Siegel, 1997). To ensure my role looked proper, I put together a well-groomed professional appearance in the academic setting, dressing in designer clothes that would make me more attractive. Youth and beauty are highly valued commodities in the gay world. I attracted many suitors, and I sexually integrated into the community, but I did not assimilate socially or with any true emotion (Cass, 1979). I sometimes felt loved by my suitors, but most of the time, I was validated only through sex. Building stable, meaningful same-sex relationships and friendships were challenging for me. Trust was always a feeling I struggled with when dealing with men. I never had a gay peer group. I was 22 years old when I started dating, and I "dated" professional men in their forties, fifties, and even sixties. I believe I exchanged sex for informal education and a lifestyle that I could not afford on my own. Some of the men with whom I became more intimate taught me about their professions and took me out to social events. I got very good at this strategy because I realized that they liked talking about themselves and it took the focus off me. In hindsight, I objectified my sexuality because I believed that I could not possibly contribute in a meaningful way to the relationships I was having. Jonathan Cassidy was not real. These professional men liked the Jonathan Cassidy persona, a well-groomed, educated, work-focused, and sexually attentive young boy. I thus cultivated an exterior shell and an unwritten script in this small gay niche. I did not fully feel integrated into the gay community; after all, I did not associate with boys my age, nor did I feel welcome. I was Asian and did not meet their masculine North American beauty standards. The gay culture does not cast Asians in "desirable roles." I struggled with feelings of marginalization and alienation (Chan, 1994), as well as self-esteem issues (Tasker & McCann, 1999). Did those feelings stem from the lack of authenticity I personified to the gay audience (Tasker & McCann, 1999)? I take partial responsibility for creating a front stage, pseudo-self. My observations and experiences confirmed that a lot of gay men were attracted to other men who fit the "beauty ideals"—or was I simply projecting my own bias? The men I found myself extremely attracted to fit the "white jock" image—like Dean. These boys rejected me because I did not fit their ideal of beauty. Maybe my father was right. The blueprint my father left me with was that gay people were useless. Maybe, for that reason, I failed to develop a peer group. Furthermore, my observations of the gay community were that it was segregated by ethnicity. One time, I recall a Chinese friend of mine saying to me that "the typical gay man will not find you attractive because you are Asian, and a typical gay man attracted to Asians will not find you attractive because you don't look Asian enough." It was the same message all over again. This time, it was clear. I just did not belong anywhere: not in my family because I am gay and not in the gay community because I am Asian. In short, I started feeling a sense of social invisibility in both communities, contributing to my feelings of isolation, marginalization, and rejection (Chan, 1994).

Gradually, I got wiser in the gay community. I realized that I did not need to get validation through sex. Slowly, a few casual sex relationships evolved into friendships, and these men were closer to my own age. But I slowly removed myself from the casual dating scene. One of the reasons I stopped dating is that the men I was seriously attracted to were not the monogamous type. I was not monogamous myself. My deviant identity forced me to engage in promiscuous sex to fill the intimacy void. I count my blessings every day that I am disease-free and healthy at a time when HIV/AIDS affects a lot of people I know in the community. In actuality, my relationships were not destined to work out for various reasons other than monogamy. I realized that I dated men who were very much like my father—emotionally uninvolved. Or was I looking for a father figure, a familiar dynamic? The invisible bubble I built was unconscious, and I slowly became a person who was just a persona of Jonathan Cassidy. My role was a script that I created: a well-mannered young male who people wanted to be around all the time. At the same time, I did not understand why people wanted to be around me. My character had no real story line, no unity; I cast myself in walk-on parts, acting in whatever way the occasion called for. I did not feel a sense of belonging, and hence I did not develop any enduring relationships.

But I had no role models for relationships. My family never talked to me about relationships; they were focused on my education. My conversations with my parents were centered on my teaching assistant job and my studies. Those were very safe topics. Soon they started asking me what I wanted to do upon graduation. I had no answers. Moreover, I got frustrated trying to find a way to fit into the gay community, a community that itself faces a lot of discrimination but at the same time is very discriminatory toward its own members. Eventually, I only engaged in casual sex, becoming more of a sexual object to fulfill the intimacy void, and I hung on to my education to negotiate between familial expectations and my exploration of same-sex activities. To maintain being the object of affection, and to prolong my family's front stage, I slowed down my undergraduate education. After all, I did not know anything about the real world outside. Who was I outside of the role of an academic student? The academic niche kept me safe from public scrutiny. My mother said to me that as long as I was in school, I would always be precious. I should have asked, "Precious to whom?" Thus, it took me six years to complete my bachelor's degree. I held on to education as a master status characteristic for as long as I could. When my mother suggested that I go to graduate school, I complied and planned for that route. For three of my undergraduate years, I did my best to improve my marks so I could apply to the University of Toronto's Master of Social Work program. I did not get accepted. I left the university with my head down. I went to convocation knowing I had disappointed my parents once again. Both Donny and Jonathan were at a standstill after the graduation. As Donny, I could not get steady, meaningful employment. I jumped from one job to another for the first two years after I graduated. As Jonathan, I had lost my marketability with professional men. I was the son who had graduated with a university degree but was still living at home with his parents, while my siblings were married and developing lives of their own.

At family dinners, my master status shifted to "the single son." This status, combined with my lack of a career direction, served to make me feel shameful. I recall one dinner at a restaurant where my parents ordered food for 10 people; that is typically the way Chinese banquet dinners are prepared—for 10, 12, and so on. There would have been 10 diners if I had brought whomever I was sleeping with at the time. The first dish came and there was one portion left over. Everyone saw the last piece on the plate. My father said to the family, "When Donny gets married, we will not have that one portion as a leftover." The comment triggered my childhood memories when at the kitchen table my family teamed up and questioned my sexuality because of my friendship with Dean. It was the same stage, but this time the actors were performing different scripts. My sister stated, "Leftover … my sons will eat it." My mother added, "Donny will have to go to and finish graduate school before he gets married." My brother, instead of teasing me as he did with Dean, jumped in and jokingly said, "Stay single as long as you can." Collectively, they were in agreement about keeping the family secret—*my* secret (Chan, 1994)! On that evening, I felt as if I had allies. However, those allies came at a cost, which was to remain silent and not reveal my true self. This silence forced me to keep my sexuality separate from family discussions. It was the same norm: to maintain the veil of silence I learned when I was a child, but do it as an adult.

The anxiety and conflict I felt was indescribable (D'Augelli et al., 2001). I felt the need to hide all the time. It was getting tiresome, and the non-genuineness was seeping into all my created roles. At home, I was camouflaging my sexuality. In the gay community, I was projecting a Euro-Asian identity. I was also attempting to find a career identity. My sense of self became fragmented just to please others. At the same time, I could not pinpoint who or what was making me anxious. Perhaps, it was the veil of silence that was around me. The veil of silence served to regulate my behaviour and shape my being (Chan, 1994). I realized that living at home was a barrier preventing me from developing any kind of meaningful relationships and a sense of self. I decided to do something unheard of in the Asian culture: I moved out of my parents' home. I was not moving out to go to graduate school or to get married. Those would have been acceptable reasons. I just wanted the space to integrate my compartmentalized selves—to synthesize my identity (Cass, 1979). I confided in my sister, and she knew of my plans to move out. Together, we constructed a story to present to my parents. I was moving out to be closer to work, and I had found a very cheap downtown Toronto apartment to rent. I told my plans to my mother and father together. My mother smiled and was sad immediately, but she did not disapprove. My father's reaction was strange. He did not look at me: his head was down and his hands were busying themselves with some stuff on the kitchen table. After a few moments, he said to me, "I don't understand what you are talking about." Two weeks later, I was out of the family closet, but still very much behind my own walls of protection.

My parents were in shock, sadness, and confusion. According to my sister, my mother thought that if I had just stayed at home, I would not be gay. The veil of silence was not so silent any more. My mother and sister were discussing my sexual orientation behind my back. My mother always knew, but she never spoke about it. I feel sad every time I think about the deception. All those times, when I went on vacations with one of my casual boyfriends, she never asked with whom I was going. All those times I stayed at a "friend's place" for the weekend, she did not query further. What I interpreted as their lack of interest was actually a type of "don't see, don't speak, don't acknowledge" strategy. The silence distanced me from my family, but it also distanced me from getting to know myself emotionally and sexually. In many ways, I felt invisible (Chan, 1994). I felt a part of me was not developed to its fullest potential. As a consequence, I did not share the "personal" part of my life with them. Did they ignore a part of my sense of self, or did they let me explore without questioning me? My feelings of alienation stemmed from hiding my sexuality. Or was the alienation a cause of my disconnection from my family? I have no answers.

Nevertheless, I am an adult now at the age of 39. I earned a master's degree by getting all A's in my courses, and I am out to my friends and family, with the exception of my parents. Career-wise, I am settled and have a good position with a recognized university as a professional administrator. I should be proud of myself. I gave my business card to my parents, and they accepted it without even glancing at it. Instead of asking me what the letters stand for behind my name, my father called my sister for her interpretations of my job and education. My sister told me that our father called her to learn about my career, and what my master's degree was all about. I asked her why he did not call me. No explanations were provided, but she ended our conversation with one statement: "He is proud of you." When I heard that line, I did not comprehend what I was feeling. My father is proud of me? What does that really mean? Do I have something to be proud of or to celebrate? After all, if my birthdays were not celebrated, what other events are worthy of celebration? I have more questions than answers.

Why am I still single at 39 years old? I have dated many men. Some of them were actually "good catches," but I always managed to let them slip away.

If my parents and family were more active in my personal life, if I had received guidance, and if they were more accepting of my choices in dates, would I have been more successful with my romantic relationships? If my parents and family had encouraged me to explore and accept my sexuality, would I have worked harder to find a life partner? If I ever dare to come out to my parents, will it make me feel more validated? Is a loving relationship with another man acceptable to me? More importantly, did the walls of protection and the created persona serve or hinder my love opportunities?

I am an adult, and my next step in life is to think about how I can be more professionally visible and respected in my chosen field. I have not given a lot of thought to finding a life partner. I have, however, given a lot of thought toward starting a second master's program or venturing toward a Ph.D. Why is it that I feel as if I don't own my life or my accomplishments? Is it because I don't have a significant partner to share them with? Next time I call home and my father answers, should I say hello and ask for my mother, the way I always do? Next time I speak with my mother, should I express to her how I feel and involve her in answering the questions I have in my head? Or would I rather maintain the aura of silence and tell her what is happening in my professional life and all the things I have accomplished at the university so that she can continue to brag to her friends about me? To the next gay man I meet, should I introduce myself as Donny or Jonathan? My gayness started this family's secret and the scripts. I played a role in constructing the closet, the walls, and the identities, and my family insisted on keeping appearances on the front stage (Goffman, 1959). Perhaps it is time for Jonathan to introduce himself to Donny and for them to start connecting the fragmented pieces of my "self." Perhaps when I actually synthesize Jonathan and Donny, I will realize that the gay and the Asian selves are not that different (Cass, 1979). Perhaps I should just continue to travel down the road I know. I end this chapter with one thought: When I am walking down the road of life, have I been blinded by the darkness, or am I choosing not to see?

The journey continues, but now I am able to turn up the volume to hear my own voice: the voice of my authenticity. Previously, I listened to the advice of closeted gay men. Their "wisdom," such as "Your family does not need to know what you do in the bedroom" or "Coming out to the family just relieves one's guilt," only served to maintain a veil of silence and foster a very sophisticated disguise. Additionally, I learned to not blame my parents for constructing an ideal persona of a son. I am certain that they know being gay is a very difficult identity to own in our society and in the Asian culture. In their own ways, they wanted the best for me. They were only equipped with a certain level of understanding and parental skills. For the reader of this chapter, regardless of your age and where you are in your life's journey, I leave you with this thought: being authentic and being blinded by the sun when you look up at the clear blue sky is preferable to a life in darkness and keeping track of the various role scripts. My journey continues. Coming out of the closet does not involve just one step; it is only the first step—recognizing that I was living life in a closet. When will I work up the courage to tell my parents about my life?

References

Berger, P., & Luckmann, T. (1966). *The social construction of reality: A treatise in the sociology of knowledge*. Garden City, NY: Anchor.

Bhugra, D. (1997). Coming out by South Asian gay men in the United Kingdom. *Archives of Sexual Behavior, 26*(5), 547–557.

Cass, V. (1979). Homosexual identity formation: A theoretical model. *Journal of Homosexuality, 4*, 219–235.

Chan, C. S. (1994) Asian-American adolescents: Issues in the expression of sexuality. In J. M. Irvine (Ed.), *Sexual cultures and the construction of adolescent identities* (pp. 88–99). Philadelphia: Temple University Press.

Cooley, C. H. (1902). *Human nature and the social order*. New York: Scribner.

D'Augelli, A. R., Patterson, C. J., & Ryan, C. (2001). Counselling lesbian, gay, and bisexual youths. In A. R. D'Augelli & C. J. Patterson (Eds.), *Lesbian, gay and bisexual identities and youth: Psychological perspectives* (pp. 224–250). New York: Oxford University Press.

Fassinger, R. E. (1991). The hidden minority: Issues and challenges in working with lesbian women and gay men. *Counselling Psychologist, 19*(2), 151–176.

Goffman, E. (1959). *The presentation of self in everyday life*. New York: Doubleday.

Goffman, E. (1963). *Stigma: Notes on management of spoiled identity*. Englewood Cliffs, NJ: Prentice-Hall.

Mead, G. H. (1964). The genesis of the self and social control. In A. J. Reck (Ed.), *Selected Writings: George Herbert Mead* (pp. 267–293). Indianapolis: Bobb-Merrill.

Morales, E. (1990). Ethnic minority families and minority gays and lesbians. In F. W. Bozett and M. B. Sussman (Eds.), *Homosexuality and family relations* (pp. 217–229). New York: Haworth Press.

Radkowsky, M., & Siegel, L. J. (1997). The gay adolescent: Stressors, adaptations, and psychosocial interventions. *Clinical Psychology Review, 17*(2), 191–216.

Tasker, F., & McCann, D. (1999). Affirming patterns of adolescent sexuality identity: The challenge. *Journal of Family Therapy, 21*, 30–54.

[8]

NOISES AND UNWANTED ODOURS IN OLD CLOSETS?

SI TRANSKEN

In this chapter, I will summarize my own experiences as an incest survivor, a working-class woman, a feminist activist, a scholar, and a creative writer. Elsewhere I have mapped some aspects of this journey of trauma and healing (Transken, 1995, 2000, 2001, 2005, 2007). My belief is that my own general pattern of hurts, oppressions, and healing is similar to the general pattern for most girls and women who are abused. In this chapter, I will give examples of how the ripples and consequences of abuse go on for decades—even absence becomes a place of consequence. Our particulars and specifics are unique, but the general patterns are worth noting. It is in these patterns that we survivors (and our allies) find our solidarity and strength, and we professionals find the ways to offer support and wisdom.

Yes, some closets stink more than others. Yes, opening the doors to those putrid closets is a dangerous deed. The rancid odour doesn't just immediately dissipate. And all the distress caused to all the noses in the neighborhood by your choosing to open the closet—well, that's the trouble you've caused by turning that door handle. It's hard on the survivor's spirit to be the freak who runs around opening closet doors. It's a tiresome, lonely, dreary, and difficult situation sometimes. For example, on any given day, I can open a newspaper and read something like this article from the Prince George *Citizen*:

Court of Appeal doubles dad's sex abuse jail time

The B.C. Court of Appeal has more than doubled the sentence for a man convicted of sexually abusing his daughter for 13 years, starting when she was a toddler. The Crown has appealed last November's sentence of two years less a day and the appeal court has agreed. "Society's condemnation reflects the utter vulnerability of an infant child, the position of trust of the parent and the lasting harm of sexual abuse," Justice Ian Donald said in a written ruling. "There must have been many times throughout the 13 years of abuse that the respondent's conscience troubled him, yet he persisted." Donald noted that while the man appears to be remorseful, he was convicted for child sexual abuse in 1992 and received a suspended sentence. (2009, June 22, p. 5)

I feel sad and then angry when I read of these cases. As I read these kinds of articles I always ask myself questions: If this man had stolen another man's toddler (perhaps a rich white man's child?) and held her hostage and sexually abused her for 13 years, what would have been the societal response? Why is it that, if the victim is the sexual abuser's "own flesh and blood," the sentences seem to be shorter, when—in my thinking/feeling/knowing—the consequences are worse or as bad for the victims? Research and biographical data (Camilleri, 2004; Herman, 1981, 1992; Poston & Young, 1989; Russell, 1984, 1986) have repeatedly shown us that, when a sexual abuser has free access to his victim, he abuses as often as he can. In the case noted above, this might mean that once a week for 13 years—676 sexual assaults—this girl was traumatized. Even with the revised sentence described above, the perpetrator is receiving about four weeks of sentencing per sexual assault. If he had raped 676 *different* victims over 13 years and then been caught, would he have been punished more severely?

My questions here are not intended to focus on retribution or revenge (these are separate ponderings). What I am trying to assess when I read these kinds of stories is what it means that our world still implicitly considers children as a man's possession, to do with as he wishes. Why do we still consider a home as a man's castle, his private sphere, his domain over which he has control for his own pleasure and preference? My own experiences and research suggest that incest is more traumatizing (than stranger assault) in many ways, in that it separates the victim from other family members, from the trust of the world, and from the sense of what "normal love" might be like. She can't really dream of someone coming to save her, can she? Running away still leaves the others of her family behind in the horrible circumstance. The perpetrator usually tells her that he will kill her, her pets, her mother, himself; that their family will be torn apart; and/or that no one will believe her. Silence is golden in a man's private home, isn't it? On any given day I can still feel waves of sadness and rage that are difficult for my "now" family to fully understand.

Most of the victims of incest, at multiple points in their journey of victimization and healing, are also chronically confused, because the dozens of daily lies and silences involved in *sustaining* the cover-up of what is or was really going on are toxic, damaging, and pernicious. For example, my father would take the van with garbage in it to the dump and claim that he needed my help. My mother seemed to appreciate having him/us out of the house. He would sexually assault me at the dump. I had to participate in this regular lie because I was afraid to do otherwise. Like most abusers of this type, if he *could* abuse me in the home, in my bedroom, in the van on the way to school, even at his place of work in the back room, he *would* abuse me. The lies required to cover up all the forms of violence in our household resulted in me always thinking in multiple directions and from multiple standpoints—something I do to this day. I always had to be prepared with a quick lie to disguise where he had been, what he had been doing, how my family had spent the night or evening or weekend.

Abuse changes the way meals are eaten (with fear and with our heads down), the way the house is cared for (always making sure that whatever would upset him was taken away or quieted down), the way money is spent (if he was in a good mood, he'd shower us with small gifts bought out of guilt; if he was in a bad mood, he'd destroy things we owned). Rarely did we have visitors in our home, because no one wanted observers around to see our dynamics. Shame and fear shaped most daily comings and goings. The emotional currents inside our home were melancholic, angry, volatile, embarrassing, tangled. Incest was, of course, tangled up with other problematic family dynamics. When I first left that house of oppression, I hardly knew how to carry on the most basic of ordinary conversations. I knew how to listen with hyper-alertness, but I didn't really know how to speak in a casual, friendly way. Being invited to dinner at someone's house is still an awkward, clumsy emotional environment for me sometimes.

Unresolved family conflicts? There's a lot I can speak to under that heading. As someone who was sexually abused by my biological father (including being rented out to his friends), was not protected by my biological mother, and was loved by my biological mother's adoptive parents (who never knew

about the dramas of our nuclear household), I am someone who has complicated thoughts and experiences to articulate. I have two younger male siblings (as you'll see below, their existence complicates and continues the story).
Six therapists over the last 30 years, multitudes of healing workshops and
processes, a doctorate in equity studies, more than a decade of registration as
a social worker, 13 years of teaching undergraduate and graduate-level university courses (such as family counselling, social work with victims of abuse,
advanced clinical intervention techniques, crisis intervention), an associate
professorship in a school of social work and a gender studies program—this
is how my intellect and spirit have muscled up on these issues. In my professional roles (as a therapist in an eating disorders clinic and a homeless women's
shelter, an activist with a variety of women's grassroots organizations, and a
therapist in an acute-care sexual assault treatment program) and as a private
practitioner specializing in women's issues, I have been pushed, prodded, and
pummelled with insights about trauma and healing. As stated earlier, I have
published elsewhere other aspects of my process of letting go of the past and
growing joyously into the healing and the future. To honour some of the scholars and activists who have assisted my journey of feeling and thinking, I feel
it is important to cite their writing (Abrams, 1997; Bane, 1999; Bender, 1998;
Breathnach, 1999; Cameron, 1992, 1996; Carlson, 1990; Ealy, 1995; Felshin,
1995; Fox, 1995; Fulton, 1999; Maisel, 1999; McNiff, 1992; Metzger, 1992;
Pinkola Estés, 1992; Spender, 1983; Terr, 1990, 1994; Turner and Rose, 1999;
Wisechild, 1991; Zweig & Wolf, 1997; Zweig & Abrams, 1991). I also have to
acknowledge everything written by bell hooks, but especially her books *Art on
My Mind* (1995), *Wounds of Passion* (1997), *Outlaw Culture* (1994) and *Teach-
ing to Transgress* (1994).

Regardless of the intellectual, spiritual, emotional, and practical progress
I have made, I have to admit that when I was asked to consider writing this
chapter, I still felt unresolved, disturbed, fragile, and unprepared. The pressure
to remain silent and ashamed is still there in some primal place in my soul and
brain. The bad dreams came again for a few days while I tried to discipline
myself to sit here and write what I know to be true. I am now safe, happy, an
effective person with a good, solid, creative life. And yet, the bad dreams come
back to me. The bad dreams come back, but, over the 49 years of my life, they
have been edited and adapted, and new twists manifest in their plot lines. The
dreams, this time around, were of men breaking into my home. In these dreams
my husband was with me, but he was asleep and I was unable to awaken him.
I could see these filthy men in rags and balaclavas with chains and cruel inten-

tions, climbing through our windows. In real life, eventually my husband woke me up and said I had been whimpering.

It has been almost 35 years since the last episode of physical/sexual abuse, yet I still dream about men breaking the glass in our home and climbing into my private bedroom space. Headaches. An urge to binge eat. An urge to seclude myself. These patterns are common among survivors. Knowing this pattern is what invokes my rage when the mainstream world suggests that victims should just get over it, have 12 sessions of therapy, and put the past behind them. Some aspects of abuse seem to be simply undeletable and unhealable. In 1973, I was 13 and had been abused for most of my life, like the girl in the newspaper article quoted above. Even if we knew then what we know now about abuse and abusers, would my father had gone to court and been found guilty? Would he have been given, like the abuser in the article, only four years? Even if he had, he might not have received any counselling during those four years of incarceration. He might not have actually changed. And when he got out, he might have done similar things to other children. These are the thoughts that haunt me as I read the newspapers and hear the stories of the abused women I still work with. Further, all the troubles of disclosure and social services involvement would have been put on me by everyone I knew.

Part of the challenge now is to tell the story that is *my own story* without becoming derailed with the thoughts and feelings of others who are peripheral to or witnesses of my story. Everyone has their standpoint. Everyone has their own configuration of the past that is most functional for their evolving selves. Humans are complicated and pitiful, and imaginations and erasures are nature's ongoing mercy. Again, this customized experience and retelling of the past is just part of the common pattern. This divide-and-conquer aspect is also part of the damage done by abuse. Many abuse victims find it impossible to ever talk about what happened to them, because the shame and stigma is too intense. Some popular works that feature these patterns include Camilleri's *I Am a Red Dress* (2004), Hosseini's *The Kite Runner* (2004), Potvin's *White Lies for My Mother* (1992), and Dorothy Allison's *Bastard out of Carolina* (1992). Also, as in these well-publicized examples, the denial from everyone around the victims can be overwhelming. Our "right now, right here" consumerist culture often wants quick fixes and prefers to leave the past in the past. "Just buy a new bauble, pill, or drink" seems to be the new motto. The pressures on women to be nice, cheerful, pleasant hostesses to the male world are still with us. These pressures are often felt especially poignantly by abuse victims.

My siblings? They experienced violence and a chaotic working-poor household during their childhood. My parents were frequently out of the house working long hours for poor pay. My father was an immigrant from a war-torn country. He suffered during his childhood. He came to northern Ontario with nothing but anger, bitterness, and a wildly unreasonable dream of a better life. He had no tools with which to make that life. He barely spoke or wrote English. He had no money and no contacts. He only ever spoke of his birth family with pain or hostility in his voice, and he had almost no contact with them after he came to Canada. He was always primed to explode, and my brothers and mother witnessed that. They each have their own hauntings, I'm sure. I have subsequently told my siblings about the peculiar sexual abuses I suffered, and they have shared words to the effect that they believe me. Yet, they still remain in some uncomfortable relationship with our parents. They prefer to leave the past in the past. The challenge for me is that the past does still live inside me, at least sometimes. My mother changes her story of what she remembers and what she believes. Maintaining contact with her hasn't been worth the disturbance. For most of my life, I have felt like an orphan. Legally and emotionally, I have become an orphan.

All the members of my nuclear family colluded to ensure that my maternal grandparents never knew about their son-in-law's rages and the abuse he inflicted. They preferred to think of the world as a controlled, tidy, and polite place, where a man's home is his castle. My grandparents only had this one adopted daughter. Their kin circle was limited just by biological circumstance. Yet, in their minds, my mother had made her bed and she must lie in it. My grandparents were Protestant working-poor folks who did their best to pay their bills on time, mind their own business, speak unkindly of no one, and say little in general to anyone. Their overt and covert pressures are why my mother married the man who had date-raped her. My mother had not wanted the life that ended up surrounding her. She was always unhappy in many ways. She had no coping skills. She retreated into herself.

Through my mother's subsequent saturation with religious doctrine, she has evolved into a person who prays hard and rewrites her own life story so that it is more palatable. In one of our last conversations, she emphatically stated that "she always had a happy marriage." The memories I have of him beating her up, threatening to kill her, throwing food and furniture around, constantly humiliating her—she has deleted these memories from her life story. His episodes of adultery? She did not talk about them then and will not talk about them now. His sexual abuse of me—which I know she walked in on, on more than one occasion—she says never happened. I understand her wish to do that rewriting of the life she has lived. Whatever her life has been, it is now near its inevitable completion. She has now lost her parents, and there is no radical reorganization possible for her from her perspective. Thus, it is more comforting to spend her time with God in her head and keep her hands busy, trying to keep her house in some kind of order and her memory shallow. My parents are still economically and culturally poor and geographically and socially isolated.

I have changed my name, changed my beliefs, moved to another province, married, and lost (or deliberately cut off) almost all contact with that era of my life. This has happened in increments. The last 10 years have been less complicated. Here, in my new province, no one knows my previous familial connections and disconnections. They just engage with me as "Dr. Transken" or "Si the poet" or "Si the social justice activist." Many people know my story; I don't hide it, but neither is it a central identity construct anymore. In Jungian therapy, it is proposed that we can decide to go to the dark mines in our subconscious and our past and refire the memories that reside there. Knowledge turns into something like a nugget of gold. It becomes a source of power and self-efficacy. I insist on being belligerently and muscularly optimistic. Many therapists have written about how strong, resilient, and quirkily content and productive many trauma survivors can be, if given appropriate support and counselling (Brown, 1994; Brown & Root, 1990; Duncan & Miller, 2000; Gilligan, Rogers, & Tolman, 1991; Malmo & Laidlaw, 1999; Rubin, 1996; Snider, 2000; Turner & Rose, 1999). Hope is always an important resource to note and celebrate.

As for intense intergenerational conflict, the children of the next generation of our family (they're all in their early twenties) are disconnected from this abusive era. I have made sure only that they know the truth I experienced, and this was done so that they would not unwittingly place themselves or their loved ones in vulnerable situations. Being warned will not necessarily make them wiser, but it will make them less likely to deny their own self-protecting intuition.

The emotional and inter-familial conflicts I experienced also prompted me to contrive ways to spend time with my maternal grandparents without also being in the same room with my parents. My grandparents, who loved me dearly, couldn't understand why I was so obstinate about never being in their home when there was a chance my father would drop in on them. Thus, every Christmas, New Year's, birthday, Father's Day, Mother's Day (I came to celebrate my maternal grandparents as my *parents*), and so on had to be planned out like spy work. At some point, long after I had changed my legal names, they stopped asking about the rift between my parents and me. They resorted to polite avoidance of whatever was going on and just tried to appreciate my company when I phoned in advance and then appeared. Their home was small and had a small parking lot right in front of the living-room window. I always sat on the chair that faced the window so I could see who drove into their driveway or parked across the street. As is usually the case in these survivor stories, it was I who became labelled as the odd person, the troubled person, the weirdo—not my mother or my father. Since I was the potential messenger of bad news and the person who disrupted the "normal," I became the problem. My efforts to keep my grandparents' lives more comfortable often made my own daily life that much more *un*comfortable.

Conflict between daughters and mothers? I miss her! I miss what I once subconsciously imagined was owed to me. I miss the idea of what she might have been. I miss the imagining of what the ideal mother is supposed to offer to her daughter through the various stages of life. Many women struggle to accept their "real" mothers, and many always long for more or what was not given (Carlson, 1990). My biological mother was and is a wounded and cramped person. I try to forgive her. In one of my distinct memories, she was sitting on the couch and I went to sit on that couch, but I sat too close to her (a couple of feet of space between us) and she jumped back, screeching, "Don't touch me! You're just like him!" I was about nine years old at the time. His sexual abuse of me had already been going on for a few years. I don't remember her cuddling me, nurturing me, caring for me. She avoided contact with me. I always felt that I was the cause of her downfall. She and my father would tell stories about how they tried to abort me. They would laugh! I never thought these stories were funny, but as an adult I feel the telling of these stories now to a child—well, this example of "playful" conversational content demonstrates how little they knew about raising a healthy child. They did not know how to be parents. They did not know how to be affectionate in the common ways that people are commonly affectionate.

Every now and then, my mother still phones and leaves a message saying that she loves me, my father loves me, it did not happen, or it happened and he is sorry it happened, and even if it did happen why can't I just put it behind me. She leaves these contradictory messages on my machine because I rarely answer my home phone. After all these years, I am still somewhat phobic about answering my home phone. And still, after all these years, that kind of message on the phone can depress me for a day or two. A deep melancholy grey-blue cloud moves around and into me. To survive her own abuse, she probably had to become emotionally unavailable and emotionally shut down. She just does not get that, by leaving that kind of message and talking about him to me (even though I have stated a hundred times that the only way we could ever have any kind of conversation would be if she *did not* talk about him), she continues to take his side, erasing my feelings and violating something in me. I have tried to build boundaries so that I might have some kind of reasonable adult conversation with her now and then, but she continues to disrespect those boundaries. I have no mother!

At my grandmother's funeral, my parents were there. I did not talk to them. My grandfather wept, and I felt I could not really be emotionally connected to and physically near him, because my parents hovered closely around him. Of course, it was their right to be with him as well. Yet, the rage and hurt I have been left with was something that set me up to leave the funeral immediately after the speaking at the podium that I was requested to do. Because my grandparents lived reclusive lives, and because my parents have been so socially odd, there were only a few people at the funeral. It is hard to lose yourself within a big, empty, gloomy room and a "crowd" of 10 or so people. All the events that most families take for granted—graduations, weddings, holidays—none of these have been a space of normal comfort for me. I never thought about or attended any of my five graduations. No one who is related to me attended my marriage ceremony. I have never attended the graduations of our next generation because of the possibility that my parents would show up. If I think about these losses, the absences become presences. I just try not to think about them.

When my grandfather was dying (the one adult figure I have been the closest to my whole life) I could not fly across the country and be with him in his last days of hospital care, because I knew I would be trapped in a small room with him and my parents. The thought of that entrapment repulsed me. Also, I knew my rage would likely burst out in that circumstance. I did not want my grandfather to go to his grave with this ugly knowledge about the abuse—instead, I spent a lot of time on the phone with him. And when he died, I spent the day alone, grieving, with no support from or for anyone from that era of my life. He was my last meaningful link with that era. My family photos are only of him and my gram. They are in a corner of my office, with a picture of their home, too. I am grateful for their examples of quiet and stable kindness. Had I not had them in my life, I am absolutely certain that I would have died of suicide or drugs before I reached the age of 20.

A few years ago, my mother decided to bus her way across the nation. When she arrived on my doorstep, I was away teaching. She arrived unannounced and told my husband that she had come to visit me. She shuffled her way into our home and began telling him things that suggested I lied a lot, had had many boyfriends in the past, and was unreliable. How could a mother invest so much in discrediting her own daughter during her first contact with her son-in-law? She may have felt it was necessary to disassemble any impression of her that he'd been given regarding the abuse and dysfunction of our childhood family. He was perplexed and uncomfortable with the whole event. She left before I returned. Her grief and emotional displacement (chaos) left with her. Well, sort of! She, too, is a victim, and she always will be a victim in my mind. However, she is also a colluder. Having a conversation with her only disrupts, disorients, and disappoints both of us.

As I approach my 50th birthday, I have peers who have grandchildren. Sometimes I feel sadness that this somewhat standard trajectory (of having grandchildren and large family gatherings) is not part of my life. Maybe if I had had a lovely and cheerful childhood, I would have had a bundle of children, and thus, a bundle of grandchildren by now. It's hard to know! Hard to know if that would have been a worse path, since much of the pain of my childhood is also tangled up with rural poverty and isolation. My parents had very little "cultural currency." Because I had to work at multiple jobs for long hours in order to get a good education, I could not also spend time as a mother. Limits! My legacy from this is also about limits. Maybe I do have moments of nostalgia, as we all do, about the paths we did not or could not take. Every path selected means that there were other paths that were not selected.

Whenever I lecture or speak about these themes of incest, abuse, and poverty, I also make note of how the abuse has affected my health. Many scholars have listed the short-term and long-term health consequences of abusive childhoods. Scholars have also noted that mental (un)health and physical (un)health are undeniably interconnected (Brown, 1994; Brown & Root, 1990; Burman, 1990; Collier, 1982; Graveline, 1998; Jordan, 1997; Kaschak, 1987; Malmo & Laidlaw, 1999; Pennington, 1988). Again, it is impossible to ascertain whether the migraines, clinical depression, incessant bouts of insomnia and bad dreams, irritable bowel syndrome, and cravings for binge eating (when under stress) would have been there if everything else had been more "standard" in my childhood. High-blood-pressure medications, antidepressants, ulcer medications, anti-inflammatory medications, and a $400-a-month (minimum) investment in supplements might have been the trajectory my body was on anyway. All those thousands of dollars and hundreds of hours of therapy and consultations with naturopaths to manage these conditions and stress—how might I discern which portions of those challenged coping skills are the result of this or that variable in a complicated life?

I am now a resilient and creative person. There are too many writers, survivors, and scholars to thank for what they have given me. I have been blessed in having always loved reading (and later, writing) as a way to grow, understand, cope, fortify, and clarify. Some of my "coaches" have been like uncles, aunties, and cousins. Some, such as Julia Cameron, bell hooks, Carol Gilligan, Judith Herman, Diana Russell, and Dorothy Smith, are authors to whom I will always be indebted. I have published poetry and creative writing in many important places. I have had over a hundred public readings of my poetry. Just last year, I was involved in art projects with homeless women and thesis students. For a decade, I have been journalling every day (Julia Cameron is one of my "sheroes"!). Perhaps all of this powerful insistence on creativity has emerged as a compensation prize for the bad years of my childhood. At least, that's what Jungian and feminist therapists might say. On the other hand, perhaps I was meant to be even more creative and confident that I am today, but somehow got hobbled or diminished through the abuse.

I know that I have a strong radar/third eye/sixth sense about people. This is a gift and a burden. Many times, I have heard clients and other abuse survivors talk about having that extra sensitivity to what is going on around us. We had to have that alert attentiveness to our abuser's moods as a way to minimize the troubles that he gave us on a day-to-day basis. No doubt, all of that has been part of the unfolding of my life as a social worker and as an activist. Is it just random coincidence that I have given all of my adult life to the women's movement? In some way—albeit a twisted and horrific one—my father (the abuser) and my mother (the silencer and neglecter) educated me into the role of organic or accidental social worker for my family. Accidents happen. Some aspects of accidents can be about salvaging and finding fortuitous outcomes. Any of us can make the decision to write happier commentaries on our lives. We can belligerently insist on optimism and positivity. One of the best revenges is simply (if possible) living a gorgeous and meaningfully engaged, successful life. I do that. Sometimes I really almost knock myself out to be happy.

Over the years, I have worried that my father and his friends have abused others. I know he did abuse others when I was a girl; this is part of the reason I did not bring friends to my home during my childhood—I knew he would abuse them. As an adult, I spoke to my siblings about the abuse and tried to have substantive conversations about it with them. I do not know how seriously they took my warnings. I also made a lengthy phone call to the Children's Aid Society at one point near the beginning of my journey to well-being. I disclosed everything to the social worker I spoke with and told her that I would be prepared to testify if anyone else ever came forward. How much of what I said that day actually got written down and stored somewhere useful, I cannot say. I did not attempt to take my father to court because, simultaneous with my own private journey, I have been an activist within many other women's journeys. I know that in the context of our patriarchal, evidence-based judicial system (Gordon, 2002; Lakeman, 2005; Schell & Lanteigne, 2000; Smith, 1999) it would be a case of my word against his word and my world view against his world view. Years of abuse, yet no collaborating evidence exists! Too many years have gone by. When my grandparents were alive, taking my father to court and the ensuing disclosures would have broken their hearts. Perhaps I also feared that if they ever had to choose between taking his side and taking mine, they would choose his. Not because they believed it had not happened, but because it would be too terrible for them to be separated from their only daughter, my mother. If they had chosen my side, it would have meant knowing and accepting that their own daughter betrayed her child for so long and in so many ways. They could not have managed that shame. They could not have managed any of this unspeakable disaster. Thus, court never seemed to be a feasible option for me. My experience has been that most incest victims are still unsupported by the legal system, and/or they choose not to use the legal system for the reasons I have listed above.

As a result of speaking publicly, writing, researching, and teaching about these issues, I have had many women send me emails and letters. Some approached me in public and told me parts of their own traumatic stories. The specifics of how, when, and by whom we were abused are different and distinct. However, the outcomes usually fit into a pattern: we feel unable to bear the burden of being the one who "breaks up the family" by "washing our dirty linen in public." We feel wounded in many inner ways and places. Every commercial or catalogue cover featuring scenes of comfy, safe, wholesome family settings has the potential to make us feel loneliness, melancholy, or deep despair. These ever-present images and imaginings of the loving family are often felt by abuse survivors as an absence. Some type of theft has occurred, and we have lost the ability to restore our inner safety, pride, and confidence. We have to consciously labour and strive to become complete, balanced, loving, resilient citizens. Long weekends are sometimes morose. The last work shift before the long holidays can be particularly difficult. Everyone is sharing stories of how they are going to visit family, be with family, miss this or that family member, celebrate this or that family tradition. To mention our authentic story of loss and trauma would only make others feel overwhelmed or awkward. But constructing a false tale would reposition us as colluders, cleaners, calm hostesses, falsifying the records of theft and abuse. Most of us witness those common conversations but remain silent. This is a form of invisible and long-term "family conflict."

Researchers have written about how the imprints of family dynamics have potential consequences in the workplace (Holly, 1989; Page, 1999; Schell & Lanteigne, 2000; White, 1997). The workplace is still one of those contexts that sometimes cause bad feelings to flicker in me. Some of my "sisters" in the workplace become people I deeply and sincerely care about. Most of the authority figures I must deal with are male. Most of these males have a different value cluster and belief system than mine. This is inevitable and standard. None of them are feminist socialist activists. None of them are Buddhist (the faith system I have chosen). None of them have or should have an interest, one way or the other, in my mental and spiritual health. They could not care less, really, if I died on the spot or on some other spot. Such is the way that large organizations and academia (patriarchal and capitalist in core assumptions and practices) flow. Countless times over the years I have been called into a "superior's" office and asked to do this or that task. Usually the asking is more like a telling. There is an implicit threat that my priority ought to be the task I have just been assigned. His word against my word ... his wishes over my wishes ... his goals over my own: this is how the adult professional workplace flows. My silencing is part of his job, and that is the norm. Yet, it sometimes triggers a really low mood (a sense of helplessness) for me for a day or two afterward. I feel that resistance is futile. This mood has meaning in my "now" family. Unless I want to be unemployed or underemployed, any workplace resistance that I do must be covert and subtle. And there is always the risk of retribution. My radar has usually served me quite well; I know how the dynamics of abuse unfold. Thus, although I have had 27 jobs and more than 65 bosses (most of whom have been male), any job I have left has been at my own timing. Each time, a better job was waiting for me. I do not trust authority. I do not believe what comes out of the mouths of authority figures. I am more convinced by their long-term behaviour. All of these work-life experiences have an impact on my present family life. It is not possible to subtract the 40 or 50 hours a week that I work from the emotional consequences my close connections feel from me. This robust paranoia has turned into an asset I have as a consequence of 15 years of abuse. This ability to walk out of a bad situation is just a repeat of leaving my father's house before it was even legal for me to do so. There is no memo that a dean can ever threaten to send me that is worst than being raped in all one's orifices for years by one's own father, is there?

In many gorgeous, wholesome, and succulent ways, the feminist movement has been my mother over the years, and hundreds of its authors have shaped my world views and values. Emma Goldman, Jane Addams, Patricia Monture-Angus, Lee Maracle, and a hundred others have helped me grow up into a person who feels I *belong* somewhere, through rituals of connection (Take Back the Night, International Women's Day, women's organizations' fundraisers, feminist research projects, December 6th commemoration ceremonies) that made me feel affirmed and cared about. My will leaves most of my (paltry but perhaps interesting) assets and resources to the women's centre at our university. I visit at least one women's organization in our town weekly. I have a national connection to many women activists like myself. I have a HERitage and a wide legacy of SHEroes. They are my "now" family and my future family. I live with an incredibly loving and sensitive husband, three Siamese cats, 30 plants, and a neighbourhood of sociable people. My missions are clear to me. A purposeful, mindful life with a muscular sisterhood is beyond revenge—it is letting go of the private, patriarchally inflicted past and tenaciously celebrating creative potential and kindness.

References
Abrams, R. (1997). *The playful self: Why women need play in their lives*. London: Fourth Estate.
Allison, D. (1992). *Bastard out of Carolina*. New York: Dutton.
Bane, R. (1999). *Dancing in the dragon's den: Rekindling the creative fire in your shadow*. York Beach, ME: Nicolas-Hays.
Bender, S. (1998). *Writing personal poetry: Creating poems from your life experiences*. Cincinnati: Writer's Digest Books.
Breathnach, S. B. (1999). *The illustrated discovery journal: Creating a visual autobiography of your authentic self*. New York: Warner Books.
Brown, L. S. (1994). *Subversive dialogues: Theory in feminist therapy*. New York: Basic Books.
Brown, L. S., & Root, M. P. P. (Eds.). (1990). *Diversity and complexity in feminist therapy*. New York: Harrington Park Press.
Burman, E. (Ed.). (1990). *Feminists and psychological practice*. New York: Sage.

Cameron, J. (1992). *The artist's way: A spiritual path to higher creativity*. New York: Jeremy P. Tarcher/Putnam.

Cameron, J. (1996). *The vein of gold*. New York: Putnam.

Camilleri, A. (2004). *I am a red dress: Incantations on a grandmother, a mother, and a daughter*. Vancouver: Arsenal Pulp Press.

Carlson, K. (1990). *In her image: The unhealed daughter's search for her mother*. Boston: Shambhala.

Collier, H. V. (1982). *Counselling women: A guide for therapists*. New York: Free Press.

Duncan, B. L., & Miller, S. D. (2000). *The heroic client: Doing client-directed, outcome-informed therapy*. San Francisco: Jossey-Bass.

Ealy, C. D. (1995). *The woman's book of creativity*. Berkeley, CA: Celestial Arts.

Felshin, N. (Ed.). (1995) *But is it art? The spirit of art as activism*. Seattle, WA: Bay Press.

Fox, J. (1995). *Finding what you didn't lose: Expressing your creativity through poem-making*. New York: Penguin Putnam.

Fulton, K. L. (1999). Put it in writing: Outgrowing the pain by creating change. In J. Turner & C. Rose (Eds.), *Spider women: A tapestry of creativity and healing*. Winnipeg, MB: Gordon Shillingford Publishing.

Gilligan, C., Rogers, A. G., & Tolman, D. L. (Eds.). (1991). *Women, girls and psychotherapy: Reframing resistance*. New York: Harrington Park Press.

Gordon, L. (2002). *Heroes of their own lives: The politics and history of family violence*. Chicago: University of Illinois Press.

Graveline, F. J. (1998). *Circle works: Transforming Eurocentric consciousness*. Halifax, NS: Fernwood Publishing.

Herman, J. L. (1981). *Father-daughter incest*. Cambridge, MA: Harvard University Press.

Herman, J. L. (1992). *Trauma and recovery: The aftermath of violence—from domestic abuse to political terror*. New York: Basic Books.

Holly, M. L. (1989). *Writing to grow: Keeping a personal-professional journal*. Portsmouth, NH: Heinemann.

hooks, b. (1994). *Outlaw culture: Resisting representations*. New York: Routledge.

hooks, b. (1994). *Teaching to transgress: Education as the practice of freedom*. New York: Routledge.

hooks, b. (1995). *Art on my mind*. New York: New Press.

hooks, b. (1997). *Wounds of passion*. New York: Henry Holt.

Hosseini, K. (2004). *The kite runner*. Toronto: Anchor/Random House.

Jordan, J. V. (Ed.). (1997). *Women's growth in diversity: More writings from the Stone Center*. New York: Guilford Press.

Kaschak, E. (1987). *Engendered lives: A new psychology of women's experience*. New York: Basic Books.

Lakeman, L. (2005). *Obsession with intent: Violence against women*. Montreal: Black Rose Books.

Maisel, E. (1999). *Deep writing: 7 principles that bring ideas to life.* New York: Jeremy P. Tarcher/Putnam.

Malmo, C., & Laidlaw, T. S. (1999). *Consciousness rising: Women's stories of connection and transformation.* Charlottetown, PEI: Gynergy Books.

McNiff, S. (1992). *Arts as medicine: Creating therapy of the imagination.* Boston: Shambhala.

Metzger, D. (1992). *Writing for your life: A guide and companion to the inner worlds.* New York: HarperCollins.

Page, S. (1999). *The shadow and the counsellor: Working with the darker aspects of the person, role, and profession.* New York: Routledge.

Pennington, S. (1988). *Healing yourself: Understanding how your mind can heal your body.* Toronto: McGraw-Hill Ryerson.

Pinkola Estés, C. (1992). *Women who run with the wolves.* New York: Ballantine Books.

Poston, C., & Young, L. S. (Eds.). (1989). *Reclaiming our lives: Hope for adult survivors of incest.* Boston: Little, Brown.

Potvin, L. (1992). *White lies for my mother.* Edmonton, AB: NeWest Press.

Rubin, L. (1996). *The transcendent child: Tales of triumph over the past.* New York: Basic Books.

Russell, D. E. H. (1984). *Sexual exploitation: Rape, child sexual abuse, and workplace harassment.* Beverly Hills, CA: Sage.

Russell, D. E. H. (1986). *The secret trauma: Incest in the lives of girls and women.* New York: Basic Books.

Schell, B., & Lanteigne, N. M. (2000). *Stalking, harassment, and murder in the workplace.* Westport, CT: Quorum Books.

Smith, D. E. (1999). *Writing the social: Critique, theory, and investigations.* Toronto: University of Toronto Press.

Snider, J. (Ed.). (2000). *Tales from the couch: Writers on therapy.* New York: Harper Collins.

Spender, D. (Ed.). (1983). *Feminist theorists: Three centuries of women's intellectual traditions.* London: Women's Press.

Terr, L. (1990). *Too scared to cry: How trauma affects children and ultimately us all.* New York: Basic Books.

Terr, L. (1994). *Unchained memories: True stories of traumatic memories, lost and found.* New York: Basic Books.

Transken, S. (1995). Reclaiming body territory. *Feminist Perspectives, 25,* 1–35.

Transken, S. (2000). How budget cutbacks to services for sexual assault victims are dissolving, dividing, and distressing. In D. Gustafson (Ed.), *Care and consequences* (pp. 127–154). Halifax, NS: Fernwood Press.

Transken, S. (2001). The stones, roses, gold and fires of reclaimed territory. In *Caring communities.* Toronto: Inanna Publications, Laurentian University, and the Canadian Research Institute for the Advancement of Women.

Transken, S. (2005). The meanings and healings that can emerge from writing to ances-
tral women (Or: What I've learned since I adopted Emma Goldman as my ances-
tral grandmother ...). The Association for Bibliotherapy and Applied Literature
home page. Retrieved from http://www.abal.laurentian.ca

Transken, S. (2007). Re/searching with art/ists: Praxis, practice, and social justice. *Open
Letter 13*(4).

Turner, J., & Rose, C. (Eds.). (1999) *Spider women: A tapestry of creativity and healing.*
Winnipeg, MB: Gordon Shillingford.

White, W. L. (1997). *The incestuous workplace: Stress and distress in the organizational
family.* Center City, MN: Hazelden.

Wisechild, L. M. (Ed.). (1991). *She who was lost is remembered: Healing from incest
through creativity.* Vancouver: Raincoast.

Zweig, C., & Abrams, J. (Eds.). (1991). *Meeting the shadow: The hidden power of the dark
side of human nature.* New York: Penguin Putnam.

Zweig, C., & Wolf, S. (1997). *Romancing the shadow: A guide to soul work for a vital,
authentic life.* New York: Ballantine.

Suggested Reading

Chesler, P., Rothblum, E. D., & Cole, E. (Eds.). (1995). *Feminist foremothers in women's
studies, psychology, and mental health.* Binghamton, NY: Harrington Park Press.

Gil, E. (1994). *Play in family therapy.* New York: Guilford Press.

Gilbert, L. (2004). *I might be nothing: A journal* (C. Itter, Ed.). Victoria, BC: Trafford
Publishing.

Gilligan, C. (1982). *In a different voice: Psychological theory and women's development.*
Cambridge, MA: Harvard University Press.

Gilligan, C., Ward, J. V., & Taylor, J. M. (Eds.). (1988). Mapping the moral domain: A
contribution of women's thinking to psychological theory and education. Cambridge, MA: Harvard University Press.

Hill, M., & Rothblum, E. (Eds.). (1996). *Classism and feminist therapy: Counting costs.*
New York: Harrington Park Press.

Rubin, T. I. (1998). *Compassion and self-hate: An alternative to despair.* New York:
Touchstone Press.

Sands, R. G. (2001). *Clinical social work practice in behavioural mental health: A post-
modern approach to practice with adults.* Toronto: Allyn & Bacon.

Terr, L. (1999). *Beyond love and work: Why adults need to play.* New York: Touchstone.

Tuhiwai Smith, L. (1999). *Decolonizing methodologies: Research and indigenous peoples.* New York: Zed Books.

Wolper, A. (1995). Making art, reclaiming lives: The artist and homeless collabora-
tive. In N. Felshin (Ed.), *But is it art?* Seattle, WA: Bay Press.

[9]
A BROTHER NO LONGER
A Real Story of Family Dysfunction and Abuse

ANONYMOUS

In my years as a sociologist, I have read about the general relationship patterns and typical behaviours of dysfunctional families, including poor communication and ineffective or punitive parenting. These types of families manifest not only negative personal outcomes but also multiple negative or even destructive interactions between family members (Paulson & Sputa, 1996; Howe & Bukowski, 1996; Claes et al., 2005). Additionally, a significant age difference between siblings may be a factor contributing to negative interactions in childhood and can result in sibling estrangement over the lifespan (DeKeseredy, 1996; Duffy & Momirov, 1997; Ambert, 2006). Family dysfunction has also been linked, in the social psychological literature, to a tendency toward traumatic bonding (Duffy & Momirov, 1997), including finding life partners whose characteristics match or may even exceed the destructive patterns established during one's formative years. Add to this the patriarchal rule that prevails in most families (Nelson & Robinson, 1999), and it gives a snapshot of my family of origin.

The emerging narrative is consciously autobiographical. Feminism has embraced the autobiographical method as a way of emphasizing the integral links between the personal and the political. In feminist epistemology, the person telling the story and giving it an interpretation is the expert (Griffiths, 1994; Jones, 2004). This means that there are multiple risks associated with engaging with the autobiographical method. I am not only opening up a chapter of my life that is painful and difficult to talk about, but I am also doing so with the realization that my account and interpretation will be subject to criticism of bias (Jones, 2004; Tenni, Smyth, & Boucher, 2003). This is part of the standard reaction in academia toward feminists in general. Furthermore, in the tradition of acceptable ("scientific") research methods, all research should be objectively verifiable. The idea of relying on personal/political narratives can result in dismissal and even ridicule. These negative reactions marginalize the experiences of the less powerful (Jones, 2004) and are the very reason why autobiographical accounts are necessary. Mine is one such account.

Even in the face of the risks involved, I will tell my family story as directly and honestly as I can. It should go without saying that the multiple subjectivities (Jones, 2004; Martindale, 1992) involved in this story mean that only I can tell this story; the stories of other family members will be different. Another implication is that, although the narrative will contain my reactions and feelings, they may not seem justified to some readers. The details of the story are sufficient to establish my personal interpretation. This is in keeping with the autobiographical method. Thus, it is possible to give multiple readings of the same data. Indeed, personal interpretations of the same narrative may change over time (Griffiths, 1994). What follows are my present narrative and my interpretation, based on the overall objectives set out for this collection of family stories.

On the surface, my family was a perfectly ordinary family. We lived in a rural setting on the outskirts of a small town. We were somewhere between poor and not-quite-poor, which showed in the hand-me-down clothing we often wore and the looks that my more well-to-do peers gave my outfits at school. My parents owned a small farm that didn't produce enough to make ends meet, so my father combined farming with wage work all his life. The farm gave us some basic staples, including milk from the one or two cows we kept and vegetables from the farm garden, which was tended by everyone in the household. My mother also obtained a low-paying manual job after raising her oldest children to school age. In addition to me, there were my mom, dad, and three brothers. I was the only girl. I was the second eldest, born in relatively close succession with two of my brothers. My parents told me in my adult years that they always planned to have four children but paused after the first three for financial reasons. Six years after the birth of my middle brother, my youngest brother was born.

The three of us were sent to my grandmother's farm from a couple of weeks before to a few weeks after my baby brother was born in order to give my parents some breathing space from the constant demands of a lively brood of four young children. I spent the summer on pins and needles, distracted from my usual farm chores, waiting for news about the long-awaited baby. When word finally reached us, I remember a feeling of excited anticipation at meeting this new addition to our family. I couldn't wait to get home. Finally, the three of us were sent back home in a train that seemed to stop unnecessarily long at every station and a bus that crawled along the dusty country road like a thirsty snail. We were met by the welcoming arms of my mother, who ran to greet us at the bus stop in an unusual fit of maternal emotion. Unaccustomed to being cuddled, since I seemed to have gotten too old for that kind of thing in my parents' eyes, I was a little shy and apprehensive. I covered up by telling my mother how I longed to see my baby brother. I found him sound asleep in a pastel blue basket in the living room. I was awed by how tiny and perfect he was, with his silky eyelashes and the pink and round fingers that curled around my little finger, even as he slept, when I touched his hand.

I was seven years old, and I remember the delight I took in looking after him. He seemed like a doll to me, someone to cuddle and look after and take for strolls bundled up in a carriage. My brothers and I would stand by my mother when she was breastfeeding him, mesmerized by this act that she told us all of us had engaged in as babies, wanting to taste the milk that the baby seemed to love so much. My mother would first object, then laugh, and finally express some of her breast milk in our small tin cups for us to taste. It was a short experiment. Our taste buds had outgrown the warm and rank sweetness of breast milk. As our parents laughed out loud, we rushed to rinse our mouths with water.

When my brother grew out of early infancy, I would feed him soft and mushy foods that I sampled and that also left a strange taste in my mouth, to be quickly washed away with gulps of juice. It was extra work to look after the baby while my mother tended to other household chores. My brothers took turns taking him for a stroll, but more of it fell to me. It seemed natural to look after the baby, who soon became a toddler, and—seemingly in a blink of an eye—a preschooler. Minding him was my sisterly responsibility, and though I do not remember ever really resenting my babysitting duties, I'm sure that I must have had moments. Especially as I grew older, there were times when I would rather have played with my other brothers and friends but was stuck looking after him.

As my kid brother grew up, he spent more of his time in the company of his brothers than me. The two oldest would usually take him along when they spent time with their peers, and they would play their boys' games, making slingshots and building huts out of tree branches in the woods in the summer. I would also participate in those activities but was equally content to play with my dolls or playhouse or to play-act being a schoolteacher with my girlfriends. In the winter, we all built snow castles, went skiing or skating, and had snowball fights. Summers were mostly spent on our bikes, going swimming, and playing different team games with other children in the neighbourhood: volleyball, badminton, baseball, table tennis. We were also occupied with farm chores in the summer, either at our home or at my grandmother's, but we got breaks during the day and time off in the evenings to play among ourselves or with our friends.

There were the usual sibling rivalries (DeKeseredy, 1996) and commotions between the three oldest and our kid brother. Compared to us, he was born into a wealthier family. Our parents' economic circumstances had improved steadily; our mother had taken paid employment outside of the home, and our father had steadily risen through the lower ranks of clerical workers. My two brothers and I remembered times when we didn't have so much, and when our requests for treats and special items were often met with a curt reply: "We don't have the money."

It was different when my kid brother was at an age to start asking for things. More often than not, he got what he wanted. Accompanying his status as the youngest was a kind of pampering by our parents that we older children had never experienced at such an early age. We responded with outbursts of jealousy and resentment. My parents' response was not the desired one as far as we were concerned; they tended to react protectively, defending their youngest against what they saw as attacks by us. "He's only a baby" was the standard reply to our grumblings. The words that really stung were "You are old enough to know better." They never explained why my baby brother was receiving the royal treatment. It was only later that I realized how my parents' financial status had made them more relaxed about money and gift-giving even outside special occasions like birthdays and Christmas.

Along with many parents of their generation, and in contrast with today's more approachable and "liberal" parents (Aapola, Gonick, and Harris, 2005), mine thought of parenting as consisting of putting food on the table and clothes on our backs and teaching us to work hard in order to prosper. I don't remember being held or cuddled, though they must have done so when I was young—too young to remember. I appreciate the work ethic they taught and the basics of life that they provided. But seeing them show affection to, give special treats to, and side with my little brother was difficult to take. In contrast, I remember that I was often fearful as a child—of the dark, or dogs, or flying insects—only to be chided for "being a baby" instead of being comforted through words or hugs. Seeing the different treatment of my youngest sibling made me feel that I was secondary to my parents.

I think we three oldest children grew close to one another partly because we took comfort in one another in the absence of parental affection and attention. Of course, I realize that my parents expected us to become more independent with age, but they certainly didn't do it through "sponsored independence," that idealized middle-class norm of gradually relinquishing parental control over children in a supportive environment (Nett, 1993, p. 196; Nelson & Robinson, 1999, pp. 130–131). I found that there was not enough support in words or deeds as I struggled to find my way as an adolescent through a web of increasing expectations. We older siblings just had to rely on ourselves and our trio to navigate the complex network of peers, schools, farm work, paid part-time work, and parental neglect. As it happens, the teen years, with their siren call of different peers and activities, diminished our threefold solidarity. In the end, each of us managed our lives the best we could, increasingly by ourselves.

As a teen, in keeping with patriarchal family patterns (Nelson & Robinson, 1999; Aapola et al., 2005), I was subjected to more controls than my brothers. They had so many more freedoms than I. They could go out and stay out late without any parental commentary. Later on I found out that all my brothers had their first sexual intercourse in their early teens. I was shocked, both at the idea that any girl would have found those geeky, pimply boys attractive and at the idea that they had actually gotten away with it! Not so for me; I was watched and controlled. It felt like I was always suspected of being up to no good. Much to my humiliation, I was dragged home from perfectly innocent peer activities if I didn't come home exactly at a designated hour. I felt that my parents never trusted me, even though I worked hard at my chores, had excellent grades at school, and had friends of whom they approved. I was a good daughter according to their expectations, yet I didn't have their trust. For my part, I tried to approach my parents with my teenage angst, only to be brushed off with "It will get better" and with no advice other than "Don't worry about it so much."

To be sure, my political activities as a teenager caused a lot of friction between my father and me. I was in high school during a time of a great awakening of young people in their teens and twenties. In my circle of friends, I found out about new and exciting political ideas and practices. I was passionate about social justice issues and became an activist in my school and community.

In my case, the "generation gap" (Koller, 1974, pp. 208–209; Nett, 1993, p. 175; Duncan, 2000) between my parents—particularly my father—and me was a very painful and daily reality over a few years. Insofar as my avid reading habit and associating with politicized peers led to my youthful activism, I also credit the injustices I felt in my home life for awakening in me a political fire to fight oppression in any shape or form. For that I am thankful, in a rueful sort of way. As it turned out, my politics did not go over very well with my father, who had been to war and hated everything that smacked of communism. I now know that his reaction was his side of the vast generational divide between us, deeply rooted in his wartime experiences.

What hurt me even more in the schism between my father and me was that my mother sided with him instead of protecting me from his verbal attacks, even as I left the dinner table regularly in tears, loudly slamming every possible door shut behind me both literally and figuratively. Much to my embarrassment, my mother would make me apologize to my father for my words, but while I lived at home, he never apologized to me for the many cruel and hurtful phrases and epithets he flung at me.

Over three decades passed before my father would apologize to me. When it finally happened, it really surprised me because I did not think he had it in him to apologize, let alone understand what he was apologizing for. However, because of how I have come to view him, I also see it as a selfish act, one that was meant to absolve him. He prefaced his apology by saying that he did not want to go to his grave knowing that I hated him. It was still all about him, a man facing his own mortality. I was moved by the gesture, nevertheless. It is difficult not to love a parent and want their love in return.

By the time I left—or really, ran away from—home, my youngest brother was 12 years old. Through my teen years, he had needed less babysitting and spent more time with our brothers, and he had many friends of his own age who shared his interests. He and I grew distant through this time, drawn away by our respective peers as is customary for teens (Delgado, 2002; Akers, Jones, & Coyl, 1998). We pretty much only saw each other at the dinner table. After I moved far away from home, I only visited my parents and brothers at most once a year, hardly enough time to build or cement a relationship. I took pride in hearing that he was doing well in school and that he had a wide circle of friends and a number of talents and interesting hobbies. At the same time, I felt pangs of jealousy when I saw that his musical and other tendencies were lavishly supported by my parents through the purchase of expensive musical instruments and other gadgets. I had wanted to take piano and singing lessons when I was his age and younger, only to be told that we couldn't afford it. That my parents sent me money to go and visit them when I was struggling as a student far away only felt to me like "too little, too late."

Yet, I felt a lot of affection for my kid brother, whether because it was expected or because it was genuine. I remembered his birthdays and Christmases with cards and gifts, wrote him letters, and took an interest in his life, just as I did with my other brothers. Nevertheless, we three oldest were quite close, and remain so today, but my youngest brother is now lost to me.

Over the years I spent away from my parental home, my kid brother was becoming a teenager and young adult. He grew up and went to university. He found a lovely girlfriend whom all of us really liked. She had a sad family situation (her father was an alcoholic) and she found my brother's shoulder to lean on. The two of them dated—happily, it seemed—for a number of years, and the rest of the family was sure that we would hear wedding bells in the not too distant future. As it turns out, the wedding bells rang instead for my brother and a young woman who had presumably been his girlfriend's best friend and confidante.

I had a conversation with my youngest brother just after he had broken off his relationship with his old girlfriend and started to date his wife-to-be. He was asking me for advice on how to deal with his feelings of guilt over having hurt his past girlfriend by getting involved with her best friend. I remember that he told me how his new-found love had explained to him, while he was still in a relationship with her supposed friend, that that relationship was founded on deceit. She had helped him understand that he didn't really love the girl but merely felt sorry for her because of her unfortunate family situation. This so-called good friend explained to my brother that the poor soon-to-be-ex-girlfriend was obviously so needy that she would only be even more trouble later on, because all the trauma of her father's alcoholism obviously made her unable to form a solid relationship.

I remember listening to my brother tell this story of how he came to realize that his new girlfriend was right and that he had to cut off his relationship with his old girlfriend to make sure that he did not end up in an unhappy relationship. I tried to tell him that perhaps his own counsel would be better, because he certainly would know his own feelings better than an outside observer. I recommended that he ask his old girlfriend directly how she herself felt about her prospects of living in a loving relationship, something that he had not thought to do. I also questioned the motives of someone who would come to him with such an analysis while professing to be the best friend of the person whose character she was so skillfully assassinating.

Of course, I did not say all of this as directly as I am describing it here. It has been a long-time family tradition not to talk about any difficult personal matters. Silences and short, vague statements are more in keeping with the way my parental family tends to deal with things, as part of its dysfunctional pattern (Paulson & Sputa, 1996; Howe & Bukowski, 1996; Claes et al., 2005): let's just brush any problems under the carpet and pretend they are not there. So, I mostly listened, said a few mild things, and in the end said what everyone in my family always says: "It's your life, and you must do what you want." It sounds supportive but is nearly always anything but. Now I think that statements of that kind absolve us from our responsibility to other people.

I remember meeting my future sister-in-law briefly after my brother had told me the news about his change in girlfriends. We had a very pleasant family visit, with my parents and all of my brothers present. Over dinner we talked about her and my brother's educational and other plans. I remember her complimenting me on my new sweater, which my mother had knitted for me. We laughed and shared stories.

Within a short time, they were married. I was unable to attend the wedding due to travel expenses. I was still going to university, had recently married, and had a new baby. It was impossible to afford the travel costs. I received a wedding album of pictures in which the newlyweds looked somber and nervous before and during the ceremony and happy and relaxed after, just like most other wedding photos I have seen, including my own. There was a picture of the couple with my parents and my middle brother. My oldest brother and his wife were in no pictures.

By this time, my sister-in-law had followed the script that she had used in separating my brother from his previous girlfriend. She explained to her husband that his other relationships were also based on faulty premises. Soon after they got together, she had convinced him to break off his relationships with his oldest and best friends. There was apparently always something wrong with them. Either they were not really his friends or they wanted something from him, in her judgment. My three brothers had friends in common from their past, all of whom tell the same story: they have little or no contact with my youngest brother, and their attempts to do so go nowhere. On the rare occasion that he sees them, it's usually on his own and outside of his home.

In the end, my sister-in-law's analysis was also extended to our sibling relationships. My oldest brother was the first one in line. He had helped the new couple—who were still in university—by getting them summer jobs in his workplace and giving them a room in his home. After a couple of weeks of this arrangement, my sister-in-law had interpreted this generosity as evidence that my oldest brother was working out his guilt over the many wrongs he had presumably committed against his younger brother while they were children. She talked my kid brother into confronting our oldest brother, with the result that the two of them got into a bitter argument. At the end of the verbal exchange, it was my sister-in-law who told my oldest brother not to ever see or contact her husband again. All of this she told my parents in the aftermath of the altercation.

When my oldest brother phoned to tell me what had taken place, both he and I asked my parents if they could do something about the situation, to try to mediate between the brothers. They said they felt that their hands were tied because both were their sons and they didn't want to take sides. When I raised the possibility that their daughter-in-law was really to blame for any of it happening, they acknowledged it but also said they could do nothing because they didn't want to cause trouble between the couple and they were afraid their youngest son would reject them if they said anything negative about his wife.

It occurred to me at that point that as much as I, as a feminist, was reluctant to acknowledge that women can be abusive in their intimate relationships, I had to give serious thought to the possibility that my own brother was involved in just that kind of a situation. The pattern of psychological control, manipulation, and isolation of my brother by his wife sounded too much like the research I had read about the topic (Johnson, 1996; Duffy & Momirov, 1997; Sev'er, 2002). My sister-in-law was gradually cutting my youngest brother off from all of his social networks. Not only that, she was successfully bullying my parents into being complicit.

I talked about my fears with my other brothers, and they reported further alarming aspects of our youngest brother's married life. Apparently, after their studies were over, our sister-in-law had convinced our youngest brother that they should buy a home out of town, with some land that they could work on. The closest neighbour lives at least a kilometre away. Since then, they have spent nearly all of their time working on the house and the land. They rarely visit either set of parents, and when they do, their visits are short. They have no friends that anyone in the family has seen or heard of. This pattern of

isolating the victim is all too familiar to those of us who know the intimate partner violence literature (Johnson, 1996; Duffy & Momirov, 1997; Sev'er, 2002).
Most often, the abusive partner is a man. In this case, it is my sister-in-law.

Up until about a decade ago, I maintained a relationship with my youngest
brother, despite the estrangement between him and my oldest brother. I found
it difficult and stressful to deal with my sister-in-law because of the family
rift, but I made an effort to remain friendly, mostly for the sake of our parents,
who find the family breakdown painful. Now, my middle brother is the only
one to remain in touch with our kid brother, and he tells us about the goad-
ing, verbal abuse, temper tantrums, and other psychological warfare directed
at him by our sister-in-law. They have never visited him, and they tell him
they have no interest in visiting him. He visits them even if he is not invited,
and our sister-in-law always makes it clear to him in words and deeds that he
is not welcome.

Despite the unpleasant pattern that was unfolding over the years between
my brothers, the breaking point in my relationship with my youngest brother—
in reality with his wife—still came as a shock. My husband, son, and I visited
them about a decade ago as part of a trip to see everyone in the family. My middle brother picked us up from the airport and drove directly to my kid brother's
home; we planned to spend the evening with them before going to stay at my
middle brother's place overnight. In the car, we all talked about how important it would be to be as pleasant as possible so as not to give any cause for our
sister-in-law to act out. Our meeting was happy and amicable. We sat down
for dinner and had a calm and friendly session of catching up with all the
news. Our hosts were pleading with us to stay overnight at their place and to
head out the next morning. We accepted the invitation, and it was decided
that my middle brother would drive over to his apartment to pick up his
overnight bag. My husband, son, and kid brother joined him on the ride. My
sister-in-law and I said we would stay behind to catch up on more family
news.

In retrospect, I should have known that any attempt to create a situation
in which I could have avoided a disaster was futile. It is a typical strategy by
victims of abuse to try to control the cycle of violence, but it is the abuser's cycle
and they don't need a reason for their negative behaviour (Johnson, 1996;
Duffy & Momirov, 1997; Sev'er, 2002). As the menfolk left amid animated
and happy chatter, my sister-in-law and I continued our conversation about
family. I let her take the lead, not wanting to say anything that would set her
off. She asked me if I had heard that my middle brother had a new girlfriend.

I said that I had but that I had not met her yet, and that I was a little concerned about their great age difference.

At that point, my sister-in-law started to become very agitated. She began pacing back and forth in the kitchen and told me that she thought that all of my side of the family was harshly judgmental and that we had no business interfering with anyone's lives. In the next few minutes she got increasingly angry and animated and proceeded to tell me what was wrong with each and every person in my family, ranging from our ignorance and inability to accept others to the way we treat everyone badly. She berated my parents for their "lack of backbone," and my other brothers and me for "being jealous of" our kid brother's and her "success," among other things. All of this was punctuated with cursing and loud shouting.

I tried to ask her to calm down and to sit down to talk about what was bothering her, but she got even louder and started hitting her fist on the kitchen counter. At that point my initial disbelief at this unnecessarily strong reaction was starting to turn to fear over my safety. Her manner was getting increasingly aggressive; at each turn on the kitchen floor she would get closer and closer to me as she punched the kitchen counter ever harder. I sat very quietly in my chair, not daring to move a muscle, making myself as contained and invisible as possible.

Finally, she stopped her ranting for a moment. At that point, I stood up slowly from my chair and left the room, telling her I needed to use the bathroom. I splashed water on my face, dried myself with a towel, walked quietly into the adjacent hallway, picked up my coat and my purse, and went outdoors, making sure I closed the door as softly as I could. In the front yard, I phoned my middle brother's cell phone; speaking very quickly and in a near whisper, I told him to get back as soon as he could. Then he passed the phone to my husband, to whom I said that I would like to leave the moment they returned because my brother's wife was totally out of control.

Meanwhile, my sister-in-law had realized that I had left the house and came out looking for me. She saw that I had my coat and purse with me and asked what I was doing. I kept my distance from her, told her that I was afraid of her, that I would not go back in, and that I thought she needed help. She seemed surprised and then began apologizing and pleading with me to come back in. I refused to go in and told her that we would leave as soon as my husband and son got back. I was frozen to my spot on the lawn, unwilling to move anywhere until the others got back but watchful of what she would do next. When she finally understood that I wasn't going to go back indoors, she picked up her verbal tirade where she had left off, and before the others returned, spewed more abuse and epithets at me, then went back to the house telling me never to contact her or her husband again. She came back out of the house only to throw on the ground all the gifts we had brought, telling me she would send us a bill for the dinner.

Shortly thereafter, the men returned, everyone with a stunned look of concern on their faces. My kid brother came out of the car, carrying some of our luggage, and asked what had happened. In a voice that I hardly recognized as my own, I replied that he should ask his wife. He looked at me for a moment, dropped the luggage on the front lawn, stopped to hold his head in his hands for a short while, and walked toward the house without saying a word. My middle brother called for him to stop, but he did not turn around; he went in the front door, closing it behind him.

The rest of us just stood there, not knowing what to do. I told them shakily what had happened, filling in the details while we put our luggage back into the trunk of the car and drove off. As we drove to my middle brother's place and through the evening, I kept on telling and retelling everyone the details of the events that had unfolded. I kept on going back to the fact that my sister-in-law had chosen a moment when I was alone with her in her home to start her physical menacing and verbal abuse. Up until the point that the men left, she had been fine, chatty, and sociable. Almost the moment they left, she went on the offensive. My middle brother told me that it was the way she behaved with him, too, and that he didn't let it get to him. I said I refused to allow her to bully me ever again, and if it meant that I could never see my youngest brother again, so be it.

After those events, I still tried to see my brother a few times, at the request of our mother. Once, when my mother and I were in his hometown visiting other relatives, I phoned him at work and asked him if he would like to join us for lunch. He told me he was not going to. I sent him an email to ask him to communicate with me, telling him that we need not talk about what had gone on but could just talk about other things. His only response was "Compost only starts to stink when you turn it over." I finally gave up, and I have only seen him and his wife twice in the last decade, at important family events that none of us could miss. Otherwise, there has been no contact or communication.

Our lives go on. I get together with my two other brothers when I visit home. We share happy times and laughter. On occasion, some bitterness will emerge from my oldest brother because it's with him that our sister-in-law's attacks on our family started. Our middle brother continues his visits with the couple even amid abuse. I have made my peace with the situation and don't think about the two of them very often. Sometimes I'm sad or angry. At the end of the day, I tend to think that just because we are born into families does not mean that we will become or stay close.

As painful as it is, I am also forcing myself to reflect on some of the personal reasons my youngest brother may have for his estrangement from the family, in addition to the abusive isolation imposed by his wife. This is not about "blaming the victim," which is a customary (and misguided) reaction in cases of intimate partner violence (Johnson, 1996; Duffy & Momirov, 1997; Sev'er, 2002). On the one hand, it should be very clear by now that I do see my brother as a victim of his wife's abusive acts, and in no way do I want to absolve her of the responsibility she must take. And I am increasingly convinced that we need to subject women's abusive behaviours and the reasons behind them to systematic and thoughtful analysis, while avoiding the standard pitfalls of those conservative scholars who propose that women and men are equally violent.

On the other hand, many domestic violence victims are driven to those types of relationships as adults because of the negative family climate they experienced as children. It is very possible that my kid brother experienced our family as a negative environment and that the sibling rivalry I describe above felt to him like emotional and psychological abuse. I will not allow myself to think that there may have been other possible types of abuse by my brothers, who, after all, spent more time with him in their teen years. This is part of the vault of silences in our family, and it is a part that I dare not delve into. Going back to the documented ideas of traumatic bonding and the cycle of family violence (Duffy & Momirov, 1997), it is possible that a dysfunctional family such as ours may have driven him into the relationship he is now enduring. The whole family is reaping the bitter fruit from the blighted seeds sown in the past.

Meanwhile, my parents live in hope that one day we will all be one big, happy family again. They try occasionally to raise the issue with the three of us. I believe that they still think it's at least partly a continuation of the childhood rivalry between their three oldest and their youngest child. They don't want to hear and I don't think they fully believe what we have told them about their daughter-in-law's acts of abuse. They try their best to hide our sibling estrangement from the extended family. They also read too much into my asking, out of politeness, if my kid brother and his wife have visited or phoned recently. They pretend that greetings are passed to me from my youngest brother and his wife at Christmas or for special birthdays and anniversaries, and vice versa. I guess that is what they need to do to make it work for them. My mother will on occasion ask me if I could try to contact my baby brother again. My answer is always the same: "I have tried. It didn't go anywhere."

As I have told this story, I have made links to sociological literature on different types of family dysfunction, neglect, and abuse. The biggest sign of dysfunction in our family is the general lack of, or poor, communication. The neglect is manifested in the withdrawal of affection and lack of mutual support. The abuse is mostly verbal and psychological, though my parents used corporal punishment, too, as a disciplinary tactic in my childhood. Yet, I still think of much of my childhood as quite happy. The difficult parts, however, have appeared in adulthood. My youngest brother is locked in an abusive relationship. My oldest brother's physical and mental health recently collapsed. My middle brother, now well into middle age, has not been able to form any significant intimate relationships. And I am a workaholic, obsessed with having to constantly reaffirm my self-worth—if not to those around me, just to myself.

I do firmly believe that the seeds of these negative and self-destructive behaviours were sown in our formative years. For whatever reason, my parents created a web of dysfunctions that were normalized for us while we were growing up. Having realized this relatively soon after escaping the tangled family web, I have tried in my own family life to maintain an open and healthy family communication; to show approval, acceptance, love, and both verbal and physical affection; and to pay attention to everyone's needs, including my own. I feel that, unlike my youngest brother, I was largely able to stop recreating the dysfunctions that plagued my family of origin, just as many children who were abused do not necessarily become abusive themselves (Duffy & Momirov, 1997). In the end, research is needed into both how and why different family lines establish specific positive or negative behaviour patterns and how and why they may be either perpetuated or changed over generations.

I would say that the key lesson I learned from my experiences is that sometimes running away is the best and only way to get away from very difficult family circumstances. With distance, I was able to re-evaluate my family relationships and to build new and healthier relationships with my significant others. I also realize that it would have been impossible to avoid the showdown that took place between me and my sister-in-law. The estrangement between my brother and me was inevitable, given the family scripts. I was shaken through the experience but not broken, thanks to help from my family of marriage and close friends who support and sustain me. In my view, families such as the one I come from are bound to self-destruct. Any therapeutic or counselling intervention would have had to have taken place many decades ago—possibly generations ago—and would have required the kind of studies I recommend above.

As family members deal with one another over time, they may be subjected to the same phenomena that face friends and acquaintances: some of them remain in your circle and others fall by the wayside. We are less likely to tolerate unpleasant and hostile behaviour in people outside the family than we are to put up with it from those who are presumably our "nearest and dearest."

I believe that family fragmentation (outside the well-documented phenomenon of divorce rates) is more prevalent than current documentation reflects, and that it would be normalized if it were not for the mythology around families that keep people together even if their interpersonal relationships are unhealthy. The unfortunate outcome of the mythology of "happy families" is the perpetuation of family dysfunction and abuse over generations.

References

Aapola, S., Gonick, M., & Harris, A. (2005). *Young femininity: Girlhood, power and social change.* London: Palgrave Macmillan.

Akers, J., Jones, R., & Coyl, D. (1998). Adolescent friendship pairs: Similarities in identity development, behaviors, attitudes, and intentions. *Journal of Adolescent Research, 13*(2), 178–195.

Ambert, A. M. (2006). *Changing families: Relationships in context* (Cdn. ed.). Toronto: Pearson.

Claes, M., Lacourse, E., Ercolani, A. P., Pierro, A., Leone, L., & Presaghi, F. (2005). Parenting, peer orientation, drug use, and anti-social behavior in late adolescence: A cross-national study. *Journal of Youth and Adolescence, 34*(5), 401–411.

DeKeseredy, W. S. (1996). Patterns of family violence. In M. Baker (Ed.), *Families: Changing trends in Canada* (3rd ed., pp. 238–266). Toronto: McGraw-Hill Ryerson.

Delgado, M. (2002). *New frontiers for youth development in the twenty-first century: Revitalizing and broadening youth development.* New York: Columbia University Press.

Duffy, A., & Momirov, J. (1997). *Family violence: A Canadian introduction.* Toronto: James Lorimer.

Duncan, S. (2000). *Is there a generation gap?* Billings: Montana State University, Communications Services. Retrieved from http://www.montana.edu/cpa/news/wwwpb-archives/home/gap.html

Griffiths, M. (1994). Autobiography, feminism and the practice of action research. *Educational Action Research, 2*(1), 71–82.

Howe, N., & Bukowski, N. W. (1996). What are children and how do they become adults? Childrearing and socialization. In M. Baker (Ed.), *Families: Changing trends in Canada* (3rd ed., pp. 180–190). Toronto: McGraw-Hill Ryerson.

Johnson, H. (1996). *Dangerous domains: Violence against women in Canada.* Toronto: Nelson Canada.

Jones, B. (2004). Telling family stories: Interpretive authority and intersubjectivity in life history research. *University of Sussex Journal of Contemporary History, 7*, 1–11.

Koller, M. R. (1974). *Families: A multigenerational approach.* Toronto: McGraw-Hill.

Martindale, K. (1992). Theorizing autobiography and materialist feminist pedagogy. *Canadian Journal of Education, 17*(3), 321–340.

Nelson, E. D., & Robinson, B. W. (1999). *Gender in Canada.* Scarborough, ON: Prentice Hall Allyn & Bacon.

Nett, E. M. (1993). *Canadian families: Past and present* (2nd ed.). Toronto: Butterworths.

Paulson, S. E., & Sputa, C. I. (1996). Patterns of parenting during adolescence: Perceptions of adolescents and parents. *Adolescence, 31*(122), 369–382.

Sev'er, A. (2002). *Fleeing the house of horrors: Women who have left their abusive partners.* Toronto: University of Toronto Press.

Tenni, C., Smyth, A.,& Boucher, C. (2003). The researcher as autobiographer: Analysing data written about oneself. *The Qualitative Report, 8*(1), 1–12.

[10]

FEMALE EXCOMMUNICATED

A Life Course and Family in Conflict with Norms and Tradition

CLARY KREKULA

It was during my earliest school days that I first heard about her. Mom had taken us kids and some visiting relatives to the village cemetery. While we cousins ran along what looked like a hilly slope in the woods surrounded by a low stone wall, the adults stood around talking in low voices. When I came closer, they stopped talking, and I was asked to go back and play with the other children. I did as I was asked, but I walked away as slowly as I could and tried to overhear what they were talking about. I heard Mom referring to a woman who had not been buried in the cemetery. Her body had been buried somewhere outside the cemetery walls; no one knew where. I could not hear what the woman had done, but I understood that it must have been something terrible; otherwise, she would not have been treated in such a way. It was not until I was a middle-aged woman that I knew the whole answer. The woman who had been buried in an unknown place had given birth to four children by the same man but had not been married to him. He was already married to someone else. The woman's name was Alma. She was my father's aunt, my paternal grandmother's sister. She had lived her life in that small village where I grew up, a village that lies among the woods and marshes and bordering rivers in the northernmost region of Sweden.

With a Borrowed Father

Alma died in 1941, almost 20 years before I was born. My story about her is based therefore on conversations with the villagers who knew her story, through family and through other social relations. Some of them had met Alma, and others had only heard stories about her. The description below of her life is based on several different retrospective interpretations. This means that each conversation about Alma that I have taken part in constitutes *one* version of how the story can be told (Danielsen, 1990). Each story should be understood as the result of the storyteller's primary values (Shenk, Davis, Peacock, & Moore, 2002) and of his or her interpretation of what took place or what was told as recalled in the present. That is, the interpretation does not necessarily reflect how it was regarded at the actual time in the past (Trost, 2005). Another way of understanding this is that the structure of each individual story is shaped by what is regarded as a concern for the storyteller in the present (Nilsen, 1996). In the case of the stories about Alma, this has led to versions that deviate from one another on a number of points. This does not affect the focus of this chapter, however: namely, reflections about how perceptions of normative family building are created in relation to the engendered life course.

Alma was born in 1892 as the oldest child in a family of 10 children (Levisdotter Kostet, 1997). At that time, approximately 200 people inhabited the village (Kaunisvaara byaförening, 2000). The principal industries were agriculture and logging, along with reindeer herding and public works financed by the state, such as digging ditches to collect runoff and dry out the bogs (Kaunisvaara byaförening, 2000). Alma's parents were farmers. While all of Alma's siblings either married or moved to the United States and left their childhood home, Alma remained with her parents. At the age of 29, she became pregnant. While she was expecting her first child as an "unwed mother," she took on temporary work as a domestic servant in a larger township in the region. She returned after a while to her parents' home with a daughter. While she lived with her parents, she gave birth to three additional children: a son in 1922 and two daughters born in 1927 and 1929, respectively. The father of her children was Albert, a married man who lived in the village. Albert was well off; he was a successful farmer and local businessman.

During the years Alma gave birth to her children, Albert also fathered children with his wife. At one point, the two women were pregnant at the same time. The so-called half-siblings came to grow up together, attending the same school and socializing. Stories recall that Alma's son often visited Albert's house to play with his siblings. He did not speak of them as brothers and sisters, but he regarded them as his friends. Neither did he call Albert, whom he met frequently, "Father." When the son met his father while in the company of his fiancée for the first time, he commented to her, "They say he is my father."

Alma later moved to a house of her own with her youngest daughters. The son remained with his grandparents and grew up there. The oldest daughter married at a young age and moved away from home. Albert's wife died during childbirth during the early 1920s. However, this did not change the relationship between Alma and Albert; they continued to live in separate households. Even after the wife's death, Alma and Albert were not regarded as an official couple by others.

Famine characterized the early 1900s in northern Sweden. This led to a major national campaign to collect funds for those in need. Another consequence of the famine was the establishment of workhouses. These northern Swedish workhouses were boarding houses where poor children received schooling and food in exchange for their hard labour (Slunga, 1993). In the village where Alma lived, the first village school was opened during the 1890s (Uusitalo, 1997). Although Alma's children were born during a period that is described as the heyday of the workhouses and of economic turmoil in the area, they were not sent to the workhouses. Alma likely received economic support from her parents and from Albert. A woman who had grown up around Alma's daughters recalled, "They were certainly not in want of anything." However, others described Alma as poor in comparison to the circumstances of others in the village during this period.

The relationship between Alma and Albert gave rise to many conflicts within their respective families. Alma's sisters argued with her often, urging her to come to her senses and end the relationship with Albert. Alma was even subjected to criticism from her own children, and it is reported that one of them repeatedly said, "There wasn't just one guilty party. She was just as guilty as him." Some commented upon the relationship with this statement: "She was a bad woman. I don't want to talk about her." The relationship also caused conflicts within Albert's family. When Albert was away for longer periods of time, his wife often sent servants to see whether his bicycle stood outside of Alma's house. Although it stood there, the person who was sent often neglected to report this in order to avoid the wife's dejected reaction. One of Albert's daughters was often seen at the window, looking toward Alma's house and crying. The conflicts sometimes turned physical. When Albert's grown sons attempted to talk sense into their father, Albert was known to reply by hitting them with a weapon.

When Alma's story is told, the word *guilty* is frequently repeated. Who, in the eyes of the village, was guilty in this relationship? Did the gossip condemn one or both of the partners for this family constellation's problems?

The image of how the village people looked upon Alma's children and upon Albert is a fractured one. Some tell of Alma's good relationships with family members, but others describe Alma as a lonely woman. "I think she only socialized with one other woman in the village," recalled a woman who remembered her. Others told the story about how she called upon a neighbour one time, frozen and covered in snow, but was not invited in for coffee, as custom suggested. She was left standing in the doorway. The image of Albert is also a conflicting one. Some say that he was a welcome guest in all the homes in the village. However, others say that, behind his back, he was not considered a "real man," living as he did with two households. Even Alma's children suffered from the guilt that was ascribed to their parents. Although they had their friends, they could not avoid being called the "bastard children."

Alma died when she was only 49 years old. It is not known what really happened. Some believe that Alma died in her own home; others claim that she died at a hospital in the nearby township. It is also plausible that, if Alma died during the winter, her body was transported to the larger town where bodies were stored until the snow melted and it became possible to bury them. In any event, when the news that Alma was to be buried reached the village, her brothers and her then 19-year-old son travelled to town to arrange for the funeral. When they arrived, however, they were met with the news that Alma had already been buried: the municipality had already arranged for it. Neither the children, whose ages ranged from 12 to 21 years old by then, nor any of the other loved ones had been called to the funeral. Neither does it seem that any of the relatives were informed by the municipality as to where her body was buried. Alma's gravesite is thus shrouded in mystery even today. When the village people talk about it, they give different answers. Some say, "Outside the church cemetery." Others claim, "She was buried by the municipality with a pauper's burial, in a mass grave for the poor, but within the church cemetery walls." In discussions, some speculation is made about the funeral and about the names of authorities who were responsible for Alma's burial. However, there are more questions than answers: Was it a conscious decision made by an individual civil servant of the municipality that the relatives were not given an opportunity to arrange a funeral? If so, why were Alma and her children treated in this way?

Condemned to a Silent Burial

Alma's funeral contradicts what was common during this period. If she was buried outside the church cemetery, this suggests she was regarded as having relinquished her right to a Christian burial. The right to be buried in a church cemetery, in so-called sacred ground, is regulated by the oldest of Christian doctrines, which state that Christians shall not be buried as pagans and that those who deviate from Christianity shall not have the right to a Christian burial. The doctrines of the Swedish Church regulate the right to burial in a similar way in the Church Canon Law of 1571 (Croneborg, 1941). With this as a point of departure, the right to be buried in sacred soil within a church cemetery was revoked from persons who had taken their own life, unbaptized children, and persons who had committed serious crimes (see Nilsson, 1989). Among the serious criminals who were forced out of sacred grounds were those who had been executed. Today, the right to burial is regulated by Swedish civil law.

Even if Alma was buried in a church cemetery, the forced silence about the funeral—that is, the revocation of the possibility for the relatives to arrange a funeral or to participate in one—can be seen as a so-called dishonourable funeral. This emerges in legislation that regulates the burial of those who commit suicide. According to the laws of 1734, the graves of those who had committed suicide were to be dug in soil in a remote place. The bodies were transported there by an "executioner"; that is, the person whose job it was to carry out death penalties and other corporal punishment. Exceptions to these rules were made, however, for those who had taken their own life while lacking mental capacity. These individuals were allowed to be buried in the church cemetery by "honest people," "in serenity, and without the usual ceremony" (Bexell, 2009). Thus, the dishonourable funeral was carried out outside the church cemetery, while a funeral carried out in silence was a milder form for disgrace.

A silent funeral was a form of punishment, and the frugal funeral can be found in the constitutional law of 1894, in which three forms of burial service are mentioned: (1) burial according to usual practices; (2) burial of a less ceremonious nature, used in the case of stillborn children; and (3) burial in silence—that is, without the ringing of church bells, a memorial service, songs, or similar elements. Relatives of the deceased could be present, as well as the necessary undertakers to carry out the funeral. This form of burial was reserved for people who had been executed, those who had been killed while carrying out heinous crimes, and those who had ended their own life. The last were only exempted if one could prove with a confirmatory physician's statement that the person in question was not in a state of full mental capacity at the time (Nordisk familjebok, 1904).

That public recognition of a person's death was a component of how one showed respect for the deceased emerges even in customs such as the so-called ringing of the death knell. Initially, this involved ringing the church bells once, as soon as possible after someone died. It was believed that this prevented evil spirits from taking the soul of the deceased. The routine was also thought to shorten the deceased's time in purgatory, which was believed to precede entrance to heaven. With time, the ringing of the death knell became a question of class, and a fee was attached to it that the poor did not have the means to pay. Even the length of time it was rung and the time at which it was rung indicated class distinctions between those who had passed away. In the case of a king, the ringing could continue for a year, for example, while for others it might only be rung on one occasion. For a simple commoner, the bell might ring early in the morning, while greater respect could be shown for someone from a higher class by ringing the bell later in the day. In large areas of Sweden, the ringing of the death knell was carried out with a large church bell for a man and with a small church bell for a woman. In the late 1800s, a common hour for the ringing of the death knell was implemented, regardless of social class (see Aries, 1978; Dellert, 2009). Later, the custom was abolished.

Consequently, the desirable burial was characterized by its public nature. Following from this, a burial in silence denoted punishment (Plejel, 1983; Åhren Snickare, 2004). When someone made the decision that Alma should be buried in silence, this was meant as an insult to her. We should, therefore, ask ourselves why—on what grounds—Alma was consigned to a silent burial. Because she had not carried out a criminal act, her "crime" must have been of another kind. Let us examine this by looking at Alma's life and how she built a family and compare it to that which was considered common practice and expected behaviour at that time.

In Conflict with the Expected Life Course for Unwed Mothers

What is presented as a norm contrary to a deviation is not a given. These positions are created in relation to one another. As has been correctly pointed out, that which commonly occurs also becomes an imperative that prescribes how something should be (Pickering, 2001). Impressions regarding wherein Alma's "crime" lay—that is, in what way she deviated from what was respectable—

should therefore be understood in relation to contextual notions of the time as well as how women's lives should be shaped and what families should look like. Below, I will discuss some aspects of how Alma's life deviated from what was expected through a life course perspective.

The life course perspective generally assumes that an understanding of an individual's life demands knowledge about the experiences it has contained but also about when these experiences took place during the life course. Accordingly, old age, for example, is not an isolated category; the experiences that follow are a result of the life lived (Giele & Elder, 1998; Hagestad, 2002). The concept encompasses at least four different aspects when it is used in studies about old age: that old age can be understood by looking at circumstances earlier in life, that an understanding of old age is improved by examining when during the life course individuals have experienced events, that old age constitutes a developmental process in which old age is the final phase, and that an understanding of old age is improved by examining how old age constitutes an integrated part of the lifestyles people have had (Tornstam, 2005).

The perspective also draws attention to the normative character of perceptions of life courses as more or less expected, depending upon the individual's social positions, such as gender, class, and age. Within these institutionalized forms, the life course is also affected by existing power structures that differentially distribute possibilities and resources. Power structures often dictate how life should be lived. In other words, they define rights, obligations, expected activities, and what is to be regarded as normal and what as deviant for individuals in different life phases (Gubrium, Holstein, & Buckholdt, 1994; Närvänen & Näsman, 2007). Family norms, with their legitimizing of some relations and questioning of others, are an example of an institution that contributes to maintaining "normative" life courses.

We can begin by stating that when Alma gave birth to her first child she was already 29 years old; that is, she was not a "young maiden." Although it is difficult to locate statistics about when women gave birth to their first child during the period in question, we can still state with confidence that Alma was a late first-time mother. What we do know about births during this period is that the birth rate was fairly stable in Sweden from 1751, when population statistics first were collected, until the early 1900s. During this period, on average, 4.5 children were born per woman. In the early 1900s, the birth rate dropped quickly, reaching the low average of 1.8 births per woman of childbearing age in the middle of the 1930s (Trost, 1993; Statistiska Centralbyrån

[SCB], 1963, 1969). The fact that Alma gave birth to four children during the 1920s means that she had well above the average number.

Alma was a single mother; she did not share parenting with anyone. She was not the first single mother in the village. The church records tell of village women who were left alone with children and farms when their husbands left to seek work in other areas (Levisdotter Kostet, 1997). These women did not lose the respect of those around them. Therefore, it is not her role as a *single mother* that should be regarded as Alma's crime against the norms.

Neither was the fact that Alma was an unwed mother, something that was unusual but not out of the question for the time. From 1921 to 1925, approximately 28 children were born per 1,000 unwed mothers. Among married women, the corresponding figure was 242.4 children per 1,000 (SCB, 1969). This means that approximately 10 percent of the children born during this period were born to unwed women. The view of premarital intercourse at that time has been described as residing amid the difference between ideal norms and behavioural norms (Trost & Levin, 1999). Ideal norms that suggest that intercourse occurs only within marriage prescribe a *desired* behaviour. This norm was not accompanied by particularly strong sanctions against those who openly broke it. Therefore, it was not regarded as particularly important to comply with the norm. In other words, the norm was regarded as a weak expression of regulations for how the life course should be lived; thus, it only weakly directed individuals' concrete actions in the form of refraining from sexual intercourse outside of marriage.

If we compare Alma's life course with the results of Øyen's (1966) Norwegian study of unwed mothers during the 1960s, we can state that Alma deviated in two ways from the typical image of unwed mothers. As Øyen notes, different age groups gave birth to children inside and outside of marriage. Among those who gave birth outside of marriage, we find predominantly younger women. Alma distinguishes herself in this case in age; she was significantly older than the majority of others who gave birth outside of marriage. Øyen also shows how it is unusual to give birth to multiple children outside of marriage. As a rule, unwed mothers generally had only one child, and her research demonstrates that this was true for 89 percent of the unwed mothers who were studied. Since the majority of unwed mothers got married after the birth of the child, either to the child's father or to another man, additional children were born within a marriage. In the Norwegian study, two-thirds of those who gave birth outside of marriage got married within one year after the birth of the child. Even in this respect, Alma deviated from what was typical; she gave birth to several children outside of marriage, and she never got married.

For a time, Alma lived with her parents with her children. Øyen's study (1966) also shows that a large portion of the maternal parents accepted the situation after the birth of the child. For example, 47 percent of those who were interviewed continued to live with their parents with their child. Against this backdrop, it is not exceptional that Alma lived with her parents with her children as an unwed mother.

Finally, Alma died when she was 49 years old. Even if we were to measure this according to the standards of the time, she was young when she died. At the time she was born, the average life expectancy in Sweden was approximately 50 years old. Given the remaining life expectancy for those who had reached 49 years of age, one could expect her to have lived another 22 years. Only 5 out of 1,000 women in that age group died at age 49 (SCB, 1969).

Thus, we can state that Alma's life deviated in several ways from the expected life course of a woman during this time period. A woman seldom gave birth to her first child at the age of 29, particularly if she was not married. Furthermore, it was unusual for women at this time to give birth to as many children as Alma did, especially this is combined with being an unmarried woman. Therefore, Alma's deviation from the accepted life course for women was not her status as a single mother and a single parent to her children, nor was it her status as an unwed mother. Her deviance rested instead in *when in the life course* she was a single parent and *in what way* she was. In contrast to the expectations of how the role of the unwed mother should be lived, Alma was *too old* when she gave birth to her children, and she gave birth to *too many children,* which also meant that she was an unwed mother for *a long period of time.* Hence, it does not appear to be her actions per se that were problematic, but rather that they were carried out by a woman of her age. In other contexts (Krekula, 2009) I have used the term *age coding* to refer to the practices of distinction that maintain perceptions of actions, phenomena, and characteristics as associated with and appropriate to demarcated ages. Following this, we could argue that the role of the unwed mother is coded as appropriate for young women but not for women of Alma's age, which in this case refers to women in their thirties and older. By breaking this code, Alma appears as a deviant from unmarried mothers and ultimately also from perceptions of what characterized respectable mothers and women.

In Conflict with Normative Families and Perceptions of the Role of the Mistress

That Alma and Albert were involved in a long-term relationship without being married was nothing unusual. Already during the late 19th century, so-called Stockholm marriages existed. Industrialization involved a rapid migration to Stockholm, and a housing shortage arose as a consequence. Thus, there were many people living in close quarters. At the time, marriage was expected to be accompanied by the establishment of a separate household. Because this was not always possible, many couples lived together until they attained their own housing and could get married (Trost, 1993). Similarly, in the Norwegian countryside during the mid-1800s, some couples who did not have the resources to get married lived common law, and even after their financial situation would have allowed them to get married, they did not bother to do so (Sundt, 1855/1975). Thus, it was not problematic that Alma and Albert had a relationship without being married; rather, it was problematic that one of them was married to someone else.

Divorce has been possible in Sweden for a long time, and a law from 1919 made it relatively easy to get divorced (Trost, 1993). Had he chosen to, Albert could have divorced his wife and moved in with Alma. However, statistics indicate that, although it was possible, divorce was uncommon. During this period, only 1.5 women per 1,000 married women ever got divorced (SCB, 1969). A divorce was therefore not a readily available alternative.

Throughout their relationship, Alma and Albert maintained separate households. Both according to the law and in the view of onlookers, their relationship was subordinate to the one Albert had with his wife. Neither formally nor informally could their relationship therefore be understood in terms of polygamy. Alma's role in the relationship was not that of a wife. Neither can she be described with the contemporary concept of a partner in a LAT (Living Apart Together) relationship. LAT relationships are based on the partners being regarded by both themselves and others as a couple (Trost & Levin, 2000). This was not the case here. Alma and Albert's relationship was not accepted by others, and opportunities to regard themselves as a couple in public contexts seem to have been limited. Based on the overarching description of her relationship as an extramarital one with a married man, Alma's role instead was that of Albert's mistress.

Only limited research attention has been paid to the role of the mistress. However, we do find rich descriptions of mistresses in both literary and historical texts. They are spoken of as mistresses, paramours, and lovers. The role of the mistress often includes an economic dependency, in which the mistress is expected to be financially supported by the married man. This is seen, for example, in the Nordic descriptions from the Middle Ages of how the mistress sometimes appeared as a second wife. This was also the case with mistresses of some members of the royal family. The economic dependency of the mistress on the married man emerges also in the current research (see Nelson, 1993). Descriptions of the mistress's life as both comfortable and free from financial worry are also expressed in historical works. The easy life of the mistress is also depicted in the tales about the paramour's life in the French court as a mistress to royalty. These mistresses not only received financial favours but could also wield considerable political influence. Maria Walewska, Napoleon's mistress, is one such example (Lindqvist, 2004). The historical depictions further show that mistresses often gave birth to the children of their partners.

Because of the mistress's financial dependency upon her partner, it has largely been well-positioned men who have kept mistresses in the Western world. Studies on working-class women and their bodies emphasize how, during the 1800s, these women were ascribed corporeal qualities (such as sexuality, grime, and odours) that the upper class felt were not part of their own culture (Johannisson, 1994). This may have contributed to the oversexualization of lower-class women and their being more likely to be considered as potential mistresses.

Alma and Albert's relationship can be regarded as a result of this class and gender interaction pattern, given that he was well off while she lived with only modest means. However, there are clear contrasts between the descriptions of Alma's sparse life and the depictions of the glamorous life of the mistress. Viewed from the present, Alma also seems to break with notions of how a mistress should behave and live. The relationship yielded her no extravagant gifts, no political platform, no position of power. She was too poor and too common to be regarded as a representation of the glamorous and desirable mistress.

Even if it is reasonable to expect that the depictions of the easy life of the mistress had not made their appearance to any great extent at that time in the little isolated village, a class perspective should not be dismissed when we seek transgressions of norms that made Alma a disreputable woman. The class-based nature of the relationship between the mistress and her partner, along with the economic dependency of such relationships upon men's means, makes it reasonable to assume that relationships of this sort were rare in this village. Most likely, the majority of men lived according to very simple means and were unable to support two households. The role of the mistress can therefore be described as a largely non-existent role in the village. Under other social conditions, a mistress role such as Alma's would not have been regarded as quite so deviant. Alma's "crime" against the institutionalized life of a woman of her time should be seen in context. She was a mistress in the *wrong place* at the *wrong time*.

Some General Reflections

In this chapter I have discussed factors pertaining to Alma—a mother of four and my father's aunt—that led to her being treated as a disreputable person. The first aspects I presented are related to her position as a woman and a mother. I argued that the decisive factor was not that she was a single mother; nor was it that she was an unwed mother. Rather, we must also consider the dimensions of *age* and *time* to uncover how Alma's life course deviated from what was expected for a woman; we must see how the role of unwed mother is age-coded. Alma's "crime" resided in her being an unwed mother in a way that deviated from normative representations of unwed mothers—she was older than most unwed mothers, she gave birth to more children than was usual for unwed mothers, and she remained unmarried for a long period of time, indeed until her death.

I have also claimed that the role Alma had in relation to Albert bore characteristics that contributed to her deviance from a normative life course among women. Here I noted aspects such as *gendered class relations* and the importance of *place* and culture. Alma was a mistress. This was a role that could only have been "correctly performed" if there had been a larger number of well-positioned men in her home village at that time. The poverty and difficult economic conditions that overwhelmingly determined the class relations among the villagers accentuated the deviant nature of Alma's and Albert's relationship. Alma certainly did not appear to be a glamorous and carefree mistress. And, we should also add, such carefree mistresses would not have been particularly welcomed within a village where everyone was expected to contribute actively to survival.

In general, the argument above suggests that an understanding of the processes by which certain life courses are constructed as the norm while others are ascribed positions as deviant demands that we move beyond deciphering an individual's actions and life choices. Our analysis must also consider how phenomena and roles are coded—that is, to what degree they can be regarded as more or less appropriate depending upon the individual's social positions, such as age, class, and gender. By doing so, we shift our focus from the individual and his or her actions to the processes by which codings become embedded in institutional contexts. The question then is no longer how Alma deviated from what was respectable, but rather, how these normative conceptions are maintained and challenged, with the aid of which actions, by whom, and why.

References

Åhren Snickare, E. (2004). *Döden, kroppen och moderniteten* [Death, the body, and modernity]. Stockholm: Carlsson Bokförlag AB.

Aries, P. (1978). *Döden, föreställningar och seder i västlandet* [Death, perceptions, and customs inVästlandet]. Stockholm: Tiden.

Bexell, O. (2009). Personal written communication, Uppsala, January 6.

Croneberg, O. (1941). *Om gravrätt: Kyrkorättslig studie* [On the right to burial: A study of church canon]. Stockholm: Svenska Kyrkans Diakonistyrelses bokförlag.

Danielsen, K. (1990). *De gammeldags piker: Eldre kvinner forteller om sitt liv* [Old-fashioned girls: Older women tell about their lives]. Oslo: Pax Forlag.

Dellert K. (2009). Själaringning och likstolsko—död och begravning i tro och tradition [Ringing of the death bell and the cow—Death and burial according to faith and traditions]. *Artikelbiblioteket.* Retrieved from http://web.comhem.se/akademin/artikelbiblioteket/index.html

Giele, J. Z., & Elder, G. H., Jr. (1998). *Methods of life course research: Qualitative and quantitative approaches.* Thousand Oaks, CA: Sage.

Gubrium, J. F., Holstein, J. A., & Buckholdt, D. R. (1994). *Constructing the life course.* New York: General Hall.

Hagestad, G. O. (2002). I det lange løp. *Aldring og livsløp, 1,* 2–5.

Johannisson, K. (1994). *Den mörka kontinenten* [The dark continent]. Stockholm: Norstedts.

Kaunisvaara byaförening. (2000). *Kaunisvaara 1800–2000.* Kaunisvaara, mimeo.

Krekula, C. (2009). Age coding: On age-based practices of distinction. *International Journal of Aging & Later Life, 4*(2), 7–31.

Lindqvist, H. (2004). *Napoleon.* Stockholm: Norstedts.

Levisdotter Kostet, E. (1997). *Kaunisvaara. Vi var de första* [Kaunisvaara: We were the first]. ABF Pajala, mimeo.

Närvänen, A., & Näsman, E. (2007). Time, identity and agency. In H. Zeiher, D. Devine, A. T. Kjørholt, & H. Strandell (Eds.), *Cost A19, Children's Welfare: Vol. 2. Flexible childhood? Exploring children's welfare in time and space* (pp. 69–92). Odense: University Press of Southern Denmark.

Nelson, E. D. (1993). Sugar daddies: "Keeping" a mistress and the gentleman's code. *Qualitative Sociology, 16*(1), 43–68.

Nilsen, A. (1996). Stories of life—Stories of living: Women's narratives and feminist biography. *NORA, 1*, 16–30.

Nilsson, B. (1989). *De sepulturis. Gravrätten i Corpus Iuris Canonici och i medeltida nordisk lagstiftning* [The sepulturis: The right to burial in canon law and in Nordic legislation of the middle ages]. Solna: Almqvist & Wiksell.

Nordisk familjebok (1904). Konversationslexikon och realencyklopedi, uggleupplagan [Projekt Runeberg's digital facsimile edition of Nordisk familjebok, Owl ed.] Retrieved from http://runeberg.org/nfbb/0646.html

Øyen, E.(1966). *Ugifte mødre* [Unwed mothers]. Oslo: Universitetsförlaget.

Pickering, M. (2001). *Stereotyping: The politics of representation*. New York: Palgrave.

Plejel, H. (1983). *Jordfästning i stillhet: Från samhällsstraff till privatceremoni. En samhällshistorisk studie* [Burial in silence: From social punishment to private ceremony. A social-historical study]. Lund: Arken.

Statistiska Centralbyrån (SCB). (1963). *Folkmängdens förändringar. År 1961.* [Changes in population size. Year 1961]. Stockholm: Author.

Statistiska Centralbyrån (SCB). (1969). *Historisk statistik för Sverige. Del I. Befolkning 1720–1967* [Historical statistics for Sweden. Part I. Population 1720–1967] (2nd ed.). Stockholm: Author.

Shenk, D., Davis, B., Peacock, J. R., & Moore, L. (2002). Narratives and self-identity in later life: Two rural American older women. *Journal of Aging Studies, 16*, 401–413.

Slunga, N. (1993). *"Skola för glesbygd." Arbetsstugor i norra Sverige* ["Schooling for rural areas": Workhouses in northern Sweden]. Luleå: Stiftelsen Norrbottens Läns Arbetsstugor.

Sundt, E. (1975). *Om giftermål i Norge* [On marriage in Norway]. Oslo: Universitetsforlaget. (Original work published 1855).

Tornstam, L. (2005). *Åldrandets socialpsykologi* [Social psychology of aging]. Stockholm: Norstedts Akademiska Förlag.

Trost, J. (1993). *Familjen i Sverige* [Family in Sweden]. Stockholm: Liber Utbildning.

Trost, J. (2005). *Kvalitativa intervjuer* [Qualitative interviews]. Lund: Studentlitteratur.

Trost, J., & Levin, I. (1999). *Att förstå vardagen.* [Understanding everyday life] (2nd rev. ed.). Lund: Studentlitteratur.

Trost, J., & Levin, I. (2000). *Särbo: ett par—två hushåll* [LAT relationships: one couple—two households]. Lund: Studentlitteratur.

Uusitalo, G. (1997). *Kaunisvaara skola, 1947–1997* [Kaunisvaara school, 1947–1997]. Kaunisvaara, mimeo.

CONCLUSION
Strategies That Work and
That Fail to Work

AYSAN SEV'ER

JAN TROST

As the editors of this unique and fascinating collection, we will try to high-light some patterns in the emergence of conflicts and how different families try to dissipate these conflicts. However, we urge our readers to also draw their own conclusions about the narratives they have read, even if their conclusions are diametrically opposed to ours. As we clearly stated in our introduction, we are not claiming that this book will become the last word in theories and meth-ods of the social analysis of family conflicts. We do not even think that such a lofty goal is attainable, given the existing patchwork knowledge about the area. Instead, we want this collection to bring about insights, through a non-tradi-tional sociological method (autonarration), and to fuel a healthy debate about what family conflict means and how to study it. Like the skeletons our authors have taken out of their own family closets and courageously shared with us, we wanted to rattle sociology's relative silence in the area of family conflict. We hope that our authors and readers will find that the rich narratives in this book help them think outside the box, both theoretically and methodologically.

Sources of Conflict

Although we do not want to make overgeneralizations, it is clear that most fam-ily conflicts are robust and persistent. Moreover, the sources of most conflicts are based on factors with which sociologists are closely familiar. Most of these conflicts are not attributable to simple "personality clashes" and cannot be explained away through individual traits. So, let us focus on conflicts that seem to arise from gender, age, sexual orientation, class, and cultural differences. Perceptions of equity and distributive justice (again, familiar sociological concepts) are also exceptionally important in engendering family conflicts.

Gender

Families are not egalitarian institutions, and gender is one of the main axes of inequality in most, if not all, family relations. Sometimes it is the gendered distribution of resources, at other times, it is the gendered distribution (and expectation) of power and influence that sets the stage for covert or overt forms of conflict. Although there are many examples to choose from, let us focus on Chapter 9. In the rural family existence of the author's childhood, there is not much space for leisure, since the parents and their growing children are engulfed by the demands of a small farm. Yet the brothers still manage some playtime, with a nod from their parents, while the only daughter is expected to care for the youngest brother. Maybe, it is this gendered inequity that has contributed to the frictions between the author and her parents.

Gender again surfaces in various other chapters. In Chapter 1, the grandmother's relentless guilt about the loss of her tiny granddaughter is gendered. This kind of torturous self-blame is very much a women's domain, especially in male-dominated societies. In Chapter 3, we see a variation of the gendered sacrifice in the mediating role the mother takes on in order to smooth out the rough edges created by the declining mental health of her son. Although the whole family is affected by the son's episodes, the mother is the one who is on call, day in and day out, to patch things up. Moreover, in Chapter 10, the social group scrutinizes and constantly judges the behaviour of the mistress to the degree that she is eventually buried in a pauper's grave. Her lover, a married man who has several children with his legal wife, continues to be mostly respected in his community despite his adulterous status. So, in many cases of conflict, the gender of individuals cannot be dissociated from the type and severity of the conflict they find themselves in.

Age

Like gender, age is also a universal basis of inequality within family relations. Age difference between individuals (brothers, sisters) and generational difference between parents and their children are closely associated with power differences. It is also important to realize that the power that is derived from age shifts across time. In early years, parents hold all resources and all decision-making power over their children. In their declining years, the same parents may find that their children are making most of their decisions for them. Although we can find many examples for age-based inequalities in the narratives in this book, let us focus on one which clarifies the point: the grandmother in Chapter 4 who lives in South Africa. Although she must have been quite a resourceful woman in her time, running a farm and raising her grandson, the aging process, coupled with a mild form of dementia, prevent her from leading an independent life. In the narrative, her caregivers are her two daughters and a granddaughter. However, the narrative also shows that the caregivers may be too demanding and controlling. Even in relatively minor points, such as when to go to bed, we see that the grandmother is given no choice in the matter: decisions are—sometimes forcefully—made for her. Of course, some of the control in her life could be justified, given the incrementally deteriorating state of her mental capabilities. However, some of the over-controlling behaviour seems to be more for the benefit of her caregivers. The caregivers are not cognizant of or sensitive to the changes in the grandmother's mental health needs. Instead, even a fleeting request for independence is interpreted as the ramblings of a "difficult" woman.

The situation of the mother in Chapter 5 is not very different. In this case, the increasing frailty of the mother seems to make her more an object that her sons and daughters make decisions about than a person in her own right. Although at least one son claims to be abiding by her wishes, the reader gets the impression that the siblings are more interested in jostling for power than truly listening to their mother's need for some independence.

Sexual Orientation

Despite the development of human rights legislation that prohibits unequal treatment of individuals based on personal characteristics, many groups still suffer from overt or covert forms of marginalization. Canada is one of the countries at the forefront of human rights legislation, with its Charter of Rights and Freedoms and its championing of UN human rights declarations and conventions. However, at a practical level, some people here may still feel "less equal" than others. Moreover, people who immigrate to Canada from more hierarchical and especially more patriarchal regions of the world may have additional difficulties with concepts of equity, tolerance, or acceptance. Chapter 7 provides a blatant example of intra-familial discrimination on the basis of sexual orientation. In this case, the parents and extended kin are the discriminators. The author, a gay man, is one of three children in a first-generation Chinese-Canadian family. He eloquently narrates the differential treatment he has received and the verbal and physical abuse he has suffered just because he has not been able to fulfill his father's expectation that he would be a heterosexual son. In a way, he has been forced to lead a double life, pretending to be a straight man in his own community but secretly leading a gay life in another. The conflict takes a toll on this family, creating much fragmentation.

Class

Studies of stratification have been the bread and butter of sociology. Social class has a major impact not only at the macro level but also at the level of family interactions. The class-based conflicts in this book are no exception. In Chapter 9, as readers will recall, there is an ideological tension between the highly educated narrator's expectations about child-rearing and what her working-class parents have been able to deliver. The ideological tension is not random, but very much linked to the respective class positions of the family members and how these divisions have led to differential expectations about equity.

An even clearer example of class tensions can be found in Chapter 10, where a well-to-do man is able to establish a long-term extramarital relationship with a poor woman. It is likely that the root of the skeletons in that particular story was the poverty of the young woman versus the relative affluence of her benefactor. Possibly due to the dire socio-economic circumstances of her life, she lives as a mistress of the wealthy man and bears four children in the process. Both she and her children endure many social sanctions and much isolation because of this arrangement. The fact that her lover/benefactor also breaks the rigid rules of "procreation within marriage" does not affect him nearly as much as it does her. In general, prosperous men have significant freedom to break rules or come up with new ones. When class combines with gender, as in the case of the mistress in Chapter 10, women are doubly vulnerable for exploitation.

Perceptions of Equity

Sociologists have been keenly invested in issues regarding equality and equity. Equality implies fair access to resources on the basis of equivalence—that is, identical treatment. Equity, on the other hand, is a concept of fairness that goes beyond treating everyone the same. Equity may involve compensating for existing inequalities by giving a little more to those who need it the most and giving a little less to those who already have a lot. In small groups and families, these concepts have been the focus of study under "distributive justice" (Ridgeway, 1983). In distributive justice, not only the actual distribution of resources but also the perceptions of equity are crucial. In different chapters of this book of narratives, we see strong reactions to *perceived* inequalities. For example, the author of Chapter 9 feels that her parents spoiled their youngest son while expecting almost adult-like behaviour from their older children. Moreover, the father is seen to be exceptionally harsh toward his daughter's youthful ideas and ideals. This author has spent most of her adult life expecting some kind of an apology from her parents (especially from her father). But when the apology comes, the author is not only shocked but also suspicious. Even when he apologizes, the father is seen as motivated by the desire to clear his own conscience rather than by the more selfless desire to admit wrongdoing toward his daughter.

Cultural Difference
In a globalized world, there are endless opportunities for people from differ-ent cultures to interact with each other. This does not mean that culture as a factor for "othering" has lost its importance. Many judgments are still made, many opportunities are still differentially appropriated, and many misunder-standings continue to occur because of cultural differences. Cultural tensions can even occur among family members from the same racial, ethnic, religious, and class backgrounds if some members establish new roots elsewhere as emi-grants or refugees. The ones who leave develop new ways of seeing the world, views that are different than those of the ones who stay within the original cul-tures. What is right, what is wrong, what is good, what is bad, what is a respon-sibility, what is an intrusion—all these may start to have different meanings on the basis of shifting versus stagnant expectations.

In this book, there are many examples of cultural clashes within the same family. In Chapter 4, the treatment of the narrator's South African grand-mother by her daughters (his mother and his aunt) appears inadequate to him because he has been exposed to the health care practices of a different cul-ture (Canada). Yet the cultural differences also seem to discourage open com-munication. As the author laments, North Americans who are not familiar with African family norms can hardly be expected to understand why a fully grown, highly educated man would have so much difficulty discussing issues with his own mother.

In Chapter 6, the agonizing death of a brother due to AIDS seems that much more of a disaster for the Americanized narrator who has learned about the easily preventable nature of this disease. We also see the impact of culture in Chapter 7, where the parents who are deeply rooted in their Chinese traditions reject the sexual orientation of their son. The ensuing fragmentation, both at the personal and family levels, is severe. In fact, the author invents a different persona for himself, to accommodate his gay and straight selves.

The Responsibility of the State

As the feminist political economy theorists inform us (Armstrong & Armstrong, 1982; Mandell, 2010), what appears as a private trouble often has public implications. The most crucial factor in failing to resolve family troubles is often a failure of the state. Some states are better than others at ensuring their citizens are protected. Examples of state failures are clear in several chapters of this book. In Chapter 4, the origins of a family trouble (the young mother's inability to care for her infant son because of her poverty) are a direct result of the South African apartheid regime, under which millions of black families lived in abject poverty. Some of the grandmother's troubles in this chapter stem from the lack of easily accessible, publicly funded health care. In Chapter 6, the young author's escape from the place of his birth was precipitated by the corrupt Ugandan state, which at the time not only failed to provide safety but instigated much of the violence perpetrated against its own citizens.

However, we do not need to go to the developing world in order to find an example of state failure to protect its citizens. For example, the author of Chapter 8, who was repeatedly molested by her father, was failed by the school system and by the so-called child-protection agencies of Canada. It is clear that analyses of family conflicts cannot be totally accounted for by the micro variables; they also require macro-level theoretical tools.

Common Strategies

Now that we have had an opportunity to summarize some of the sociologically relevant variables as possible contributors to conflict, it is time to turn our attention to the strategies that members of families in this book have used. As we have seen, some of these strategies did help to diffuse family tensions. Others, however, may have exacerbated the original conflict rather than help solve it. In the worst-case scenario, the strategies themselves may have been poorly chosen, ineffective, or even destructive. At this sociologically embryonic stage of studying intense family conflict through narratives, we make no claims about arriving at some "ultimate truth" about which strategies work and which do not. We simply want to summarize some for the intellectual curiosity of our readers.

The literature on small groups shows that people who are caught up in conflict have numerous options (strategies) available to them. For example, they may physically withdraw from the situation or they may use silence to put psychological distance between themselves and what they perceive to be the source of conflict (Folger, Poole, & Stutman, 2009). Given the fact that family relations are complex, intense, often ascribed, and expected to have longevity, physical distancing may not be an easy option for many family members. For example, one may easily stop socializing with a friend or stop interacting with a neighbour or co-worker, but it is much more difficult to sever one's complex ties with a parent, sibling, or grandparent. So, both actual and symbolic distances between family members play important roles in the continuation or escalation of family conflicts. Using silence (that is, maintaining psychological rather than physical distance) may be easier, but it may nevertheless slowly gnaw at feelings of closeness and intimacy. Moreover, silences cannot solve family conflicts; they can only place such conflicts in a closet. In the following pages, we will review numerous strategies and provide examples of how they were used by different families. Again, we urge our readers to draw their own conclusions.

Silences

We discussed the use of silence, as an act, in our introduction. Whether it was self-imposed or imposed by others, what we observed in the previous chapters was a thick layer of silence surrounding the family secrets. Brothers not talking to sisters, parents ignoring their own children, in-laws silently pushing their relatives away from their intimate circles, sons keeping their sexual orientation secret for decades—all are examples of silences in the lives of the contributors to this book. In Chapter 1, we see the silent "blame" for the death of the baby girl. The unspoken blame reverberates in the family, enveloping the grandmother, the father, the sister, and even the niece. We also see an impenetrable silence surrounding the topic of child mortality in general. In that family, these silences reign across decades. Moreover, we also read about the silencing of others, whether they are friends or neighbours. However, rather than providing an opportunity to heal, the silences keep the original pain smouldering.

In Chapter 2, we read about another application of silencing, one that results in the outright rejection of the grandson. After the suicide of her daughter, the grandmother and some of her brothers refuse to talk to the grandson and bar him from attending family functions. Even after another brother (the author) tries to bring an end to this long-term silence and rejection, the opportunity to unify the family is sadly missed. In fact, a larger wall of silence is created when the grandmother stops communicating with two of her own brothers in addition to her grandson.

In Chapter 7, we read about the highly controlling behaviours of the parents, which silence any discussion of the sexual orientation of their son. The controlling behaviour of the father includes physical and psychological abuse. The young author's struggle to find his sexual identity is tantamount to an epic battle. Everyone in his immediate surroundings rejects who he is, relegating him to the status of an outcast because of his appearance and a "deviant" because of his sexual orientation. From an early age, he feels he is being forced to play dramaturgical games rather than being allowed to develop an integrated self. Silences and accusations fragment him and his interpersonal relations. This fragmentation also makes him vulnerable to exploitation by others (particularly by older men, including an older professor). It is a tribute to him that he manages to grow into an insightful, caring individual, despite the hostile silencing he experiences.

In Chapter 8, we see that the mother most likely knew about the sexual molestation of her daughter (the author), yet she chose to remain silent. Even after the daughter has told her about her victimization, her position is "It did not happen, and even if it did, why can't we just go on?" This type of conspiracy of silence is common in families where violence occurs, and it ultimately emboldens the abuser's unacceptable—criminal—behaviour (Sev'er, 1997, 2002).

In Chapter 3, especially during the early stages of their son's bipolar episodes, the parents' socially constructed stories and justifications are attempts to avoid mentioning the illness. The shame that is often attached to mental illness could be seen as one of the culprits that make families turn inward and become increasingly isolated when their loved ones exhibit behaviours that fall outside of the "normal" realm (Goffman, 1963). Unfortunately, silences may shroud troubles but rarely make them go away. In Chapter 9, numerous attempts are made to talk to the youngest brother about his wife's offensive attitudes and behaviour. The brother's response is to prefer silence over communication: he says, "Compost only starts to stink when you turn it over." To come back to our metaphors, not only what lies inside the closets but the silences required to keep those closet doors closed seem to be common—albeit dysfunctional—strategies. Although one can find many socially desirable reasons motivating the examples of silences in these narratives, the toll on families is nevertheless steep (Perls, 1970).

In some chapters, we also see more benevolent uses of silences. For example, in Chapter 4, the "Canadianized" son goes out of his way to avoid confronting his mother, sister, and aunt on their lack of knowledge about a relatively common disease of the aged (dementia). In this silence, what is preserved is cultural relativity, and what is gained is the continuation of family relations. What is sacrificed is the possibility of a positive change. In Chapter 6, the Ugandan author does not confront the blatant racism he experiences in Kenya or the much more subtle, but just as insidious, forms of racism in the United States. His mild, non-confrontational approach toward his host country helps him when he meets a mentor/benefactor under conditions that can only be described as miraculous. In Chapter 9, the three older siblings do not openly confront their parents about the unequal treatment they received throughout their childhood. In contrast to their experiences, the youngest brother had a much more carefree childhood. These silences, especially for the author, provide the mental space in which to rethink and re-evaluate the past. She comes to realize that, perhaps, after all, her parents did the best they could with the little they had.

Cliques and Coalitions

Cliques and coalitions have a very special function in small group or family interactions. For example, in Chapter 6, a total stranger walks into the life of the author and becomes a source of emotional and economic strength during a time of major transition (from Uganda, to Kenya, to the United States). Cliques and coalitions have many important functions, possibly the most important being the balancing of power for those who have no power in isolation (i.e., children in relation to parents, immigrants in a new country). However, coalitions also have the potential to set groups against groups and to radiate existing conflicts outside of their original source. Therefore, formation of cliques is an important strategy in management of conflict, but the results may not be uniform. In Chapter 7, the author who is struggling with his sexual identity finds a strong ally in his sister. At one point, the sister says, "You don't need to defend yourself" (meaning that he has nothing to be ashamed of), thereby bestowing—perhaps for the first time in his life—

legitimacy on his gay identity. This alliance is that much more important because the rest of the family members are unrelenting in considering only heterosexuality as the norm. We also find a positive coalition in Chapter 9, where the older children take some solace in establishing close ties among themselves to counterbalance the emotional unavailability of their parents. However, in the same family, there is also a clique formed by the brothers that sometimes excludes the only sister (the author). Even when cliques work in relatively positive ways, by their nature they include some and exclude others.

On the more negative side, the grandmother in Chapter 2 justifies her total rejection of her son-in-law and grandson because a couple of her brothers and their wives go along with her jaundiced view of the son-in-law. Eventually, the grandmother enlarges her targets of rejection by including two of her brothers in the list of outsiders. Again, her exclusionary choices are reinforced because of the clique she has established for herself. The two remaining brothers (one being the author) and the grandson form their own clique, but they are not able to reverse the tide of rejection the grandmother has bestowed on them.

In Chapter 5, we again witness the dysfunctional workings of cliques. On the one side, the four brothers, and on the other side, the two sisters, seem to be fighting over how to provide the best care for their aging mother. However, the reader sometimes gets the impression that, rather than protecting the best interests of the mother, the two sides may be caught up in a struggle for power and dominance. In this family, preconceived notions about what "that sister" or "that brother" is like have also blocked possibilities for clear and candid communication. Some of these stereotypes are heavily gendered.

Distances

Often, not only the level of psychological involvement but also physical distance is a factor in the development of the stories. Sometimes, family distances are artifacts of mostly benign considerations (marriage, jobs, etc.), but at other times, they are used as a strategy to deal with family conflict. For example, shortly after the traumatic death of her baby niece, the author of Chapter 1 immigrated to Canada. This move put thousands of miles between herself and her mother's and sister's inferno of pain. The latter two are the main characters in the sad story she narrates, but we see their lives though the eyes of the author, who lives on another continent and in a much different day-to-day reality. As readers, we can never know what would have happened if the author had stayed in Turkey. We will never know if the family fragmentation would have slowed down or been reversed. Without her aunt's example to follow, would the niece have moved to the United States? This, too, will remain unanswered. More obvious are the deep wounds that were created by the move, because the mother and grandmother, rightly or wrongly, have seen it as an emotional betrayal. Clearly, at least two family members in Chapter 1 made a choice to use distance as a mechanism for coping with ongoing family pressures and control.

In Chapter 9, we meet another author who chose to leave her country of origin and take up residence in Canada. It is possible to see her move as a partial reaction to her father's aloofness and hurtful style of interaction. We also see the disintegration of her bond with her youngest brother. Could she have sustained a better relationship with him if she had not moved so far away? On the other hand, would her relationship with her parents have been even more troubled if she had stayed? Of course, no one can know the answer to these questions. What is clear is that, like cliques, distances can also play sometimes positive and sometimes negative roles in family affairs.

The author of Chapter 4 resides in Canada, while the rest of the members of his family in his narrative live in South Africa. The author is highly cognizant of cultural differences in his interactions with his family. Physical distance is also a factor in these interactions. For example, although he loved his grandmother as his "mother," the great distance prevents him from attending her funeral. A similar process is also true for the author of Chapter 6, whose remaining family members still live in Uganda while he resides in the United States. In this case, the author's move away from Uganda might have been a life-or-death choice, since many of his peers who stayed back lost their lives. However, the distances have had their own costs. For example, the author feels a deep emptiness as he sits beside his dying brother and realizes he knows little of his brother's now-ending life since his own departure. In all of these cases, physical distances between family members have created additional psychological distances. The shared portions of their lives have dwindled; the "lived lives" are no longer shared. These distances, at many levels, undermine a sense of family unity.

We must also keep in mind that distances can be important even when they are relatively short. For example, after being rejected by his grandmother, the grandson in Chapter 2 moves to another town. After the public conflict and humiliation he experiences at a major family reunion, he is not likely to come back to his birthplace. The sisters and brothers in Chapter 5 have, in part, apportioned the care of their mother on the basis of physical proximity. Even in dimensions where the division of labour is not clear, those who are living closer to the mother seem to be demanding executive privileges on the basis of their proximity. Those who are living at a distance seem to feel that their ideas and concerns are challenged and ignored.

In Chapter 3, we yet again see how distances, either by choice or through necessity, figure in family lives. In this case, the author lives at a distance, and his involvement with the family is erratic. The interaction is mostly confined to times of crisis engendered by the bipolar episodes of the brother. The author admits that his distance may not have allowed him an objective or reliable perspective in the unfolding of his brother's mental illness. Maybe just the opposite is true: due to the distance, the author may have been the most reliable observer of the family conflicts.

In Chapter 7, we see the author's desire to put some distance between his heterosexist family and himself by leaving the family home and renting his own apartment. He feels that this distance is absolutely necessary for him to reconcile his gay identity and the socially constructed heterosexual identity that his family demands. Nevertheless, even such a seemingly minor move within the same city is difficult for the author, because his Chinese culture expects unmarried sons and daughters to remain in the parental home. In a way, a distance necessary to heal his segmented selves can only be accomplished by the creation of additional tensions within the family. As we mention above, his ability to form a clique with his sister helps to smooth some of the ruffled cultural expectations.

Communication

Although an old English saying declares that sticks and stones may break bones but words can never hurt, there are numerous proverbs in different cultures that liken spoken words to swords. In social analysis, we see that words can and do inflict real injury. In the Universal Declaration of Human Rights (1948), two of the most important and protected rights are those of freedom of speech and expression. It is no wonder that oppressive, dictatorial regimes first do away with freedom of speech. However, although spoken (and written) words have the potential to hurt, they also have the ultimate power to clarify, explain, express, appeal, appease, and even heal.

A most desirable way to deal with conflict is to openly communicate, negotiate, and if need be, engage in bargaining to resolve the conflict (Folger et al., 2009; Ford, 1994). In theory, this strategy has the potential to provide a way out—to use Goffman's (1959) terms, to save face—for all parties. However, when the emotions that surround a conflict are intense and are knowingly or unknowingly fuelled by the vested interests of other family members, open communication, let alone bargained resolutions, may be hard to reach. Especially in the West, the privatization of the family domain has worked against reaching transparency in family affairs (Eichler, 1997). More often than not, privatization has turned family strife into a closeted problem.

Effective communication requires the dovetailing of at least three components: the sender, the receiver, and the message. At the simplest level, the sender should be perceived as credible and either neutral or well meaning. The receiver is also expected to be neutral or well meaning. Moreover, the message should be clear. If not, the receiver should be able to ask for clarification, and the sender should be able and willing to provide clarification. The trouble is that, in most communications, something that sociologists call "noise" blocks clear and effective communication. The noise can be submersed in any one or all three of the components (sender, receiver, message).

Ineffective communication may create new difficulties rather than resolving existing problems (Folger et al., 2009). The language may become a weapon rather than an ointment to facilitate healing. Since this book is about family conflict, we see more examples of ineffective, rather than effective, communication in the narratives. For example, in Chapter 7, the father calls his young son a "faggot" when the little boy does not even understand the word. At the time, the boy is not clear about his own sexual orientation; however, he senses that the word is meant to degrade and hurt him. It is no wonder that this particular son's relationship with his father, within a milieu of disrespect and fear, is stunted.

In other instances, the noise in communication may be a by-product of cultural differences. In Chapter 4, the Canadianized son reacts negatively to the treatment of his grandmother in South Africa. In contrast, his mother is not able to understand what "dementia" means and how it is different from simple aging and "being difficult." In this case, the fact that the mother and son do not even share the same vocabulary about the grandmother's health is a further impediment to resolving their different views about what type of care she should receive.

The noise in communication can also be due to the interaction of gender and culture. In Chapter 1, both sisters have difficulty with how their respective husbands deal with the family tragedy (the death of the baby girl). Both perceive their husbands as non-caring and emotionally unavailable men. Both marriages end in divorce shortly after. However, the patriarchal culture they live in (in late-1960s Turkey) is notorious for socializing men to act "strong" and be unemotional. If either of the husbands had openly revealed emotional vulnerability, it is highly likely that they would have again been seen as inadequate, as failing to act like pillars of strength. In the same chapter, the inconsolable guilt and blame that plagues the grandmother is also a product of the interaction of culture and gender. It is no wonder, for whatever happens to their children, society blames women, and women blame themselves. Both communication and perception are overlaid with cultural and gender expectations.

At times, communication breaks down and interaction is no longer possible. Sometimes, the culprit is mental or physical illness. In Chapter 6, due to the sheer exhaustion of the dying man, the author can no longer have a meaningful conversation with his brother. He has so many questions that will never be answered. Likewise, in Chapter 4, the author can no longer converse with his grandmother, whose dementia has robbed her of many of her mental capabilities. In Chapter 3, the author can only carry out a shallow level of interaction with his brother, who is suffering from bipolar disorder. Even these shallow conversations often end in mutual frustration.

In addition to the above examples of communication problems, there is yet another danger of noise in family interactions. This unique noise derives from the intimacy of family members and their absolute certainty that they each know what the others are like. Of course, no person can know another person totally, and even if this were possible, the self is not static. Yet stereotyping family members into rigid categories is common in families, and it is often the culprit in communication breakdown. Statements such as "That's just typical of him!" or "She always acts that way!" or "What else can you expect!" create a destructive noise in family communication. In Chapter 5, we see one of the brothers classify his sisters as being dominant and wanting things their own way. When people are classified, their legitimate concerns are not likely to be heard. Ironically, the sisters in the same family also classify their brothers as domineering, stating that it's hard to be "a female" in this family. In this example, there is noise in the communication on both sides, and effective communication is blocked by both parties.

In Chapter 7, we see that the author has classified his father as cold and abusive. Of course, the narrative contains clear examples of how this perception has developed over time. Nevertheless, once the classification is established, it is very hard to break the mould. For example, the author feels suspicious even when his father shows him warmth and affection. In Chapter 1, we see that the author regards her mother as dependent and childlike. Although there is sympathy and affection, the level of respect the author has for her mother may have been compromised. In Chapter 9, we see that the author classifies her youngest brother as a victim of abuse. That being the case, the brother's own agency in staying in his marriage is not fully explored. Thus, in all these family narratives—as in many other family relations—there are countless pigeonholes and counter-pigeonholes used by the interactants. Although there may be a kernel of truth to each categorization (i.e., the sister may indeed be domineering, or the father may indeed be cruel, or the mother may indeed be childlike, or the brother may indeed be a victim), each categorization will also cloud the possibility of hearing a clear message about or by that person.

If messages are not clear, and if the senders and receivers of the messages do not have at least a neutral expectation from each another, there will be little chance for an effective communication to resolve differences. We see the clearest example of this total failure in communication in Chapter 8, where the author has changed her name, has moved to another province, and has basically cut off all communication with her birth family. It is interesting that her mother has made numerous attempts to rekindle the relationship, by leaving messages on the author's telephone and by making a trip to the author's home. Yet, these attempts have not engendered a better relationship, because the author views her mother as in collusion with her abuser (her father). In a way, both the message and the sender are seen as unreliable and untrustworthy, and the past wrongs of one continue to shadow the present relationships of many.

Impression Management and Face-Saving

Most family members in the narratives have probably never heard of Erving Goffman, although most of the authors who are sociologists would know Goffman's body of work (1959, 1963, 1967). Some even use Goffmanian concepts such as face-saving, stigma, backstage, and other dramaturgical mechanisms to explain some of the events in their own narratives. In Chapter 7, the author, who is pressured to behave as a heterosexual man, finds a female friend who is willing to pose as his girlfriend at family events. This way, he helps his family to save face in their highly traditional Chinese community by presenting their son as a straight man. These dramaturgical strategies also help the author to establish a life of his own, since the parents stop asking him about his whereabouts all the time. They assume—or at least can pretend they assume—their son is with his girlfriend. The relaxation of family pressures provides the author some breathing space to explore his true sexual identity. Thus, despite the internal complexities, appearances are maintained and faces are saved.

Goffman's conceptualizations again come alive in explaining family behaviour in Chapter 3. First, the parents of a son suffering from bipolar episodes engage in impression management, and in doing so, they are able to ward off the acknowledgement of their son's illness—for a while. When the manic dimension of the disorder becomes too severe to ignore, we see the family's self-imposed isolation to protect their son from further stigmatization. Moreover, the mother undertakes many ritualized activities to avoid conflict and retain some form of normalcy in the interactions between the father and the son. Until the last stages of her life, the mother defends the family unity by personally, materially, and emotionally sacrificing for her son. Even the much more realistic father seems to refrain from openly challenging these dramaturgical performances.

Confrontation and Violence

One undesirable strategy in conflict situations is that of escalated confrontation, intimidation, or even violence. Unfortunately, this strategy is not uncommon. Often, the confrontation is gender- and/or age-based. Sociologists have long studied full-blown violence against women and children under the rubric of "domestic conflict" (Gelles, 1972; Straus, 1979). However, there is nothing "domestic" about any conflict when it involves violence (Sev'er, 2002, 2010a). Violence can be physical, psychological, sexual, or economic. In this book, although physical violence is rare, there are still a few examples. For example, as little boys growing up in very different parts of the world, two authors recall being subjected to physical violence by their parents (by a South African mother in Chapter 4, and by a Chinese father in Chapter 7). These early experiences set the stage for the manifestation of other family conflicts in the authors' adult lives. Yet, family violence is not exclusive to the developing world; it can also be found in countries where the general tolerance for violence is low. In Chapter 5, a woman in Canada strikes her sister-in-law in the face, resulting in a police report. In Chapter 9, the wife of the youngest brother threatens the author to the extent that she ends up waiting outside the home for her husband and son to rescue her; the family in this case lives in an affluent European country. In Chapter 3 (again, in Canada), a mentally ill man breaks off a large branch from a tree and physically threatens the brother who is trying to help him. So, although rare, physical violence or threats of violence can be part and parcel of family conflicts everywhere. The authors of Chapters 4 and 6 (originally from South Africa and Uganda, respectively) also provide us a glimpse of state violence against the citizenry.

Sexual violence, especially when it takes place against an innocent child, is one of the most abhorrent forms of violence. It is estimated that about one in four girls and about one in eight boys are sexually molested, often by someone they know well, before they reach the age of 16. Moreover, sexual violence against children is one of the most under-reported forms of family violence. Child victims are often too afraid to complain, and their adult custodians and/or witnesses are too eager to question the child rather than the perpetrator. In Chapter 8, Si Transken courageously shatters the social silences surrounding this loathsome crime.

Although the issue is contentious, the most common form of family violence is psychological. This type of violence often occurs through acts of domination, degradation, subjugation, and marginalization (Dobash & Dobash, 1979). Ignoring, belittling, embarrassing, and using prolonged silences as a psychological weapon are destructive and hurtful tactics that prolong conflict (Sev'er, 2002, 2010b). In the family narratives of this book, psychological violence is the most common and the most destructive strategy used by many family members. In Chapter 2, the grandmother totally rejects the son-in-law after her daughter commits suicide. She accuses the son-in-law of murdering his wife, despite numerous hospital and police reports that refute the accusation. In Chapter 4, as a little boy, the author is left with his grandmother for many years, then is plucked out of his relatively happy rural life by an emotionally remote set of biological parents. His feelings of uprootedness, rejection, and loss are never taken into account or properly addressed. His acting up against what he sees as abandonment brings him no consolation, but only leads to additional punishment.

In Chapter 7, calling the little boy appalling and disparaging names, rejecting his friends, and pressuring him about his emerging sexual orientation lead to a severe fragmentation of the self. The fragmentation is so intense that the young man actually feels the need to create an alternate identity for himself, with a different first and last name. In a way, he can only be true to himself as a gay man within this alternate identity. In Chapter 5, despite the goodwill and love they share towards their aging mother, brothers and sisters are caught up in their own power battles. They do not seem to be aware of the psychological angst they may be causing their mother—or each other—through psychological games. In Chapter 1, the bereaved mother and the grandmother bestow infinite love and care on the daughter that follows the one who died as an infant. Yet, there seems to be a psychological price for this endless love: there are expectations of proximity and loyalty. When the daughter moves away and settles in the United States, both the mother and the grandmother feel anger and betrayal.

Belief Systems

Critical sociology's approach to religion is full of contestation. As Marx once forcefully stated, "Religion … is the opium of the people" (Marx, 1978). Yet, starting with Durkheim (1912/1976), functionalists have been keenly aware of the positive impact of religion in providing solidarity among believers. In Durkheim, solidarity is seen as a panacea for many social ills (divorce, suicide, crime, alienation, etc.). In his *The Protestant Ethic and the Spirit of Capitalism* (1904/1958), Weber also acknowledges the importance of belief systems. In the latter, the work ethic and frugality of Protestants are seen as absolutely important prerequisites for the accumulation of capital and the eventual triumph of capitalism. So, social scholars in general, and sociologists in particular, have a long tradition of acknowledging the power of religion, differing only in their opinions as to how that power will affect people. Marx saw religion as a device designed to subjugate the disgruntled masses, whereas both Weber and Durkheim saw religion as a force for collective unity, achievement, and order.

In some of the narratives in this book, we see a reflection of this sociological polarity on religion. On the negative side, we see a working-class mother's inability to understand, accept, and move beyond her daughter's suicide as the result of her very orthodox religious beliefs (Chapter 2). The religion, in that narrative, is Orthodox Catholicism. The believers are socialized into interpreting suicide as a major sin. In that narrative, the mother's intense love for her daughter, and her intense and unquestioning belief in the religious teachings she thought the two of them shared, did not permit her to accept her daughter's suicide. Instead, she chose to accuse, blame, and reject everything and everyone (including her brother, son-in-law, and grandson). In this mother's inability to question the religious teachings she was socialized in, we find reasons for Marx's skepticism about the role of religion.

However, two other narratives attest to either a dual role or a much more constructive role that belief systems can play in family interactions. In Chapter 3, the brother who suffers from a serious bipolar disorder finds an accepting religious community for himself (in this case, Orthodox Judaism). This community, in the Durkheimian sense, seems to protect the brother from experiencing further bipolar episodes by providing a strong sense of support and solidarity in his life. On the less positive side, his extreme form of religiosity may heap further pressures upon his relationships with his brother and father, who are much more secular in their approach to religion. His rigid rules also inconvenience his mother, who has to prepare his food separately and cover parts of the kitchen with aluminum foil to keep his food uncontaminated. His ultra-orthodox community may also create additional pressures by preaching the necessity of marriage and procreation. Despite much effort and expenditure, the brother's religiously fuelled aspiration for marriage has remained unattainable, due at least in part to the condition of his mental health.

In Chapter 6, we see the purest, and the most positive, workings of a deep-rooted spirituality in the face of conflict. In an incident that can only be seen as miraculous, and after much heartache as a refugee, the author finds a friend and mentor, internal peace, hope, and economic stability—all at the same time. In turn, he learns to bring hope and help to others who are in dire need in his country of birth, Uganda. Even his approach to the wrenching death of his brother appears to be one of internal acceptance and peace. Through this extraordinarily moving story, maybe others will be inspired to find new ways of reducing the impact of their family struggles on their lives and sustaining hope for better outcomes in the midst of adversity.

Conflicts in the family are not unique. What is unusual, and commendable, is the mammoth courage that it has taken for each of the 10 authors in this collection to visit publicly the secrets and skeletons in their family closets. As the editors, we are deeply grateful for their decision to allow all of our readers a glimpse of their family strife. At this point, we no longer want to speak for family skeletons, since they have already spoken so candidly and so eloquently for themselves. It is up to our readers to pick and choose what makes sense for them and what does not, what to keep from these chapters and what to discard. It is up to our readers to decide whether these meaningful visits to other people's closets will help them to garner the courage to revisit some of their own family skeletons, and put some to rest.

References

Armstrong, P., & Armstorng, H. (1982). *The double ghetto.* Toronto: McClelland & Stewart.

Dobash, R. E., & Dobash, R. P. (1979). *Violence against wives: A case against patriarchy.* New York: Routledge.

Durkheim, E. (1976). *The elementary forms of the religious life.* Glencoe, IL: Free Press. (Original work published 1912).

Eichler, M. (1997). *Family shifts.* Toronto: Oxford.

Folger, J. P., Poole, M. S., & Stutman, R. K. (2009). Working through conflict. Boston: Oxford.

Ford, R. (1994). Conflict and bargaining. In M. Foschi & E. J. Lawler (Eds.), *Group processes: Sociological analysis* (pp. 231–256). Chicago: Nelson Hall.

Gelles, R. (1972). *The violent home: A study of physical aggression between husbands and wives.* Beverly Hills, CA: Sage.

Goffman, E. (1959). *The presentation of self in everyday life.* New York: Doubleday.

Goffman, E. (1963). *Stigma: Notes on management of spoiled identity.* Englewood Cliffs, NJ: Prentice-Hall.

Goffman, E. (1967). *Interaction ritual: Essays on face-to-face behavior.* New York: Aldine.

Mandell, N. (2010). *Feminist issues* (5th ed.). Toronto: Pearson.

Marx, K. (1978). In R. C. Tucker (Ed.), *The Marx–Engels Reader.* New York: Norton.

Perls, F. S. (1970). *Gestalt therapy verbatim.* Moab, UT: Bantam.

Ridgeway, C. L. (1983). *The dynamics of small groups.* New York: St. Martin's.

Sev'er, A. (1997). Current feminist debates about woman abuse: Some policy implications. ZIF: Sonderbulletin [Special issue], 121–137. Berlin: Humboldt University Press.

Sev'er, A. (2002). *Fleeing the house of horrors: Women who have left their abusive partners.* Toronto: University of Toronto Press.

Sev'er, A. (2010a). All in the family: Violence against women, children and the aged. In D. Cheal (Ed.), *Canadian families today* (2nd ed.). Toronto: Oxford.

Sev'er, A. (2010b). Marriage go-around: Divorce and re-marriage in Canada. In N. Mandell & A. Duffy (Eds.), *Canadian families: Diversity, conflict, and change* (4th ed.). Toronto: Nelson.

Straus, M. (1979). Measuring intrafamily conflict and violence: The conflict tactics scale. *Journal of Marriage and Family, 41,* 75–88.

Weber, M. 1958. The Protestant ethic and the spirit of capitalism (T. Parsons, Trans.) New York: Scribner. (Original work published 1904).

APPENDIX
Call for Chapters

Skeletons in the Closet: A Sociological Analysis of Family Conflicts. Edited by Aysan Sev'er (Professor of Sociology, University of Toronto, sever@utsc .utoronto.ca) and Jan Trost (Professor of Sociology, Uppsala University, Jan .Trost@soc.uu.se)

Family feuds and grudges probably date back to the origins of humankind. They also form a common thread in religious teachings. Prophets of all major religions have stipulated tolerance, respect, and honour among people who are closely related. It is not coincidence that religions repeat the obligations to love and honour one's mother and father. None of the religions have forgotten the lessons learned from the Cain story.

Strife between parents and their children, siblings, husbands, wives, and in-laws also serve as the backdrop of many Hollywood movies, whether they are within the comic, adventure, thriller, or drama genre; sometimes funny (*Are We There Yet? Meet the Fockers*), sometimes tragic (*The War of the Roses, Burning Bed, Gone with the Wind, Kramer vs. Kramer, Sophie's Choice*), stories form the staple of the silver screen. Conflict among people who are (or are normatively expected to be) part of a family group reeks trouble.

Other forms of mass media also give us a glimpse of what bitter conflict among intimates looks like. The media is heavily skewed toward famous people, and the consumers of the media expect peculiar, eccentric, even bizarre behaviour from the rich and the famous. Nevertheless, when Bill Clinton's

DNA was found on the blue dress of a young intern and the information was zoomed into millions of households through TV, newspapers, and tabloids, the audience also saw the excruciating pain on his wife's well-groomed face. When Paul McCartney was accused of abusive and controlling behaviour and was sued for multiple millions of dollars after a relatively short marriage to Heather Mills, he appeared to age right in front of the cameras. When Princess Diana was killed in a traffic accident along with her new lover, deep lines of worry sketched even the otherwise stoic face of Queen Elizabeth. Even the material riches of these men and women and the admiration they have garnered throughout their lives were not sufficient to inoculate them against this kind of intimate anguish. The question is, how do the rest of us deal with wrenching conflict?

Ironically, and despite the possibly lifelong disintegration effects of serious conflict among members of families, sociology in general and sociology of the family in particular have been mostly mute on the topic (with the exception of violence research). This collected book will attempt to fill this gap. We will roughly categorize intense family strife under the following parts. The categorization is for analytical purposes alone, since we realize there may be strong overlaps in individual cases:

I. Intense intergenerational conflict
- conflict between parents and their daughters and/or sons
- incest, abuse, violence
- conflict arising from severe disability and/or unnatural death
- conflict arising from the "sandwich generation" caught between the demands of aging parents while still in the position to care for their own children

II. Intense intra-generational conflict
- sibling rivalry
- conflict arising from unfair apportioning family resources/opportunities
- inheritance issues
- fraternal incest

III. Intense cultural conflict
- conflict arising from cultural, faith-based, or ideological grounds
- conflict arising from race/ethnicity/mix-race
- conflict arising from gender/culture intersections
- dowry-related conflicts
- honour-related conflicts

Instructions to the Contributors

We propose to have 15 chapters, each based on a single author's narration of a strong family conflict, each told from the point of view of the author. Authors can add an analysis of their family conflicts, by citing social scientific literature. However, authors are urged to avoid turning their narrations into an objective "data" to be evaluated from a distance.

- *Length:* Each chapter should be 15–20 pages in length.
- *Format:* Double-spaced; 12 pt. font; references should follow APA style.
- *Deadline:* Actual submission of the FINAL chapter: June 2008 (VERY IMPORTANT).
- *Acceptance:* As editors, A. Sev'er & J. Trost will have the final say in acceptance. The editors also retain the right to make suggestions, revisions, and/ or minor corrections to the final version.

Guidelines for the Contributors

- Please note that this is *not* a call for creative story writing, but a call for a collection of "narrations." Authors should use first-person accounts and should try to capture any/all processes and outcomes of the conflict/conflicts they address as accurately as they can remember. Narrations should also include attempts (successful or unsuccessful) to resolve the conflict.
- Since the book is aimed at, for example, higher-level classes in family sociology, social psychology, social work, and women's or gender studies, as well as to an educated audience, interpretations with the help of theoretical perspectives are welcome. Such interpretations should, however, be understandable for a lay audience, too.
- Authors can use real names or pseudonyms or relational terms (my wife, my aunt, etc.) for any/all characters. It is also up to the authors to request the publication of the story under their real name/title or under anonymous authorship.
- Whether or not to get permission from others in the story is up to individual authors. Since *each* contribution is not "research" but "personal narration," the stories are not subject to the stringent ethical requirements of "doing research with human subjects." However, as editors, we expect clarity, honesty, balance, non-judgmentality, and non-abusive, non-demeaning language.

- Author's should avoid
  - making moral judgments
  - blaming people
  - deciding who was wrong/right
  - showing their own stance in a good/bad light
  - condemning any one, regardless of what he/she may have done
  - condoning/inciting any type of abuse or violence
- Authors should also avoid
  - turning the story into a literary piece
  - weaving in events or add characters that were not part of the actual case
  - analyzing their own stories
  - trying to turn their narration into research and their story into a research paper
- Authors will not receive monetary compensation for their submission/publication.

Please submit your intention and the following information to either editor.
Full Name:
Title/University Affiliation:
Contact Information:
    Full Address:
    Email:
Title of Proposed Paper:
Expected Completion Date:

ABOUT THE EDITORS

Aysan Sev'er is Professor of Sociology at the University of Toronto Scarborough. She is the recipient of numerous national and international awards for her work on violence against women. Her current research focuses on extreme forms of violence against women in India and in southeastern Turkey. She is the founding editor of the journal *Women's Health & Urban Life* and the recipient of the Canadian Person's Day Award (1998), the Canadian Sociology & Anthropology Association Service Award (2001), the Daughters of Ataturk Award (2003), and the Canadian Women's Studies Book Award (2004). Her forthcoming book is on honour killings in southeastern Turkey. Aysan Sev'er has presented papers and reports in Canada and in many other countries across the world, and has organized numerous national and international conferences in the areas of violence against women, health, family, and gender.

Jan E. Trost is Professor Emeritus of Sociology at Uppsala University, Sweden. He is Honorary President of the Committee on Family Research of the International Sociological Association. In 1999 the National Council on Family Research inaugurated its Jan Trost Award for outstanding contributions to comparative family studies. He has published hundreds of articles and chapters in international journals and books and more than forty books in various languages. His work has mainly been on theory development of symbolic interaction and focused in application on family and disaster studies as well as sexology. He has also been Distinguished Visiting Professor at University of North Carolina and visiting professor at the University of Minnesota, the Kinsey Institute, and universities in Belgium, Israel, Lithuania, and Norway.